致青春
中英双语读物

与青春有
关的日子

砥砺派

主编 青闰

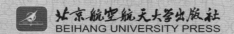

北京航空航天大学出版社
BEIHANG UNIVERSITY PRESS

图书在版编目（CIP）数据

与青春有关的日子．砥砺派：英汉对照 / 青闰主编
．－－北京：北京航空航天大学出版社，2016.12
ISBN 978-7-5124-2296-4

I.① 与…　II.① 青…　III.① 英语—汉语—对照读物
IV.① H319.4

中国版本图书馆 CIP 数据核字（2016）第 277616 号

与青春有关的日子　砥砺派

主　编　青闰

责任编辑　秦　莹

*

北京航空航天大学出版社出版发行

北京市海淀区学院路 37 号（邮编 100191）　http://www.buaapress.com.cn
发行部电话：（010）82317024　传真：（010）82328026
读者信箱：bhwaiyu@163.com　邮购电话：（010）82316936
涿州市星河印刷有限公司印装　各地书店经销

*

开本：700×1 000　1/16　印张：16.5　字数：391 千字
2017 年 1 月第 1 版　2017 年 1 月第 1 次印刷
ISBN 978-7-5124-2296-4　定价：40.80 元

编委会

前　言

　　一滴水珠折射出太阳的光辉，一朵小花蕴含着人生的美好，生活中的平凡小事点点滴滴往往包含最深刻的人生哲理。

　　"与青春有关的日子系列"包括《青春派》、《幸福派》、《砥砺派》、《逆旅派》和《幽默派》五本。

　　这是值得用心品味的人生宝典，是让亿万人获得幸福的心灵密码，是按摩情感的心灵圣经，也是温暖千万心灵、改变千万人生的传世佳作。所选篇章丰富、全面、隽永、经典，所选内容发人深省、耐人寻味、引人入胜、励人奋进。

　　"与青春有关的日子系列"涉及青春、幸福、心态、宽容、尊重、亲情、爱情、友谊、善良、感恩、做人、做事、挫折、成功、幽默、诙谐等重大人生课题，涵盖人生的上上下下方方面面，文章短小精炼、字字珠玑，包含深刻的生活内涵和无穷的人生智慧，既能点燃我们内心深处的智慧火花，又能使我们感到心灵震撼，还能让我们从容自信，端正人生态度，找到人生方向，成就美满人生。

　　这里选译的文章或经典优美、百读不厌，或震撼心灵、耐人寻味，或自然和谐、生动有趣，或陶冶情操、净化心灵，或美仑美奂、动人心扉，或幽默风趣、博人一粲……她们像一颗颗珍珠、一粒粒钻石、一泓泓清泉；她们像一缕缕阳光、一处处圣火、一座座灯塔；她们像一只只神奇灵动的手拨动着你的心弦，使你如沐春风、如逢甘霖；她们像鲜花一样芬芳，月色一样柔和，微风一样清新，春雨一样滋润。

　　在选材上，我们披沙拣金，尽可能多方位、多角度、多层面地展现其风姿和魅力。

　　在翻译上，我们反复斟酌推敲，力求准确到位，传神达韵，流畅优美，让你体味到汉语言的博大精深和独特韵味。

　　在设计上，我们追求精美韵致、别出心裁，让你一见倾心、爱不释手、

1

一读难忘。

　　朋友，每当华灯初上，白天的喧哗与骚动渐渐平息，伴着明月清风，和着舒缓旋律，携一卷美文，品一杯香茗，坐在属于自己的空间，体验文字带给你的优美、睿智、灵动与流畅，感受时间从指缝间悄然滑过，体味一种纯净、充实和有趣的生活，是何等美妙和惬意！

　　朋友，来吧，这里有你的青春，有你的记忆，有你的梦想，有你的希望，有你的幸福……让我们在此相会，让我们的人生得到心灵的滋润。

　　在翻译过程中，我们得到了北京航空航天大学出版社秦莹编辑的悉心指导和鼎力支持，在此深表谢忱。

焦作大学　青闰

2016 年 12 月 10 日

目 录
Contents

old man told the traveler. "I've planted over 100,000 acorns. Perhaps only tenth of them will grow."

老人告诉那个旅行者："我已经种了 10 万颗橡子 大概只有十分之一的橡子能够成长。"

The Old Oak-Planter

A young traveler was **exploring**① the Alps. He came upon a vast stretch of **barren**② land. It was **desolate**③. It was the kind of place you hurry away from.

Then, suddenly, the young traveler stopped dead in his tracks. In the middle of this vast wasteland was a bent-over old man. On his back was a sack of **acorn**④. In his hand was a four-foot length of iron pipe.

The old man was using the iron pipe to **punch**⑤ holes in the ground. Then from the sack he would take an acorn and put it in the hole. Later the old man told the traveler. "I've planted over 100,000 acorns. Perhaps only tenth of them will grow." The old man's wife and son had died, and this was how he chose to spend his final years. "I want to do something useful," he said.

Twenty-five years later the now-not-as-young traveler returned to the same place. What he saw amazed him. He could not believe his own eyes. The land was covered with a beautiful forest two miles wide and five miles long.

生词有约

① explore
vt. 探索；探险
② barren
adj. 贫瘠的；不生育的
③ desolate
adj. 荒凉的；无人烟的
④ acorn
n. 橡子；橡实
⑤ punch
vt. 开洞；打出孔

种橡树的老人

一个年轻的旅行者在阿尔卑斯山探险。他来到一块一望无际的不毛之地。那里荒无人烟，是一种让人匆匆离开的地方。

后来，年轻的旅行者突然停住了脚步。只见辽阔的荒地中央一位老人正在弯腰播种。他背着一大袋橡子，手里拿着一根 4 英尺长的铁管。

老人用那根铁管在地上打洞，然后从袋子里掏出一颗橡子，放进洞里。后来，老人告诉那个旅行者："我已经种了10万颗橡子。大概只有十分之一的橡子能够成长。"老人的妻儿都已经故去，而这就是他选择度过晚年的一种方式。"我想做一些有用的事儿，"他说。

25年后，那个已不再年轻的旅行者故地重游。而眼前的景象却让他惊叹不已。他无法相信自己的眼睛。那块土地覆盖上了5英里长、2英里宽的美丽森林。

 诵读经典 >>>>>
Read classic

Twenty-five years later the now-not-as-young traveler returned to the same place. What he saw amazed him. He could not believe his own eyes. The land was covered with a beautiful forest two miles wide and five miles long.

25年后，那个已不再年轻的旅行者故地重游。而眼前的景象却让他惊叹不已。他无法相信自己的眼睛。那块土地覆盖上了5英里长、2英里宽的美丽森林。

 妙语连珠 >>>>>
Sparkling discourse

✪ Formal courtesy between husband and wife is even more important than it is between strangers.

夫妻间在形式上讲究礼貌甚至比陌生人之间更重要。

✪ Often the difference between a successful marriage and a mediocre one consists in leaving about three or four things a day unsaid.

通常，成功婚姻和普通婚姻之间的区别在于：一天中留下三四件事情不说。

The Eagle and an Iceberg

Once a proud eagle **perched**① on the tip of an **iceberg**② floating swiftly down the river. The big bird seemed **oblivious**③ to the **tremendous**④ waterfall that lay ahead. At the same time, a hunter was walking down a path along the river's edge. Seeing the huge bird perched on the iceberg, the hunter clapped his hands and cried out, "Brother Eagle, fly away, fly away. There's danger ahead!"

The eagle **merely**⑤ shrugged its great wings as if to say, "Don't **bother**⑥ me. I know what I'm doing."

As the iceberg floated closer to the waterfall, the hunter again cried out, "Fly away, Brother Eagle! There's a waterfall ahead!"

Again the eagle merely shrugged its wings, as if to say, "Don't bother me. I can take care of myself."

At the moment, the eagle looked down just in time to see that the iceberg had reached the brink of the waterfall and was about to go over the edge. It spread its **mighty**⑦ wings and prepared for immediate takeoff. But the eagle was unable to rise. Its claws were frozen to the ice and it went down with the iceberg.

生词有约

① perch

vi. 站（坐）在高处；栖息

② iceberg

n. 冰山

③ oblivious

adj. 不在意的；忘却的

④ tremendous

adj. 极大的；巨大的

⑤ merely

adv. 仅仅；只；不过

⑥ bother

vt. 烦扰；打扰

⑦ mighty

adj. 强大的；有力的

鹰与冰山

从前，一只傲鹰站在正在飞速漂浮的冰山顶端。这只大鸟好像对前方那个巨大的瀑布毫不在意。与此同时，一个猎人正沿着河边的一条小路行走。看着卧在冰山上的大鸟，猎人拍着手大声喊道:"鹰弟,快飞走,快飞走。前面有危险!"

鹰只是耸了耸巨大的翅膀,好像是要说:"别烦我! 我知道自己在干什么。"

这时,冰山距离瀑布越来越近了,猎人又喊道:"快飞走,鹰弟! 前面有瀑布!"

鹰只是又耸了耸翅膀,好像是要说:"别烦我! 我自己能照顾自己。"

这时,鹰低头一看,恰好看到冰山已经到达瀑布边缘,眼看就要掉下去。它展开有力的翅膀准备马上起飞,但它无法起飞了。它的爪子和冰冻结在了一起。鹰和冰山一起掉了下去。

诵读经典 >>>>>
Read classic

At the moment, the eagle looked down just in time to see that the iceberg had reached the brink of the waterfall and was about to go over the edge. It spread its mighty wings and prepared for immediate takeoff. But the eagle was unable to rise. Its claws were frozen to the ice and it went down with the iceberg.

这时,鹰低头一看,恰好看到冰山已经到达瀑布边缘,眼看就要掉下去。它展开有力的翅膀准备马上起飞,但它无法起飞了。它的爪子和冰冻结在了一起。鹰和冰山一起掉了下去。

妙语连珠 >>>>>
Sparkling discourse

✪ A statesman who keeps his ear permanently glued to the ground will have neither elegance of posture nor flexibility of movement.

总是将耳朵贴在地上的政治家既不会有优美的姿态,也不会有灵活的动作。

✪ Politics is like show business; you have a hell of an opening, coast for a while, and then have a hell of a close.

政治如同娱乐业,漂漂亮亮开张,顺顺当当经营一阵子,然后体体面面收场。

Before long, many customers complimented her to her boss, "The girl is the most intelligent girl with best temperament."

不久，许多顾客都对老板称赞她：“这位小姑娘是你店中最有才智、最有气质的女孩。”

画龙点睛

Success Comes from a Dream

Many years ago, a young girl was hired by a tailor shop in New York, working as a **charlady**①. When at work, she often saw the ladies ride luxury cars to the shop to try on beautiful clothes. They dressed and behaved very well. So the girl thought, this was the real life for a lady! After thinking this, a strong desire came up from her heart: I also want to be a boss, to become a member of them.

Since then, every day before she started work, she would smile to the mirror so happily, so gently and so confidently. Although in coarse clothes, she imagined herself to be a lady wearing beautiful **garment**②. Being polite, natural and graceful in dealing with people, she was well received by customers. She was only a charlady, but she always **conceived**③ she herself was the owner of the shop. She worked actively and **spared no effort**④ as if the tailor shop was of her own. Consequently she won the deep trust of her boss.

Before long, many customers **complimented**⑤ her to her boss, "The girl is the most intelligent girl with best **temperament**⑥."

"She is indeed very excellent," the boss also said.

After another period of time, the boss handed over the tailor shop to the girl for management.

Gradually, the girl got a **resounding**⑦ name— "Annette," then "Costume Designer Annette," and finally "Famous Costume Designer Mrs. Annette."

生词有约

① charlady
n. 打杂女工

② garment
n. 衣服
③ conceive
v. 设想
④ spare no effort
不遗余力

⑤ compliment
vt. 称赞；褒扬
⑥ temperament
n. 气质

⑦ resounding
adj. 响亮的

成功来自梦想

多年前，一个小姑娘受雇到纽约市的一家裁缝店打杂。上班时，她常常看到女士们乘着豪华轿车来店里试穿漂亮衣服。她们穿着讲究，举止得体。于是，姑娘想道，这才是女士的真正生活！想到这个之后，一股强烈的欲望从她的心里升起：我也要当老板，成为她们中的一员。

从那以后，每天开始工作前，她都要对着镜子微笑，是那样开心、那样温柔、那样自信。尽管她穿着粗布衣服，但她把自己想象成身穿漂亮衣服的女士。她待人接物彬彬有礼、自然优美，受到了顾客的好评。尽管她只是一名打杂女工，但她总想象着自己就是店主。她工作积极，不遗余力，好像裁缝店就是她自己家的。因此，她赢得了老板的深信。

不久，许多顾客都对老板称赞她："这位小姑娘是你店中最有才智、最有气质的女孩。"

"她确实非常出色，"老板也说道。

又过了一段时间，老板把裁缝店交给了这个女孩管理。

渐渐地，女孩有了一个响亮的名字——"安妮特"，然后成了"服装设计师安妮特"，最后成了"著名服装设计师安妮特夫人"。

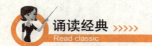

诵读经典 >>>>>
Read classic

Being polite, natural and graceful in dealing with people, she was well received by customers. She was only a charlady, but she always conceived she herself was the owner of the shop. She worked actively and spared no effort as if the tailor shop was of her own.

她待人接物彬彬有礼、自然优美，受到了顾客的好评。尽管她只是一名打杂女工，但她总是想象着自己就是店主。她工作积极，不遗余力，好像裁缝店就是她自己家的。

妙语连珠 >>>>>
Sparkling discourse

✪ A strong man will struggle with the storms of fate.
强者能同命运的风暴抗争。

✪ Energy and persistence conquer all things.
能量加毅力可以征服一切。

They went ahead, and then, as if by a stroke of magic, the secret was discovered.

他们继续努力，随后，像是得到魔力一般，终于发现了其中的奥秘。

画龙点睛

Know What One Wants

When he decided to produce his V-8 motor, Henry Ford chose to make an engine with the entire eight cylinders cast in one block. The engineers said that it was simply impossible to cast an eight-**cylinder**[①] **engine-block**[②] in one piece.

Ford said, "Produce it anyway."

"But," they replied, "it is impossible."

"Go ahead," Ford commanded, "and stay on the job until you succeed, no matter how much time is required."

Six months passed and nothing happened. Another six months passed, and still nothing happened. The engineers tried every **conceivable**[③] plan to carry out the orders, but the thing seemed out of the question.

At the end of the year the engineers again informed Ford they had found no way to carry out his orders.

"Go right ahead," said Ford. "I want it, and I'll have it."

They went ahead, and then, as if by a stroke of magic, the secret was discovered.

Ford's **determination**[④] had won once more!

Henry Ford was successful because he understood and applied the principles of success. One of these is desire: know what one wants. If you can do this, you can accomplish his achievements in any calling for which you are suited.

生词有约

① cylinder
n. 圆筒；圆柱体；汽缸

② engine-block
n. 发动机组

③ conceivable
adj. 可想到的；可能的

④ determination
n. 决心；决定

知道自己想要什么

亨利·福特决定生产 V-8 汽车时，想造一台 8 个汽缸合在一块的发动机。工程师们说要把 8 个汽缸全浇铸在一起根本不可能。

福特说："无论如何要生产出来。"

"可是，"他们回答说。"那是不可能的。"

"只管做就是了，"福特命令道。"无论需要多少时间，直到做成为止。"

6 个月过去了，没有做成。又过了 6 个月，还是没有做成。工程师们试过了每一种想得出来的计划去执行命令，但事情好像仍不可能。

一年结束时，工程师们再次告诉福特说，他们找不到什么办法来执行他的命令。

"继续做，"福特说。"我要的东西，就一定会得到。"

他们继续努力，随后，像是得到魔力一般，终于发现了其中的奥秘。

福特的决心又一次取得了胜利！

亨利·福特之所以成功，是因为他了解并运用了这些成功的法则。其中一个法则就是渴望：知道自己想要什么。如果你能做到这一点，就可以在适合自己的任何行业取得像他那样的成就。

诵读经典 >>>>>
Read classic

Henry Ford was successful because he understood and applied the principles of success. One of these is desire: know what one wants. If you can do this, you can accomplish his achievements in any calling for which you are suited.

亨利·福特之所以成功，是因为他了解并运用了这些成功的法则。其中一个法则就是渴望：知道自己想要什么。如果你能做到这一点，就可以在适合自己的任何行业取得像他那样的成就。

妙语连珠 >>>>>
Sparkling discourse

★ Man's greatness lies in his power of thought.

人的伟大之处在于他的思想的力量。

★ The good life is one inspired by love and guided by knowledge.

美好的生活是一种由爱激励和由知识指导的生活。

Suddenly, from the balcony, a little boy stood up and shouted, "Daddy, you are wonderful!"

突然，一个小男孩从剧院楼厅上站起来，大声喊道："爸爸，你真棒!"

画龙
点睛

You Are Wonderful, Daddy!

Several years ago in the Paris opera house, a famous singer had been **contracted**① to sing and ticket sales were **booming**②. The night of the concert found the house packed and every ticket sold.

The feeling of **anticipation**③ and excitement was in the air as the house manager took the stage and said, "Ladies and gentlemen, thank you for your **enthusiastic**④ support. I am afraid that due to illness, the singer you've all come to hear will not be performing tonight. We have found a suitable **substitute**⑤ who we hope will provide you with comparable entertainment."

The crowd groaned in disappointment and failed to hear the announcer mention the **stand-in**⑥'s name. The environment turned from excitement to **frustration**⑦.

The stand-in performer gave the performance everything he had. When he had finished, there was nothing but an uncomfortable silence. No one applauded.

Suddenly, from the balcony, a little boy stood up and shouted, "Daddy, you are wonderful!"

The crowd broke into thunderous applause.

生词有约

① contract
vt. 签约

② booming
adj. 急速增长的

③ anticipation
n. 期待

④ enthusiastic
adj. 热情的；热烈的

⑤ substitute
n. 代替者

⑥ stand-in
n. 替身

⑦ frustration
n. 沮丧

爸爸，你真棒!

几年前，在巴黎的歌剧院，一位著名歌唱家签约要来演唱，门票卖得非常火爆。音乐会的当天晚上，所有门票都销售一空，剧院里座无虚席。

在观众充满期待和激动之情的气氛中，剧院经理走上舞台说："女士们、先生们，感谢你们的热情支持。因为我们邀请的歌唱家身体欠佳，恐怕他今晚不能演出。我们已经找到一位合适人选替代他，希望能给你们提供同样的娱乐。"

观众发出了失望的抱怨声，连替代演员的名字都没有听清。剧院里的气氛由激动变成了沮丧。

替代演员使出浑身解数进行演唱。演出结束后，全场只是令人不快的沉默。没有一个人鼓掌。

突然，一个小男孩从剧院楼厅上站起来，大声喊道："爸爸，你真棒！"

观众们爆发出了雷鸣般的掌声。

诵读经典 >>>>>
Read classic

✪ The night of the concert found the house packed and every ticket sold.

音乐会的当天晚上，所有门票都销售一空，剧院里座无虚席。

✪ The crowd groaned in disappointment and failed to hear the announcer mention the stand-in's name. The environment turned from excitement to frustration.

观众发出了失望的抱怨声，连替代演员的名字都没有听清。剧院里的气氛由激动变成了沮丧。

妙语连珠 >>>>>
Sparkling discourse

✪ People are lonely because they build walls instead of bridges.

人们孤独，是因为他们为自己筑墙，而不是桥梁。

✪ Love is an active power in man, a power which breaks through the walls which separate man from his fellow men, which unites him with others; love makes him overcome the sense of isolation and separateness, yet it permits to be himself, to retain his integrity.

爱是活跃于人心中的一种力量，冲破人与人之间的隔阂，使我们紧紧相连；爱使我们战胜孤独无助，却仍使我们保持自我个性的独立完整。

His life was really too hard, for the Fates seemed never smile to him.

他的一生真是太苦了，命运女神似乎从来不曾对他微笑过

画龙
点睛

The Life of Van Gogh

Almost every one knows the great painter Van Gogh's name, which not only represents a **pinnacle**① of human art, but also represents the difficulties and hardships of life.

His life was really too hard, for the Fates seemed never smile to him.

When he was very young, Van Gogh fell in love madly with his cousin much older than him. Although he was so spoony that he put his hands into the burning **furnace**② to express his love, his cousin still refused him.

Later, because of a minor joke, he cut off his right ear. This made all the townspeople think he wais mad, so when he was walking in the street, everyone **dodged**③ him, and urged the government to put him in the **asylum**④.

In fact, Van Gogh was a spirit of art as well as a strange genius, but in his short life, no matter how he worked his heart out, people didn't understand his **profoundness**⑤.

Because no one showed any interest in his paintings, Van Gogh not only led a most **tough**⑥ life, but also had a nervous breakdown because of the extreme loneliness. In desperation, he repeatedly chose to commit suicide. But he was even deprived of the right to end his own life, for he failed to kill himself. Finally, the painter had to consume away with grief.

But now, every one of his painting is **invaluable**⑦.

生词有约

① pinnacle

n. 顶峰；尖顶

② furnace

n. 熔炉；火炉

③ dodge

vt. 躲闪；回避

④ asylum

n. 避难所；精神病院

⑤ profoundness

n. 深刻；深奥

⑥ tough

adj. 艰苦的；难办的

⑦ invaluable

adj. 非常宝贵的；无价的

梵高的一生

几乎没有人不知道大画家梵高的名字，这个名字不仅代表着人类艺术的一个巅峰，也代表着艰难困苦的生命。

他的一生真是太苦了，命运女神似乎从来不曾对他微笑过。

年轻的时候，梵高疯狂地爱上了大他许多的表姐。尽管他痴情到了把手伸进熊熊燃烧的炉膛里宣誓的地步，但表姐还是拒绝了他。

后来，因为一个小小的玩笑，他竟然割下了自己的右耳朵。这使全镇人都认为他是疯子，走在大街上人人都躲避他，并曾强烈要求政府把他关进疯人院。

事实上，梵高是一个艺术精灵，是一个异类天才，只是在他短短的一生里，无论他如何呕心沥血，人们都不懂得他的深邃。

因为一直无人问津梵高的画作，所以他不仅生活极为艰难，还曾因极度孤独而一度精神崩溃。万般无奈之下，他多次选择自杀。但是，他连结束自己生命的权利都被剥夺了，每次自杀都未能致命。最后，绝望的画家不得不郁郁而终。

而现在，他的每幅画都价值连城。

诵读经典 >>>>>
Read classic

✪ In fact, Van Gogh was a spirit of art as well as a strange genius, but in his short life, no matter how he worked his heart out, people didn't understand his profoundness.

事实上，梵高是一个艺术的精灵，是一个异类的天才，只不过在他短短的一生里，无论他如何呕心沥血，人们都不懂得他的深邃而已。

✪ Because no one showed any interest in his paintings, Van Gogh not only led a most tough life, but also had a nervous breakdown because of the extreme loneliness.

因为一直无人问津其画作，梵高不仅生活极为艰难，还曾因极度孤独一度精神崩溃。

妙语连珠 >>>>>
Sparkling discourse

✪ The man with a new idea is a crank until the idea succeeds.

具有新想法的人在其想法被接受之前是怪人。

✪ The only man who is really free is the one who can turn down an invitation to dinner without giving any excuse.

唯一真正自由的人是能够拒绝宴会邀请而不用提出理由的人。

The Opportunity of a Boulder

In ancient times, a King had a **boulder**① placed on a roadway. Then he hid himself and watched to see if anyone would remove the huge rock.

Some of the king's wealthiest merchants and **courtiers**② came by and simply walked around it. Many loudly blamed the king for not keeping the roads clear, but none did anything about getting the stone out of the way.

Then a farmer came along carrying a load of vegetables. Upon approaching the boulder, the farmer laid down his burden and tried to move the stone to the side of the road. After much pushing and **straining**③, he finally succeeded. After the farmer picked up his load of vegetables, he noticed a purse lying in the road where the boulder had been.

The purse **contained**④ many gold coins and a note from the king indicating that the gold was for the person who removed the boulder from the roadway.

The farmer learned what many of us never understand. Every **obstacle**⑤ presents an opportunity to improve our condition.

生词有约

① boulder
n. 大圆石

② courier
n. 朝臣

③ strain
vi. 紧拉

④ contain
vt. 装有

⑤ obstacle
n. 障碍

巨石的机遇

古时候，一位国王把一块大石头放在路上，然后躲起来，看是否有人愿意搬开这块巨石。

国王的一些最富有的商人和朝臣路过时只是绕了过去。许多人大声谴责国王没有让路保持通畅，但没有人从路上搬开石头。

这时，一个农夫担着蔬菜走了过来。这个农夫走近巨石时，放下担子，设法把石头移到路边。好一番推拉之后，他终于成功了。农夫挑起蔬菜担子后，注意到巨石原来所在的地方有一个钱袋。

袋子里装有许多金币和国王写的一张纸条，上面写着金币是送给把石头从路上搬开的人。

这个农夫领悟到了我们许多人绝不会明白的道理。每个障碍都呈现出一种改善我们自身条件的机遇。

诵读经典 >>>>>
Read classic

The farmer learned what many of us never understand. Every obstacle presents an opportunity to improve our condition.

这个农夫领悟到了我们许多人绝不会明白的道理。每个障碍都呈现出一种改善我们自身条件的机遇。

妙语连珠 >>>>>
Sparkling discourse

★ Wherever valor true is found, true modesty will there abound.

真正的勇敢，无论到哪里都包含谦虚。

★ To a chain, the weakest part determines its hardness; to a barrel, the shortest part determines its capacity; to a man, the worst aspect determines his development.

一条锁链，最脆弱的一环决定其强度；一只木桶，最短的一片决定其容量；一个人，素质最差的一面决定其发展。

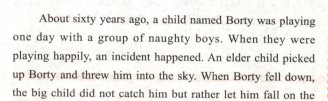

When they were playing happily, an incident happened.

当他们正玩得开心时，一个突发事件发生了。

画龙点睛

A Turning Point

About sixty years ago, a child named Borty was playing one day with a group of naughty boys. When they were playing happily, an incident happened. An elder child picked up Borty and threw him into the sky. When Borty fell down, the big child did not catch him but rather let him fall on the ground. As a result, Borty's leg broke.

He had to wear heavy **plaster**① while lying in bed for several months. The worst thing was that his leg bone did not **heal**②. It was a terrible thing to a little child. Little Borty screamed in pain and fear.

This was a tragedy, but now Borty had a new idea that he was now one of the most famous writers in the world. Maybe you are not familiar with the name of Borty, but when I mention the name Wells, you must know it. Maybe you have read some books of his. He wrote more than 75 books.

Wells thought that breaking his leg was a lucky thing for him. It made him stay at home for one year. In the year he read many books, because he had nothing to do except that. It made him very interested in literature. He became **enlightened**③ by these books. So his staying at home was a turning point for him. Later he became one of the writers in the world whose income were the highest.

生词有约

① plaster
n. 石膏

② heal
vi. 痊愈

③ enlighten
vt. 启发

转折点

大约 60 年前的一天，一个名叫宝迪的孩子正在和一群顽童玩耍。当他们正玩得开心时，一个突发事件发生了。一个大孩子抓起宝迪，抛到了空中。宝迪落下来时，这个大孩子没有接他，而是让他直接摔在了地上。结果，宝迪摔断了腿。

与 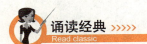 有关的日子　砥砺派

他不得不绑上了沉重的石膏，在床上躺了好几个月。最糟糕的是，他的腿骨没有康复。对小孩子来说，这是一件可怕的事儿。小宝迪常常在痛苦和恐惧中尖叫。

尽管这是一个悲剧，但如今宝迪有了新的想法，他现在是世界上最著名的作家之一。也许你不熟悉宝迪这个名字，但我提到韦尔斯，你一定知道。你可能已经读过他的一些书。他写过75本书之多。

韦尔斯认为摔断腿对他是一件幸运的事儿。这使他在屋里待了一年。在这一年里，他阅读了许多书，因为除此以外他无事可做。这使他对文学深感兴趣。他从这些书中得到了启迪。于是，待在家里成了他一生的转折点。后来，韦尔斯成了全世界收入最高的作家之一。

诵读经典 >>>>>
Read classic

Wells thought that breaking his leg was a lucky thing for him. It made him stay at home for one year. In the year he read many books, because he had nothing to do except that. It made him very interested in literature. He became enlightened by these books.

韦尔斯认为摔断腿对他是一件幸运的事儿。这使他在屋里待了一年。在这一年里，他阅读了许多书，因为除此以外他无事可做。这使他对文学深感兴趣。他从这些书中得到了启迪。

妙语连珠 >>>>>
Sparkling discourse

★ The throne is but a piece of wood covered with velvet.
皇帝的宝座不过是一块盖着天鹅绒的木头。

★ Politicians think of vote; statesmen think of the future of their country.
政客想的是选票，政治家想的是国家的前途。

When one block of prefabricated part weighing several tons was suspended on the roof, John felt relieved at last.

当一块重达数十吨的预制构件吊上楼顶时，约翰悬着的心也随之落地。

画龙
点睛

The First-Class Designer

On a coastal city of the United States rose another skyscraper, which was the designer Mr. John's top-notch work.

Tom was a high-school student. One day, he came to the building John designed and made a deep impression on the light and thin framework of the main building.

Back home, Tom searched for the material of this building from his computer. To his wonder, he suddenly found that the upwind side of the building was right on the edge of the triangle corner, but when the strong wind met the edge, it would **inevitably**① change the direction and rotate, and then the thin and weak wall was **precisely**② the largest zone of bearing the wind. He wrote a letter to Mr. John telling his discovery.

On receiving the letter, John used the computer to make a **pneumatic**③ **simulation**④ test. It turned out that Tom's **inference**⑤ was entirely correct.

John proved himself to be a first-class designer, for in the short term he actually found a solution. When one block of **prefabricated**⑥ part weighing several tons was suspended on the roof, John felt relieved at last. His unique approach not only avoided the danger of the building, but also turned over a new page in the **architectural**⑦ history of preventing and resisting the wind.

生词有约

① inevitably
adv. 不可避免地；必然地

② precisely
adv. 精确地；恰好

③ pneumatic
adj. 装满空气的；气动的

④ simulation
n. 模仿；模拟

⑤ inference
n. 推理；推断

⑥ prefabricated
adj. （建筑物、船等）预制构件的

⑦ architectural
adj. 有关建筑的；建筑学的

一流设计师

美国的一个海滨城市又一座摩天大楼拔地而起。这是设计师约翰先生的拔尖之作。

17

与 **青春** 有关的日子 *砥砺派*

汤姆是一名在校中学生。有一天，他来到约翰设计的大楼下，对主楼的轻薄构架留下了深刻印象。

一回家，汤姆就从电脑里调出了该楼的资料。让他惊叹的是，他突然发现，这幢大楼的迎风面正好落在三角形棱边上，但强风碰上棱边，势必会改变方向产生旋转，这时单薄的墙体正好是受力最大的区域。他把自己的发现写了一封信，寄给了约翰先生。

收到信后，约翰用电脑进行了风动模拟测试，结果汤姆的推测完全正确。

约翰不愧为一流设计师，短期内就找到了解决办法。当一块重达数十吨的预制构件吊上楼顶时，约翰悬着的心也随之落地。他的独到方法不仅避免了大楼的危险，而且翻开了建筑史上防风和抗风划时代的一页。

诵读经典 >>>>>
Read classic

To his wonder, he suddenly found that the upwind side of the building was right on the edge of the triangle corner, but when the strong wind met the edge, it would inevitably change the direction and rotate, and then the thin and weak wall was precisely the largest zone of bearing the wind.

让他惊叹的是，他突然发现，这幢大楼的迎风面正好落在三角形棱边上，但强风碰上棱边，势必会改变方向产生旋转，这时单薄的墙体正好是受力最大的区域。

妙语连珠 >>>>>
Sparkling discourse

❂ Kicks only raise dust and not crops from the earth.
踢脚只会扬起灰尘，却不能从泥土中得到收获。

❂ When a man is lost in a labyrinth, what he needs badly is a hint.
一个人迷失在迷宫时，他最需要的是提醒。

The God's Station

Over a hundred years ago, Wellington was a remote and desolate place in South Africa. As there were no roads, goods outside couldn't be transported here and it was also very difficult to ship out crops produced here.

In order to change such a bad situation, the government decided to build a railway here. But the biggest headache to the Railways Bureau was, a farm owner, who almost had all the ownership of land where the railway line **traversed**① Wellington, no matter what high price the government and the Railways Bureau offered, he doggedly insisted that he would definitely not transfer any inch of the land.

He said, "Now that the God asked my **ancestor**② to pass this land to me, absolutely there is no reason for me to sell any inch of the land here!"

The government and the Railways Bureau felt helpless because if the railway **bypassed**③ Wellington, it would make little sense to build this railway; if it passed through Wellington, maybe the high land price and the **uncompromising**④ farm owner would make all construction of the whole railway given up halfway.

Just when the government and the Railways Bureau lost their **bearings**⑤, the farm owner's teenage son came. He said, "Perhaps I could persuade my father."

He found his father with a group of people and asked him, "Why couldn't we sell a shade of the land?"

His father said, "This piece of land was handed down

生词有约

① traverse
vt. 越过；穿过

② ancestor
n. 祖先

③ bypass
vt. 绕过

④ uncompromising
adj. 不妥协的；不让步的

⑤ bearing
n. 方向；方位

from generation to generation. I think it might be God that enabled us to have this land. How dare we make it reduced even a tiny bit?"

The boy thought for a while and said, "Is our family born with these land?"

"No. It belongs to the God. He just temporarily left it to our management," said the father.

"Now the God would take some land back, but why do we refuse to sell?" the boy said.

His father **retorted**[6] at once, "But they are not the God. They are the government and the Railways Bureau."

⑥ retort
vt. 反驳

"But," said the boy, "according to the common prayer of the *Bible*, the will of God will be done on earth as it is in heaven."

After hearing this, everyone, including the boy's father, was stunned.

At last, the boy's father decisively agreed to transfer part of their land to the Railways Bureau for free. "My son made me understand all this is God's will," he said.

After the Wellington Railway Station was built up, it was called "The God's Station" by people. To pay **tribute**[7] to the boy, each train should stop a little passing here.

⑦ tribute
n. 敬意；称颂

上帝的车站

100 多年前，威灵顿是南非一个偏僻荒凉的地方。因为没有路，所以外面的货物运不到这里，这里出产的农作物也很难运出去。

为了改变这种糟糕状况，政府决定在此修一条铁路。但最让铁路局头疼的是，一位几乎拥有铁路线穿过威灵顿时全部土地所有权的农场主，无论政府和铁路局出多高的价格，他都固执坚持绝不出让一寸土地。

他说："上帝既然让祖先把这块地传给我，我就毫无出售这里每一寸土地的理由！"

政府和铁路局感到无奈，因为如果铁路绕过威灵顿，这条铁路修建就会没有多大意义；如果穿过威灵顿，也许高昂的地价和强硬的农场主会让整条铁路的修建半途而废。

就在政府和铁路局一筹莫展时，农场主十几岁的儿子来了。他说："也许我能说服父亲。"

他发现父亲跟一群人在一起，就问父亲："我们为什么不能出售一些土地呢？"

他的父亲说："这片土地是一代代传下来的。我想可能是上帝让我们拥有这片土地。我们怎敢让它丝毫减少呢？"

男孩想了一会儿，说："我们家生来就拥有这些土地吗？"

"不，这是上帝的土地。他只是暂时交给我们管理，"他的父亲说。

男孩说："现在上帝要收回一些土地，可我们为什么拒绝出售呢？"

他的父亲马上反驳说："可是，他们不是上帝。他们是政府和铁路局。"

"可是，"男孩说，"《圣经》的公祷文上说，上帝的旨意奉行在地上，就像奉行在天上。"

听了这话，包括男孩父亲在内的所有人都目瞪口呆。

最后，男孩的父亲果断同意无偿转让给铁路局一部分土地。他说："我的儿子使我明白，这一切都是上帝的旨意。"

威灵顿车站建成后，被人们称为"上帝的车站"，为了对那个男孩表示敬意，每列火车经过这里时都要停一小会儿。

诵读经典 >>>>>
Read classic

After the Wellington Railway Station was built up, it was called "The God's Station" by people. To pay tribute to the boy, each train should stop a little passing here.

威灵顿车站建成后，被人们称为"上帝的车站"，为了对那个男孩表示敬意，每列火车经过这里时都要停一小会儿。

妙语连珠 >>>>>
Sparkling discourse

✪ The pessimist complains about the wind; the optimist expects it to change; the realist adjusts the sails.

悲观者抱怨风向；乐观者盼望倒风；现实者调整风帆。

✪ What is memory? Not a storehouse, not a truck in the attic, but an instrument that constantly refines the past into a narrative, accessible and acceptable to oneself.

记忆是什么？它不是仓库，不是阁楼上的货车，而是一件乐器，不断将过去梳理叙述下来，让你自己接受和通过。

All Your Strength

A little boy was spending his Sunday afternoon playing in his sandbox. He had with him his box of cars and trucks, his plastic pail, and a shiny, red plastic shovel. In the process of creating roads and tunnels in the soft sand, he discovered a large rock in the middle of the sandbox.

The boy dug around the rock, managing to **dislodge**[①] it from the dirt. With no little bit of struggle, he pushed and nudged the rock across the sandbox by using his feet. He was a very small boy and the rock was very huge. When the boy got the rock to the edge of the sandbox, however, he found that he couldn't roll it up and over the little wall.

Determined[②], the little boy shoved, pushed, and **pried**[③], but every time he thought he had made some progress, the rock **tipped**[④] and then fell back into the sandbox. The little boy grunted, struggled, pushed, shoved—but his only reward was to have the rock roll back, cutting his **chubby**[⑤] fingers.

Finally, he burst into tears with **frustration**[⑥]. All this time the boy's father watched from his living room window as the drama unfolded. At the moment the tears coursed down, a large shadow fell across the boy and the sandbox. It was the boy's father.

Gently but firmly he said, "Son, why didn't you use all the strength that you had **available**[⑦]?"

Defeated, the boy sobbed back, "But I did, Daddy, I did! I used all the strength that I had!"

"No, son," corrected the father kindly, "You didn't use all the strength you had. You didn't ask me."

生词有约

① dislodge
vt. 取出

② determined
adj. 下定决心的

③ pry
vt. （用杠杆等）撬；撬起

④ tip
vi. 倾斜

⑤ chubby
adj. 圆胖的

⑥ frustration
n. 挫折；失败

⑦ available
adj. 可利用的

尽全力

星期六的早上，一个小男孩在玩沙箱。沙箱里有小汽车、卡车、塑料桶和又红又亮的塑料铲。他在柔软的沙子里铺路和开道时，发现沙箱中间有一块大石头。

小男孩在石头周围挖着，想设法把它从沙土中挖出来。他费了九牛二虎之力，脚蹬肘推想把石头移出沙箱。他人小力单，石头巨大。然而，等把石头移到沙箱边时，男孩发现他无法让石头向上越过那堵小墙。

小男孩下定决心，挤推铲撬，但每当他认为有些进展时，那块石头就侧翻着滚回沙箱。他吭吭哧哧，苦苦挣扎，又推又挤，但他得到的唯一回报就是石头又滚回沙箱，划破了胖乎乎的手指。

最后，他因沮丧而放声大哭。在此期间，男孩的父亲透过客厅的窗户注视着事情的进展。当男孩眼泪滚下来时，一个巨大的身影横过了小男孩和沙箱。是男孩的父亲。

他温和而坚定地说："儿子，你为什么不用全力呢？"

男孩像被打败似的，哭着回答说："可我尽全力了，爸爸，我尽全力了呀！我用上了所有的力量呀！"

"没有，儿子，"父亲亲切地纠正说，"你没有用上所有的力量。你没有请我哟。"

诵读经典 >>>>>
Read classic

The little boy grunted, struggled, pushed, shoved—but his only reward was to have the rock roll back, cutting his chubby fingers.

他吭吭哧哧，苦苦挣扎，又推又挤，但他得到的唯一回报就是石头又滚回沙箱，划破了胖乎乎的手指。

妙语连珠 >>>>>
Sparkling discourse

⭐ Nothing great was ever achieved without enthusiasm.

缺乏热情是完成不了伟业的。

⭐ In science the credit goes to the man who convinces the world, not to the man to whom the idea first occurs.

在科学上，功劳归于使全世界信服的人，而不归于首先有这种想法的人。

The Secret of Wealth

Ayer lived a rich life, so his friends wanted to know the secret of his wealth.

One day, Ayer would go to the market to handle affairs, when one of his friends happened to go the same way. So they went along.

It was terribly sultry. When they went halfway, they were so tired and thirsty that they stopped and sat down under a big tree by the roadside. Ayer took out two bowls from his **backpack** [1], placed before them, then untied the water bag and filled the bowls with water.

They carried the bowls and were about to drink off when a gust of wind suddenly blew, making them not open their eyes. After the wind stopped, his friend found a lot of sand dropped in his bowl, even with some leaves on it. The friend frowned, poured away the water in the bowl without hesitation, picked up Ayer's water bag **conveniently** [2], poured himself another bowl and drank off without a break. When he put down his bowl, he found Ayer's bowl was also muddy, but Ayer only carefully picked up the fallen leaves, threw them off and put the bowl on the ground.

After a while, the water was gradually clean and clear, when Ayer carried the bowl and drank slowly.

His friend laughed at his **misery** [3], for he even regarded a bowl of water as a treasure. After hearing that, Ayer said with a smile, "Each bowl of water is drawn by me from the well, which I took pains to dig. How can't I regard it as a treasure?"

生词有约

① backpack
n. （指登山者、步行者使用的）背包

② conveniently
adv. 方便地；便利地

③ misery
n. 不幸；穷困

When sand and leaves dropped into a bowl, what Ayer's saw was still the water, but what his friend was nothing but the sand and leaves. Maybe it was the secret of Ayer's wealth.

致富的秘诀

阿耶尔生活富裕，朋友们很想知道他致富的秘诀。

有一天，阿耶尔要到集市上办事，他的一位朋友正好同路。于是，俩人结伴而行。

天气非常闷热。走到一半，俩人又累又渴，就停下脚步，在路边的一棵大树下坐了下来。阿耶尔从随身携带的背囊里取出两只碗，摆放在两人面前，然后解下水囊，向碗里倒满了水。

他们端起碗，刚要一饮而尽，突然刮来一阵风，吹得人睁不开眼。风停后，朋友发现碗里落了不少沙子，水面上还多了几片树叶。朋友皱了皱眉，没多想就把碗里的水倒了，顺手拿起阿耶尔的水囊，给自己重新倒了一碗，一口气就喝干了。等他放下手中的碗时，发现阿耶尔的碗里也是一片浑浊，但阿耶尔只是小心地将碗里的落叶拈起扔掉，再把碗放到地上。

过了一会儿，水渐渐澄清了，阿耶尔这才端起碗，慢慢地喝了起来。

朋友笑阿耶尔吝啬，连一碗水都当成宝贝。阿耶尔听完，微微一笑说："每碗水都是我从井里打上来的，而井又是我辛辛苦苦亲手挖的。我怎么能不把它当成宝贝呢？"

一碗水落进沙子和树叶，阿耶尔的眼里看到的还是水，而朋友的眼里看到的却只是沙子和树叶，这可能就是阿耶尔致富的秘诀。

 **诵读经典** >>>>>
Read classic

They carried the bowls and were about to drink off when a gust of wind suddenly blew, making them not open their eyes. After the wind stopped, his friend found a lot of sand dropped in his bowl, even with some leaves on it.

他们端起碗，刚要一饮而尽，突然刮来一阵风，吹得人睁不开眼。风停后，朋友发现碗里落了不少沙子，水面上还多了几片树叶。

 **妙语连珠** >>>>>
Sparkling discourse

❂ The highest possible stage in moral culture is when we recognize that we ought to control thoughts.

道德修养有可能达到的最高境界是认识到我们应该控制自己的思想。

★ Errors, like straws, upon the surface flow; he who would search for pearls must dive below.

错误就像浮在水面的稻草；要想寻找珍珠，就得潜到下面。

The Grandfather's Diaries

Two Mexicans went along the Mississippi River for panning. When they came to a mouth of the river, they parted because one thought he could pan more gold in the Arkansas River and the other thought he would have a greater chance in the Ohio River.

Ten years later, the man who went to the Ohio River really made a fortune. There he not only found a lot of gold sand but also built the docks and roads while he made the place where he stayed a large market town. Now the business **prosperity**[①] and industrial development of Pittsburgh along the Ohio River are thanks to all his pioneering and early development.

The man who went to the Arkansas River seemed not to be so lucky, for there was no news about him since they parted. Some said he had **gone to Davy Jones' locker**[②] and some said he had returned to Mexico. Until 50 years later a **nugget**[③] of 2.7 kilograms caused a stir in Pittsburgh, so people had come to know about him. At that time, a reporter of *Pittsburgh Newsweek* wrote, "The largest nugget in U.S.A. came from Arkansas. A young man in the fish pound behind his house picked it up. From the diaries his grandfather left, this nugget was thrown into the pound by his grandfather."

Afterwards, the *Newsweek* published the grandfather's diaries, one of which wrote: Yesterday, I again found a piece of gold in the stream, greater than the piece of gold panned last year. Will I go into the city to sell it? Then there will be hundreds of people swarming here. The log shed my wife and

生词有约

① prosperity
n. 繁荣；兴旺；成功

② go to Davy Jones' locker
葬身鱼腹

③ nugget
n.（天然）块金；块

27

I built with our own hands, the garden and the pond behind the house we opened up sweating all over, along with the campfire at nightfall, the loyal hound, the delicious **stewed** ④ meat, the **chickadees** ⑤, the trees, the sky, the grassland as well as the precious peace and freedom will no longer exist. I would rather see the spray when it is thrown into the pound than just sit watching all these disappear from my eyes.

④ stew
vt. 炖；煨
⑤ chickadee
n.（美洲所产的）山雀

The 1760s were the age that the United States began to create millionaires, so everyone was in a **frenzied** ⑥ pursuit of money. But this gold miner threw away the panned gold. A lot of people thought it an **incredible** ⑦ story. Until now some people still doubt its authenticity. However, I always believe it is true because in my mind this gold miner was a real one who panned the gold.

⑥ frenzied
adj. 慌乱的；狂热的
⑦ incredible
adj. 不可思议的；难以置信的

祖父的日记

　　两个墨西哥人沿密西西比河淘金，走到一个河汊各奔东西，因为一个人认为阿肯色河能淘到更多金子，另一个人认为去俄亥俄河发财的机会更大。

　　10 年后，入俄亥俄河的人果然发了财，他在那里不仅找到了大量金沙，而且建了码头，修了公路，还使他落脚的地方成了一个大集镇。现在俄亥俄河岸边的匹兹堡市商业繁荣，工业发达，起因都与他的拓荒和早期开发有关。

　　进入阿肯色河的人似乎没有那么幸运，分手后就没了音讯。有的说已经葬身鱼腹，有的说已经回了墨西哥。直到 50 年后，一个重 2.7 公斤的自然金块在匹兹堡引起轰动，人们才知道他的一些情况。当时，《匹兹堡新闻周刊》的一位记者写道："这颗全美最大的金块来源于阿肯色，是一位年轻人在他屋后的鱼塘里捡到的，从他祖父留下的日记看，这块金子是他的祖父扔进去的。"

　　随后，《新闻周刊》刊登了那位祖父的日记。其中一篇是这样的：昨天，我在溪水里又发现了一块金子，比去年淘到的那块更大，进城卖掉它吗？那就会有成百上千的人涌向这里，我和妻子亲手用一根根圆木搭建的棚屋，挥汗开垦的菜园和屋后的池塘，还有傍晚的火堆、忠诚的猎狗、美味的炖肉、山雀、树木、天空、草原、大自然赠给我们的珍贵的静谧和自由都将不复存在。我宁愿看到它被扔进鱼塘时荡起的水花，也不愿眼睁睁地望着这一切从我眼前消失。

　　18 世纪 60 年代正是美国开始创造百万富翁的年代，每个人都在疯狂地追求金钱。但是，这位淘金者却把淘到的金子扔掉了，许多人认为这是天方夜谭，直到现在还有人怀疑它的真实性。而我始终认为它是真的，因为在我的心中，这位淘金者是一位真正淘到金子的人。

诵读经典 >>>>>
Read classic

The largest nugget in U.S.A. came from Arkansas. A young man in the fish pound behind his house picked it up. From the diaries his grandfather left, this nugget was thrown into the pound by his grandfather.

这颗全美最大的金块来源于阿肯色，是一位年轻人在他屋后的鱼塘里捡到的，从他祖父留下的日记看，这块金子是他的祖父扔进去的。

妙语连珠 >>>>>
Sparkling discourse

❍ No man is useless in this world who lightens the burden of someone else.

在这个世界上能为别人减轻负担的人都是有用的。

❍ The profoundest thought or passion sleeps as in a mine until an equal mind and heart finds and publishes it.

最深的思想或感情就如同深睡的矿藏，在等待着同样深沉的头脑与心灵去发现和开采。

God told him with a smile, "In fact, you've almost succeeded. You only need a final leap."

上帝微笑着对他说："其实，你已经快成功了，只需最后一跃。"

画龙点睛

The Ticket for Success

A knowledgeable man met the god. He asked God angrily, "I am erudite. Why don't you give me an opportunity to come to fame?"

God answered helplessly, "You're erudite, but you just tried everything a little, not deep enough, so how can you come to fame?"

Having heard this, the man started practising the piano hard. Afterwards, he had played the piano very well, but he still didn't become famous.

He went to ask God again, "My God! I have mastered the piano, but why don't you give me any chance to win a name yet?"

God shook his head and said, "It's not that I wouldn't like to offer you any chance but you can't grasp the chance. For the first time, I helped you in secret take part in the piano contest, but you lacked **confidence**①; for the second time, you lacked courage. How can you blame me?"

After hearing God's words, the man trained hard for more years. He built up his self-confidence and **mustered up**② the nerve to **participate in**③ the competition. He played extremely well, but due to the **referee**④'s injustice, the chance of fame was seized by the other.

Downhearted⑤, the man said to God, "God, I've tried my best this time. It seems doomed that I won't be able to rise to fame."

God told him with a smile, "In fact, you've almost succeeded. You only need a final leap."

"A final leap?" His eyes opened wide.

生词有约

① confidence
n. 信心

② muster up
振作；召集

③ participate in
参加；分担

④ referee
n. 裁判员；公断人

⑤ downhearted
adj. 沮丧的；灰心丧气的

30

God nodded and said, "You've got the ticket for success—**frustration** [6]. Now you've got it, the success will be a gift that **setbacks** [7] will give to you."

This time, that man bore in mind God's words. As expected, he succeeded.

[6] frustration

n. 挫折；失意

[7] setback

n. 阻碍；挫折

成功的入场券

一个博学的人遇见上帝，生气地问上帝："我是个博学的人，为什么你不给我成名的机会呢？"

上帝无奈地回答："你虽然博学，但样样都只尝试了一点，不够深入，用什么去成名呢？"

听后，那个人开始苦练钢琴，后来虽弹得一手好琴，但还是没有出名。

他又去问上帝："上帝啊！我已经精通了钢琴，为什么您还不给我机会让我出名呢？"

上帝摇摇头说："并不是我不给你机会，而是你抓不住机会。第一次我暗中帮助你去参加钢琴比赛，你缺乏信心，第二次缺乏勇气，又怎么能怪我呢？"

听完上帝的话，那个人又苦练数年，建立了自信，鼓足勇气去参加比赛。他弹得非常出色，却因裁判不公而被别人夺去了成名的机会。

那个人心灰意冷地对上帝说："上帝，这一次我已经尽力了，看来上天注定，我不会出名了。"

上帝微笑着对他说："其实，你已经快成功了，只需最后一跃。"

"最后一跃？"他瞪大了双眼。

上帝点点头说："你已经得到了成功的入场券——挫折。现在你得到了它，成功便成为挫折给你的礼物。"

这次，那个人牢记住了上帝的话，果然取得了成功。

诵读经典 »»»»
Read classic

After hearing God's words, the man trained hard for more years. He built up his self-confidence and mustered up the nerve to participate in the competition. He played extremely well, but due to the referee's injustice, the chance of fame was seized by the other.

听完上帝的话，那个人又苦练数年，建立了自信，鼓足勇气去参加比赛。他弹得非常出色，却因裁判不公而被别人夺去了成名的机会。

妙语连珠 >>>>>
Sparkling discourse

❂ Have an aim in life, or your energies will all be wasted.

人生要有目标，否则你的精力会白白浪费。

❂ Don't believe that winning is really everything. It's more important to stand for something. If you don't stand for something, what do you win?

不要相信取胜真的就是一切，更重要的是要有信念。如果你没有信念，你又能赢什么呢？

A Shortcut to Success

A Swedish rich family gave birth to a daughter in 1858.

However, it was not long before the girl had an **indecipherable**① **paralysis**② and was unable to walk.

Once, the girl went to take a boat trip with her families. The captain's wife told the child that the captain had a bird of paradise. The girl was so **fascinated**③ by the description of the bird that she longed to have a look at it herself. So the nurse made the girl stay on the deck and went to look for the captain herself. The girl was impatient to wait and asked a waiter on board to take her to see the bird. The waiter didn't know that she couldn't walk and only took into consideration taking her to see the beautiful bird. A **miracle**④ happened: the child seized the waiter's hand and walked slowly because of her **excessive**⑤ desire. The girl recovered from her illness from then on. After she grew up, she devoted herself to the creation of literature and became the first woman who won the Nobel Prize for literature finally. That was Selma Lagerlof.

Ecstasy⑥ is a shortcut to success and only in this condition can people surpass their **constraint**⑦ to release the greatest energy.

生词有约

① indecipherable
adj. 破译不出的；难辨认的

② paralysis
n. 瘫痪；中风

③ fascinated
adj. 着迷的；极度迷人的

④ miracle
n. 奇迹

⑤ excessive
adj. 过度的；过多的

⑥ ecstasy
n. 狂喜；出神；忘形

⑦ constraint
n. 强制；约束

成功的捷径

1858年，瑞典的一户富豪人家生下了一个女儿。

然而，不久，孩子染患了一种无法解释的瘫痪症，丧失了走路的能力。

有一次，女孩和家人一起乘船旅行。船长的太太给孩子讲船长有一只天堂鸟。女孩被这

只鸟的描述迷住了，很想亲自看看。于是，保姆把孩子留在甲板上，自己去找船长。孩子耐不住性子等待，要求船上的服务生立刻带她去看天堂鸟。服务生并不知道她的腿不能走路，只顾带着她一道去看那只美丽的小鸟。奇迹发生了，孩子因为过度渴望，竟拉住服务生的手，慢慢地走了起来。从此，孩子的病便痊愈了。女孩子长大后，又忘我地投入到文学创作中，最后成为第一位荣获诺贝尔文学奖的女性，也就是塞尔玛·拉格洛夫。

忘我是走向成功的一条捷径，只有在这种环境中，人才会超越自身的束缚，释放出最大的能量。

 诵读经典 >>>>>
Read classic

The girl was impatient to wait and asked a waiter on board to take her to see the bird. The waiter didn't know that she couldn't walk and only took into consideration taking her to see the beautiful bird. A miracle happened: the child seized the waiter's hand and walked slowly because of her excessive desire.

孩子耐不住性子等待，要求船上的服务生立刻带她去看天堂鸟。服务生并不知道她的腿不能走路，只顾带着她一道去看那只美丽的小鸟。奇迹发生了，孩子因为过度渴望，竟拉住服务生的手，慢慢地走了起来。

妙语连珠 >>>>>
Sparkling discourse

✪ The challenge of life is to overcome.
人生的挑战就是征服。

✪ The aim of life is to develop oneself and realize one's nature perfectly.
生活的目标就是不断发展自我，并彻底认清自我。

Dare to Show

On the course, the first step of the lead is likely to mean the final victory, so the success and failure, or gain and loss of your life may lie in whether you dare to show yourself.

As a student, I was most afraid to answer questions in class, and I found that the students around were just like me. At the beginning of each class, when the professor asked a question, I always lowered my head, for fear that the professor saw me.

In a foreign language class, an expert from the Commercial Bank **delivered**① a lecture. The speaker always wanted someone to be in concert with him, so he asked how many students in the classroom learned Economics, but no one responded. The expert said with a wry smile, "Let me tell you a story first.

"When I came to the United States to study, there are often lectures delivered in the university. Each time they invite an **executive**② from Wall Street or a **transnational company**③ to make a speech.

"Before the beginning of every lecture, I found an interesting **phenomenon**④. The students around me always took a cardboard folded in half, wrote their names in bold with the most eye-catching color, and then placed on the seat. So when the speakers need the response, he could see and call listener's name directly.

"I couldn't understand, so I asked the student in front of me. He told me with a smile, the speakers are all **top-**

生词有约

① deliver
vt. 发表；传送

② executive
n. 主管；总经理
③ transnational
company
跨国公司
④ phenomenon
n. 现象；事件

ranking [5] people, who mean opportunity. When your answer is to his satisfaction or surprised, it is very likely that presupposes he will give you more opportunities. This is a very simple reason.

⑤ top-ranking
adj. 一流的

"The fact was also like that. I really saw a few students around me went to serve in the first-class company because of the excellent **insights** [6]. This thing had a great impact on me. The chance will not find you **automatically** [7]. You must show yourself constantly to attract others' attention for you to find a chance on the cards."

⑥ insight
n. 眼光；洞察力

⑦ automatically
adv. 自动地；不自觉地

敢于亮剑

跑道上第一步的领先很可能意味着最终的胜利，所以决定你一生中的成败得失，或许在于你是否敢亮出你自己。

作为学生，我最害怕在课堂上回答问题，而且我发现周围的同学也和我一样。每次上课时，当教授提问时，我总是习惯把头低下去，生怕教授的眼光扫到自己。

一次外语课上，一位来自商业银行的专家讲演。做讲演的人总是希望有人配合自己。于是，他问道，教室内有多少学经济的同学。可是，没有一个人响应。专家苦笑了一下说："我先给你们讲个故事。

"我刚到美国读书时，大学里经常有讲座，每次都是请华尔街或跨国公司的高级管理人员来讲演。

"每次开讲前，我发现一个有趣的现象，我周围的同学总是拿一张硬纸，中间对折一下，用极其醒目的颜色的笔大大地用粗体写上自己的名字，然后放在座位上。于是，讲演者需要听者响应时，就可以直接看名字叫人。

"我不解，便问前面的同学。他笑着告诉我，讲演人都是一流人物，他们就意味着机会。当你的回答让他满意或吃惊时，很有可能就预示着他会给你提供更多机会。这是一个简单道理。

"事实也是这样，我确实看到我周围的几个同学因出色的见解而到一流公司供职。这件事对我影响很大。机会不会自动找到你；你必须不断亮出自己，吸引别人关注，才有可能找到机会。"

诵读经典 >>>>>
Read classic

I really saw a few students around me went to serve in the first-class company because of the excellent insights. This thing had a great impact on me. The chance will not find you automatically. You must show yourself constantly to attract others' attention for you to find a chance on the cards.

我确实看到我周围的几个同学因出色的见解而到一流公司供职。这件事对我影响很大。机会不会自动找到你；你必须不断亮出自己，吸引别人关注，才有可能找到机会。

妙语连珠 >>>>>
Sparkling discourse

✪　A book is like a portable garden.
一本书就像一座随身携带的花园。

✪　A home without books is like a kitchen without food.
没有书的家就像没有食物的厨房。

I'll Fly to My Beloved

Once upon a time, there was a bird in a cage who sang for her merchant owner. He took delight in her song day and night, and was so fond of her that he served her water in a golden dish. Before he left for a business trip, he asked the bird if she had a wish, "I will go through the forest where you were born, past the birds of your old neighborhood. What message should I take for them?"

The bird said, "Tell them I sit full of sorrow in a cage singing my **captive**① song. Day and night, my heart is full of **grief**②. I hope it will not be long before I see my friends again and fly freely. Bring me a message from the lovely forest. I long for my beloved, to fly with him, and spread my wings."

The merchant traveled on his donkey through the forest. He listened to the **melodies**③ of many birds. When the merchant reached the forest where his bird came from, he stopped, pushed his **hood**④ back, and said, "Oh you birds! Greetings to you all from my pretty bird in her cage. She sends her love to you. She asks for a reply that will **ease**⑤ her heart. She wants to join her beloved and sing her songs through the air with a free heart, but I would miss her beautiful songs and cannot let her go."

All the birds listened to the merchant's words. Suddenly one bird shrieked and fell to the ground. The merchant froze to the spot where he stood. Nothing could shock him more than this did. One bird had fallen down dead!

The merchant wend on his way to the city and traded his goods. At last he returned to his home. He did not know

生词有约

① captive

adj. 被束缚的；被俘获的

② grief

n. 悲痛；伤心事；忧愁

③ melody

n. 悦耳的音调；美妙的音乐；旋律

④ hood

n. 头巾；兜帽

⑤ ease

vt. 减轻；和缓

what to tell his bird. He stood before her cage and said, "Oh, nothing to speak of."

"No, no," the bird cried, "I must know at once."

"I do not know what happened," said the merchant. "I told them your message. Then, one of them fell down dead."

Suddenly the merchant's bird let out a terrible shriek and fell on her head to the bottom of the cage. The merchant was horrified. "Oh, what have I done?" He cried, "Now my life means nothing."

He opened the cage door, reached in, and cupped took her in his hands gently and carefully. "I will have to bury her now," he said, "the poor thing is dead."

The moment he lifted the bird out of the cage, she **flapped**⑥ up, flew out of the window and landed on the nearest roof. She turned to him and said gratefully, "Thank you for **delivering**⑦ my plea. I fly to my beloved who waits for me. To my beloved I'll fly. Goodbye, my master."

"My bird was wise. She taught me secret of life," the merchant reflected.

⑥ flap
vi. 鼓翼而飞
⑦ deliver
vt. 递送

我要飞向我的爱

从前有一只笼中鸟，总是为从商的主人歌唱。商人整天以她的歌声为乐，是那样喜爱她，居然用一只金碟为她盛水喝。他外出经商前，问鸟儿有没有心愿："我要穿越你出生的那片森林，路过你以前居住地的那些鸟儿。我该为他们带去什么口信呢？"

鸟儿说："告诉他们，我卧在笼子里，充满忧伤，唱着囚歌。我的心整天充满愁伤。我希望再见到朋友们、自由飞翔的日子不会太久。从那片可爱的森林给我带个口信。我渴望见到心上人，同他一起展翅飞翔。"

商人骑驴穿越森林，倾听鸟儿们优美的歌声。商人走到那只鸟生长的树林时，停下来，把风帽推到脑后，说："噢，你们这些鸟儿！我那只漂亮的笼中鸟向你们问好，把爱送给你们。她请求答复来会安抚她的心灵。她想和心上人在一起，自由自在把歌声送入云霄，但我常常想念她美妙的歌声，所以不能放她走。"

所有的鸟儿都在倾听商人说的话。突然，一只鸟尖叫一声，落在了地上。商人僵立在原地。再没有什么能比这更让他震惊的了。一只鸟落地而亡！

商人继续赶路，到城里卖掉了货物，最后回到了家里。他不知道该告诉鸟儿什么。他立在鸟笼前说："噢，没什么可说的。"

"不，不，"鸟儿大声说道，"我必须马上知道。"

"我不知道发生了什么事儿，"商人说。"我把你的口信告诉了他们。接着，其中一只鸟就落地而亡了。"

突然，商人的鸟儿发出一声可怕的尖叫，一头栽落在笼底。商人大惊失色。"噢，我都做了些什么啊？"他哭道，"现在我的生活毫无意义。"

他打开笼门，伸进手，轻轻地、小心地把她捧在手里。"我现在不得不把她埋葬，"他说，"这个可怜的东西死了。"

就在他把鸟儿捧出笼子的那个时刻，她振翅而起，飞出窗外，落在了最近的屋顶上。她转向他，感激地说："谢谢你送去了我的请求。我要飞向我的爱。再见，主人。"

"我的鸟儿非常聪明。是她教给了我人生的秘诀，"商人细想道。

诵读经典 >>>>>
Read classic

All the birds listened to the merchant's words. Suddenly one bird shrieked and fell to the ground. The merchant froze to the spot where he stood. Nothing could shock him more than this did. One bird had fallen down dead!

所有的鸟儿都在倾听商人说的话。突然，一只鸟尖叫一声，落在了地上。商人僵立在原地。再没有什么能比这更让他震惊的了。一只鸟落地而亡！

妙语连珠 >>>>>
Sparkling discourse

✪ Make your life a mission, not an intermission.

让你的生命成为使命，而不是一次停顿。

✪ Life is so brief and time is fleeting. Grasp it and it will be an opportunity; depict it and it will be a rainbow.

生命如此短暂，光阴飞逝如箭。抓住它，它就是机会；描绘它，它就是彩虹。

> I opened her door, and the moonlight from the window spilled over her sleeping form. In her hand I could see the remains of a crumpled paper. Slowly, I opened her palm to see what the item of our disagreement had been.
>
> 我打开她的门，窗外的月光洒在她熟睡的身上。我可以看到她手里还剩有一张揉皱的纸片。我慢慢地掰开她的手掌，想看看我们的分歧到底是什么。

The Most Important Part

"Mommy, look!" cried my daughter, Darla, pointing to a hawk soaring through the air.

"Uh, huh," I murmured, driving, lost in thought about the tight schedule of my day.

Disappointment filled her face. "What's the matter, sweetheart?" I asked.

"Nothing," my seven-year-old said. The moment was gone. Near home, we slowed to search for the **albino**① deer that came out from behind the thick mass of trees in the early evening. She was nowhere to be seen.

Dinner, baths and phone calls filled the hours until bedtime.

"Come on, Darla, time for bed!" She raced past me up the stairs. Tired, I kissed her on the cheek, said prayers and **tucked**② her in.

"Mom, I forgot to give you something!" she said.

My patience was gone. "Give it to me in the morning," I said, but she shook her head.

"You won't have time in the morning!" she **retorted**③.

"I'll take time," I answered. Sometimes no matter how hard I tried, time flowed through my fingers like sand in an hourglass, never enough. Not enough for her, for my husband, and definitely not enough for me.

She wasn't ready to give up yet. She wrinkled her little

生词有约

① albino
n. 白化病患者

② tuck
vt. 塞；使隐藏

③ retort
v. 反驳；反击

nose in anger and tossed away her **chestnut**④ brown hair.

"No, you won't! It will be just like today when I told you to look at the hawk. You didn't even listen to what I said."

I was too tired to argue. "Good night!" I shut her door with a resounding **thud**⑤.

My husband asked, "Why so **glum**⑥?" I told him.

"Maybe she's not asleep yet. Why don't you check?" he said.

I opened her door, and the moonlight from the window spilled over her sleeping form. In her hand I could see the remains of a **crumpled**⑦ paper. Slowly, I opened her palm to see what the item of our disagreement had been.

Tears filled my eyes. She had torn into small pieces a big red heart with a poem she had written, "Why I Love My Mother?"

I carefully removed the pieces. Once the puzzle was put back into place, I read what she had written:

"Why I Love My Mother? Although you're busy, and you work so hard, you always take time to play with me. I love you Mommy, because I am the biggest part of your busy day!"

The words were an arrow straight to the heart.

Ten minutes later I carried a tray to her room, with two cups of hot chocolate and two peanut butter and jelly sandwiches. When I softly touched her smooth cheek, I could feel my heart filled with love.

She woke from the sleep. "What is that for?" she asked.

"This is for you, because you are the most important part of my busy day!"

She cracked a sweet smile.

④ chestnut
adj. 栗子色的；红棕色的；褐色的

⑤ thud
n. 砰击声；重击

⑥ glum
adj. 闷闷不乐的；愁眉不展的

⑦ crumpled
adj. 摺皱的；弄皱的

最重要的部分

"妈咪，快看！"女儿达拉指着一只空中翱翔的鹰喊道。

"嗯，呃，"我一边开车，一边咕哝道，沉思着排得紧紧的日程。

她一脸失望。"怎么了，宝贝？"我问。

"没什么，" 7 岁的女儿说。那个时刻转瞬即逝。快到家，我们放慢速度寻找那只患白化病的鹿。傍晚时分，它会从茂密的树丛后面走出来。哪儿也不见它的踪影。

晚饭、沐浴和电话占满了就寝前的所有时间。

"快点，达拉，该睡觉了！"她跑过我，上了楼梯。我疲惫不堪，吻了吻她的脸颊，祈祷，给她掖好被子。

"妈妈，我忘记给你一件东西！"她说。

我没有了耐心。"明天早上给我吧，"我说，但她摇了摇头。

"明天早上你不会有时间的！"她反驳道。

"我会抽时间的，"我回答说。有时无论我如何努力，时间还是像沙漏中的沙粒一样从指间流过，总是不够用。不够陪她，不够陪丈夫，当然对我也不够。

她还不准备放弃，气呼呼地皱起小鼻子，把红棕色的头发甩到了一边。

"不，你不会！就像今天我让你看那只鹰时一样。你就连我说什么都不听。"

我太累了，不想辩解。"晚安！"我砰的一声关上她的房门。

我的丈夫问道："为什么闷闷不乐？"我告诉了他。

"可能她还没睡着。你为什么不去看看呢？"他说。

我打开她的门，窗外的月光洒在她熟睡的身上。我可以看到她手里还剩有一张揉皱的纸片。我慢慢地掰开她的手掌，想看看我们的分歧到底是什么。

泪水溢满了我的眼眶。她撕成碎片的原是一颗大大的红心，上面是她写的一首诗："为什么我爱我的妈妈？"

我仔细移动那些纸片。纸片一拼回原样，我就读出了她写的那首诗：

"为什么我爱我的妈妈？尽管你很忙，工作很辛苦，但你总是抽时间陪我玩。我爱你妈咪，因为我是忙忙碌碌一天中最重要的部分！"

这些话像箭一样直射我心。

10 分钟后，我端着一只托盘来到她的房间，托盘上放着两杯热巧克力饮料和两块花生酱果冻三明治。我温柔地抚摸着她光洁的脸蛋，能感觉到自己心里充满了浓浓爱意。

她从睡梦中醒来。"这是干什么？"她问。

"这是送给你的，因为你是我忙忙碌碌一天中最重要的部分！"

她露出了甜蜜的微笑。

诵读经典 >>>>>
Read classic

Ten minutes later I carried a tray to her room, with two cups of hot chocolate and two peanut butter and jelly sandwiches. When I softly touched her smooth cheek, I could feel my heart filled with love.

10 分钟后，我端着一只托盘来到她的房间，托盘上放着两杯热巧克力饮料和两块花生酱果冻三明治。我温柔地抚摸着她光洁的脸蛋，能感觉到自己心里充满了浓浓爱意。

妙语连珠 >>>>>
Sparkling discourse

✪　If you have a garden and a library, you have everything you need.

拥有一座花园和一座图书馆，你就拥有了所需的一切。

✪　A book is a miracle where the author's soul is hidden. Open the book and release this soul and it will talk with you mysteriously.

书是一种奇迹，那里藏着作者的灵魂。打开书把这个灵魂释放出来，它就会神秘地同我交谈。

He asked the wise man, "How can I become a person who can make myself and others happy?"

他问智者："我怎么才能成为一个既让自己愉快，也让别人愉快的人呢？"

画龙点睛

The Youngster and the Wise Man

A youngster went to visit an old wise man.

He asked the wise man, "How can I become a person who can make myself and others happy?"

The wise man looked at him and said, "My son, you're one in a thousand to have such an **aspiration**① at this age. I give you four sentences. The first sentence is to regard you as others. Can you explain its meaning?"

The youngster replied, "That is to say, when I feel **distressed**②, regard myself as others, so that I will reduce the distress naturally; when I'm ecstatic, regard myself as others, the ecstasy will become **placid**③."

The wise man nodded slightly and went on, "The second is to regard others as you."

The youngster thought for a while and said, "In this way you may truly **sympathize with**④ others' misfortune, understand the others' **requirements**⑤ and give them proper help when they need."

The wise man's eyes glowing, he continued, "The third is to regard others as others."

The boy said, "It means is that we should fully respect each person's independence and can never **infringe**⑥ their core territory in any case."

The wise man laughed, "Very well. The fourth is to regard you as yourself. It is too hard for you to understand, so keep it for you to taste it slowly in future."

The youngster said, "What can I use to unify them?"

生词有约

① aspiration
n. 渴望；抱负

② distressed
adj. 痛苦的；忧虑的

③ placid
adj. 平静的；沉着的

④ sympathize with
同情

⑤ requirement
n. 要求

⑥ infringe
vt. 侵犯；违反；破坏

The wise man said, "Very simple, with your life and experiences."

少年与智者

一位少年去拜访一位年长的智者。

他问智者："我怎么才能成为一个既让自己愉快，也让别人愉快的人呢？"

智者看着他说："孩子，在你这个年龄有这样的愿望，已经很难得了。我送你四句话。第一句话是，把自己当成别人。你能说说这句话的含义吗？"

少年回答说："也就是说，在我感到痛苦时，就把自己当成别人，这样痛苦就自然减轻了；当我欣喜若狂时，把自己当成别人，那种狂喜也会变得平和。"

智者微微点头，接着说："第二句话，把别人当成自己。"

少年沉思一会儿，说："这样就可以真正同情别人的不幸，理解别人的需求，在别人需要时给予恰当的帮助。"

智者两眼发光，继续说道："第三句话，把别人当成别人。"

少年说："这句话是说，要充分尊重每个人的独立性，在任何情况下都不可侵犯他人的核心领地。"

智者哈哈大笑说："很好。第四句话是，把自己当成自己。这句话理解起来太难了，留着你以后慢慢品味吧。"

少年说："我用什么才能把它们统一起来呢？"

智者说："很简单，用一生的时间和经历。"

诵读经典 >>>>>
Read classic

The youngster replied, "That is to say, when I feel distressed, regard myself as others, so that I will reduce the distress naturally; when I'm ecstatic, regard myself as others, the ecstasy will become placid."

少年回答说："也就是说，在我感到痛苦时，就把自己当成别人，这样痛苦就自然减轻了；当我欣喜若狂时，把自己当成别人，那种狂喜也会变得平和。"

妙语连珠 >>>>>
Sparkling discourse

❂ Excellent books, like a wise and good elder, support me to move forward step by step and gradually know the world.

优秀的书籍像一个智慧善良的长者搀扶着我，使我一步步向前走，并逐渐懂得了世界。

★ Books are the nutrient of the whole world. A life without books is like a life without sunlight; wisdom without books is like a wingless bird.

书籍是全世界的营养品。生活里没有书籍，就像没有阳光；智慧里没有书籍，就像小鸟没有翅膀。

画龙
点睛

The Lit Light

Some of my sisters work in Australia. On a **reservation**①, among the **Aborigines**②, there was an elderly man. I can assure you that you have never seen a situation as difficult as that poor old man's. He was completely **ignored**③ by everyone. His home was **disordered**④ and dirty.

I told him, "Please let me clean your house, wash your clothes, and make your bed."

He answered, "I'm okay like this. Let it be."

I said again, "You will be still better if you allow me to do it."

He finally agreed. So I was able to clean his house and wash his clothes. I discovered a beautiful lamp, covered with dust. Only God knows how many years had passed since he last lit it.

I asked him, "Don't you light your lamp? Don't you ever use it?"

He answered, "No. Nobody comes to see me. I have no need to light it. Who would I light it for?"

I asked, "Would you light it every night if my sisters came?"

He replied, "Of course."

From that day on my sisters **committed themselves to**⑤ visiting him every evening. We cleaned the lamp and my sisters would light it every evening.

Two years passed. I had completely forgotten that man. He sent this message: "Tell my friend that the light she lit in my life continues to shine still."

I thought it was a very small thing. We often **neglect**⑥ the small things.

生词有约

① reservation

n. （美）保留地；居留地；专用地；禁猎地

② aborigines

n. 土著；原居民；澳大利亚土著居民

③ ignore

vt. 不理睬；忽视

④ disordered

adj. 混乱的

⑤ commit oneself to 专心致志于；致力于

⑥ neglect

vt. 忽视；疏忽；漏做

点亮那盏灯

我的几个姊妹在澳洲工作。在一片保留地上的土著居民中有一位上了年纪的人。我可以向你保证，你从未见过有比这个可怜老人处境更艰难的人。大家都对也完全熟视无睹。他的家又乱又脏。

我告诉他说："请让我帮你打扫房子、洗衣服、铺床吧。"

他应道："我这样很好。随它去吧。"

我又说道："如果你允许我这么做，你会觉得更好。"

他最终表示同意。于是，我才能帮他收拾房子、洗衣服。我发现一盏漂亮的灯，上面积满了灰尘。只有上帝晓得他最后一次点着是多少年前的事儿。

我问他："你不点这盏灯吗？你从没用过它吗？"

他回答说："没有。谁也不来看我。我没必要点亮它。我为谁点亮它呢？"

我问："如果我的姊妹们来，你愿意每天夜里点亮它吗？"

他答道："当然愿意。"

从那天起，我的姊妹们一心一意每天晚上都来看望他。我们把灯擦净，姊妹们每天晚上都把它点亮。

两年过去了。我已经完全忘记了那个人。他捎口信说："告诉我的朋友，她在我生命中点亮的那盏灯仍在继续闪耀。"

我原以为这是一件区区小事。我们常常会忽视那些小事。

诵读经典 >>>>>
Read classic

I discovered a beautiful lamp, covered with dust. Only God knows how many years had passed since he last lit it.

我发现一盏漂亮的灯，上面积满了灰尘。只有上帝晓得他最后一次点着是多少年前的事儿。

妙语连珠 >>>>>
Sparkling discourse

✪ Life is just a bowl of cherries.
生活就是一碗樱桃。

✪ The secret of living is to find the pivot of a concept on which you can make your stand.
生活的秘诀在于找到一个能够支撑你的思想支点。

She scattered some of the most common seeds and took good care of them. A year later, when the marigold bloomed, she chose one faintest from those golden and brown flowers and made it wither naturally in order to get the best seed.

她撒下了一些最普通的种子，精心侍弄。一年后，金盏花开了，她从那些金色的、棕色的花中挑选了一朵颜色最淡的，任其自然枯萎，以取得最好的种子。

画龙点睛

The Miracle of Marigold

One year, a newspaper of the United States published an announcement the horticultural institute offered a reward at a high price for the pure white **marigold**①. The high reward attracted so many people, but in the **kaleidoscopic**② nature, besides golden, the marigold is brown, but it is not easy to cultivate the white one. So after they were excited for a time, many people had forgotten the announcement.

20 years flew away.

One normal day after 20 years, the horticultural institute that had published the announcement accidentally received a zealous letter and 100 seeds of pure white marigold. On that day the news spread like wildfire.

It turned out to be an old woman of over 70 years old. The institute had always been hesitating over the fact that the letter asserted with certainty that the seeds could bloom pure white marigold, and the need for **verification**③ became the focus of the debate. Whether they would make an experimental verification became the focus of **controversy**④ at one time.

Some said you would never live up to the old man's wish. Those seeds finally took root in the earth. The miracle appeared after one year: large patches of pure white marigold swayed in the breeze.

Accordingly, the old woman who was always unknown to the public became a new focus.

生词有约

① marigold
n. 金盏草；万寿菊
② kaleidoscopic
adj. 千变万化的；五花八门的

③ verification
n. 验证；证实
④ controversy
n. 争论；论战；争吵

Originally, the old woman was an out-and-out flower-lover. When she occasionally read the announcement 20 years ago, her heart kept thumping. But her eight children **unanimously**⑤ opposed her decision. After all, a woman who never knew the seed **genetics**⑥ couldn't complete what the experts could never accomplish, so her thought was only a lunatic **raving**⑦!

Still, the old woman didn't change her mind and went on working without hesitation. She scattered some of the most common seeds and took good care of them. A year later, when the marigold bloomed, she chose one faintest from those golden and brown flowers and made it wither naturally in order to get the best seed. The next year, she again grew them and chose the faintest from these flowers to plant...day after day, year after year, through many cycles of spring sowing and autumn harvest, the old woman's husband died, her children flew far and high, a lot of things happened in her life, but only the desire to grow the pure white marigold took root in her heart.

Finally, after 20 years on the day we all know, in the garden she saw a marigold, which was not nearly white, but as white as silver or snow.

A problem even experts couldn't cope with was readily solved by an old woman who didn't understand genetics. Was it a miracle?

To take root in the heart, even the most common seed can grow into a miracle!

⑤ unanimously

adv. 全体一致地；无异议地

⑥ genetics

n. 遗传学

⑦ raving

n. （常用复数）语无伦次；胡说

金盏花的奇迹

当年，美国一家报纸曾刊登了一则园艺所重金悬赏征求纯白金盏花的启事。高额赏金让许多人趋之若鹜，但在千姿百态的自然界中，金盏花除了金色的，就是棕色的，能培植出白色的不是一件易事。所以，激动了一阵后，许多人就把那则启事抛到了九霄云外。

20 年飞快地过去了。

20 年后一个平常的日子，当年那家曾刊登启事的园艺所意外地收到了一封热情的应征信和100粒"纯白金盏花"的种子。当天,这件事就不胫而走。

寄种子的原来是一位年已古稀的老人。对信中言之凿凿能开出纯白金盏花的种子,园艺所一直举棋不定,该不该验证一时成了争论的焦点。

有人说:绝不应该辜负了一位老人的心意。那些种子终于落土生根。奇迹是在一年之后才出现的,大片大片纯白色的金盏花在微风中摇曳。

一直默默无闻的老人因此成了新的焦点。

原来,老人是一个地地道道的爱花人。她20年前偶然看到那则启事后,便怦然心动。她的决定却遭到了8个儿女的一致反对。毕竟,一个压根就不懂种子遗传学的人,一件让专家都不能完成的事儿,她的想法岂不是痴人说梦!

老人还是痴心不改,义无反顾地干了下去。她撒下了一些最普通的种子,精心侍弄。一年后,金盏花开了,她从那些金色的、棕色的花中挑选了一朵颜色最淡的,任其自然枯萎,以取得最好的种子。第二年,她又把它们种下去,然后再从这些花中挑选出颜色最淡的花的种子栽种……日复一日,年复一年,春种秋收,周而复始,老人的丈夫去世了,儿女远去,生活中发生了许多事儿,但唯有种出白色金盏花的愿望在她的心中生了根。

终于,在我们今天都知道的那个20年后的一天,她在那片花园中看到一朵金盏花,它不是近乎白色,而是如银似雪的白。

一个连专家都解决不了的问题,在一个不懂遗传学的老人手中迎刃而解。这是奇迹吗?

种在心里,即使一粒最普通的种子,也能长出奇迹!

诵读经典 >>>>>
Read classic

❂ Day after day, year after year, through many cycles of spring sowing and autumn harvest, the old woman's husband died, her children flew far and high, a lot of things happened in her life, but only the desire to grow the pure white marigold took root in her heart.

日复一日,年复一年,春种秋收,周而复始,老人的丈夫去世了,儿女远去,生活中发生了许多事儿,但唯有种出白色金盏花的愿望在她的心中生了根。

❂ A problem even experts couldn't cope with was readily solved by an old woman who didn't understand genetics.

一个连专家都解决不了的问题,在一个不懂遗传学的老人手中迎刃而解。

妙语连珠 >>>>>
Sparkling discourse

✪ Man is a reed that is the most fragile in nature, but he is a thinking reed.
人是自然界中最脆弱的一棵芦苇，但却是一棵会思考的芦苇。

✪ The orbit of life is unforeknowable, so no one can finish his autobiography in advance.
人生的轨道无法预知，谁也不能事先写好自传。

The Goal of the Mind

It was an unforgettable night. The noisy Mexico City gradually calmed down. The main **stadium**① of Olympic track and field competition was **enveloped**② in the darkness.

After he finished making the scenes the marathon winners received the trophies and marked the victory, Greenspan, the world famous newsreel producer, found the stadium empty. It was time for him to return to the hotel for a rest. He was about to leave when he suddenly saw a bandaged man with his right leg stained with the blood ran into the stadium. This man ran lamely out of breath, but he didn't stop. After he ran along the runway for a circle and got to the goal, he **collapsed**③ on the ground.

Greenspan guessed this was a marathon athlete. Out of curiosity, he went over to ask why the athlete wanted to run to the goal with such a difficulty.

The young man called Kowari from Tanzania replied gently, "That my country sent me here from more than 20,000 kilometers is not let me get off the mark in the competition, but makes me complete the game. I want to run to the goal, though I have fallen behind all other runners, but I have a **sacred**④ goal like them: I will run to the goal. Though the audience won't cheer me any more, my motherland is watching me from behind..."

Tears welled up in Greenspan's eyes. Soon, he spread the

生词有约

① stadium
n. 露天大型运动场

② envelop
vt. 包围；围绕；掩盖

③ collapse
vi. 衰竭；衰弱；突然体力不支

④ sacred
adj. 庄严的；神圣的

most touching scene in the history of the Olympic Games to every corner of the world.

Life should have a dream of reaching the peak, yet we should understand not everybody has the ability to do it. The most important is not whether we can reach the peak but whether we have made the greatest efforts—to reach the goal in the mind is a success.

心灵的目标

那是一个难忘的夜晚，喧嚣的墨西哥城终于渐渐安静下来，奥运会田径比赛的主体育场被笼罩在夜色之中。

世界著名的纪录片制作人格林斯潘将当天马拉松比赛优胜者们领取奖杯、庆祝胜利的镜头制作完毕，才发现体育场内已空无一人，自己该回宾馆休息了。他刚要离开体育场，突然看到一个右腿沾满血污、绑着绷带的人跑进了体育场。这个人一瘸一拐地跑着，气喘吁吁，却没有停下来。他顺着跑道跑了一圈，抵达终点后，一下子瘫倒在地。

格林斯潘猜想，这是一名马拉松运动员。在好奇心的驱使下，他走了过去，询问这名运动员为什么要这么吃力地跑到终点。

这位来自坦桑尼亚、名叫埃克瓦里的年轻人轻声回答说："我的国家从两万多公里外送我来这里，不是叫我在这场比赛中起跑，而是派我来完成这场比赛的。我要跑向终点，尽管我已经落在奔跑队伍的最后面，但我有着和他们一样神圣的目标：我要跑到终点，尽管已经不再有观众为我加油，但我身后有祖国的凝望……"

格林斯潘泪如泉涌。很快，他就用镜头将奥运史上这最动人的一幕传递到世界上的每个角落。

人生应该拥有登临峰顶的梦想，但更应该懂得不是每个人都有攀抵峰顶的能力。最重要的不是能否到达峰顶，而是是否尽到了最大努力——抵达心灵中的目标，便是一种成功。

诵读经典 >>>>>
Read classic

✪ He was about to leave when he suddenly saw a bandaged man with his right leg stained with the blood ran into the stadium.

他刚要离开体育场，突然看到一个右腿沾满血污、绑着绷带的人跑进了体育场。

✪ Life should have a dream of reaching the peak, yet we should understand not everybody has the ability to do it. The most important is not whether we can reach the peak but whether we have made the greatest efforts—to reach the goal in the mind is a success.

人生应该拥有登临峰顶的梦想，但更应该懂得不是每个人都有攀抵峰顶的能力。最重要的不是能否到达峰顶，而是是否尽到了最大努力——抵达心灵中的目标，便是一种成功。

妙语连珠 >>>>>
Sparkling discourse

★ Even though one string is broken, the other three will play on. This is life.

即使断了一根弦，其余的三根弦还是要继续演奏。这就是人生。

★ Life is a grindstone. It depends us whether it grinds us down or polishes us up.

生活就是磨刀石。我们是被磨碎还是被磨亮，取决于我们自己。

When he was about to enter the shop, he saw a girl crying on the road. The gentleman walked to the little girl and asked her, "Little girl, why are you crying?"

绅士正要走进店门时，发现有个小女孩坐在路上哭，绅士走到小女孩面前问："孩子，为什么坐在这里哭？"

A Rose for Her Mother

A gentleman stopped his car at the door of a flower shop. He wanted to order a **bunch**① of flowers and asked them to **deliver**② them to his mother who was far in his hometown. When he was about to enter the shop, he saw a girl crying on the road. The gentleman walked to the little girl and asked her, "Little girl, why are you crying?"

"I want to buy a rose for my mother, but I haven't enough money," said the girl.

Hearing that, the gentleman felt sympathetic to the girl. "It was so..." Then he grasped the girl's hand and entered the flower shop. He first ordered the **bouquet**③ for his mother and bought a rose for the girl. Walking out of the shop, the gentleman **proposed**④ driving the girl home.

"Would you really drive me home?"

"Of course!"

"Then drive me to my mother. But uncle, the place where my mother lives is very far from here."

Following the way the girl showed, the gentleman drove out of the urban district along the **winding**⑤ mountain road and finally came to the cemetery.

The little girl put the flower close to a new grave. In order to present a rose to her mother who just passed away a month ago, she took a long journey.

The gentleman drove the girl to her home, returned to the flower shop. He **cancelled**⑥ the bouquet that would be mailed

生词有约

① bunch
n. 群；串

② deliver
vt. 交付；递送

③ bouquet
n. 花束

④ propose
vt. 提议；建议

⑤ winding
adj. 弯曲的；蜿蜒的

⑥ cancel
vt. 取消

to his mother but bought a big bunch of fresh flowers instead. He directly drove to his mother's home, five-hour drive from here. He would send the flowers to his mother in person.

献给母亲的玫瑰

　　一位绅士在花店门口停下车，打算向花店订一束花，请他们给远在故乡的母亲送去。绅士正要走进店门时，发现有个小女孩坐在路上哭，就走到她面前问："孩子，为什么坐在这里哭？"

　　"我想买一朵玫瑰花送给妈妈，可我的钱不够。"孩子说。

　　绅士听了，感到心疼。"这样啊……"于是，绅士牵着小女孩的手走进花店，先订了要送给母亲的花束，然后给小女孩买了一朵玫瑰花。走出花店时，绅士向小女孩提议，要开车送她回家。

　　"真的要送我回家吗？"

　　"当然啊！"

　　"那你送我去妈妈那里好了。可是，叔叔，我妈妈住的地方离这里很远。"

　　绅士照小女孩说的一直开了过去，没想到走出市区大马路后，随着蜿蜒山路前行，竟然来到了墓园。

　　小女孩把花放在一座新坟旁边。她为了给一个月前刚过世的母亲，献上一朵玫瑰花，而走了一大段远路。

　　绅士将小女孩送回了家中，然后再次返回了花店。他取消了要寄给母亲的花束，而是改买了一大束鲜花，直奔离这里有5小时车程的母亲家里，他要亲自将花献给妈妈。

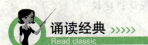

诵读经典 >>>>>
Read classic

The gentleman drove the girl to her home, returned to the flower shop. He cancelled the bouquet that would be mailed to his mother but bought a big bunch of fresh flowers instead. He directly drove to his mother's home, five-hour drive from here. He would send the flowers to his mother in person.

　　绅士将小女孩送回了家中，然后再次返回了花店。他取消了要寄给母亲的花束，而是改买了一大束鲜花，直奔离这里有5小时车程的母亲家里，他要亲自将花献给妈妈。

妙语连珠 >>>>>
Sparkling discourse

★ Often success is depended on whether you can get up the courage to fight fear.

成功常常取决于你是否能鼓足勇气去战胜恐惧。

★ The sudden disappointment of a hope leaves a scar which the ultimate fulfillment of that hope never entirely removes.

一个希望的突然失落会留下一处伤痕，即使那希望最终会实现，也决不能完全平复。

Hearing this, the little girl said unhappily, "What you carry is a weight, but what I carry is not a weight, he is my little brother."

小女孩听了很不高兴地说："你背的是一个重量，但我背的不是一个重量，他是我的弟弟。"

画龙
点睛

Love Has No Weight

A Hindu walked to the **sacred**[①] shrine in the Himalayas for **pilgrimage**[②]. The journey was long and the mountain road was hard to walk. So though he carried little baggage, he still walked hard. Just ahead of him, he saw a little girl, less than 10 years old, carrying a **chubby**[③] boy on her back and also moving on slowly. She **panted**[④] heavily and kept sweating, but her hands still firmly protected the boy on her back.

When passing by the little girl, the Hindu said to her **sympathetically**[⑤], "My girl, you must be very tired because what you carry is so heavy!" Hearing this, the little girl said unhappily, "What you carry is a weight, but what I carry is not a weight, he is my little brother."

It is true, on the scale, whether it is a brother or a burden, there is no difference, for it will show the actual weight, but for a heart, what the little girl said is right: what she carried was her little brother, not a weight, for the burden was the weight. She loved her little brother from the heart.

Love has no weight, so love is not a burden but the happy **solicitude**[⑥] and selfless devotion.

生词有约

① sacred
adj. 神圣的；庄严的

② pilgrimage
n. 朝圣之行

③ chubby
adj. 圆胖的；丰满的

④ pant
vi. 喘息；气喘

⑤ sympathetically
adv. 怜悯地；同情地

⑥ solicitude
n. 关怀；热心

爱没有重量

一位印度教徒步行到喜马拉雅山的圣庙去朝圣。路途遥远，山路难行，他虽然携带很少的行李，但沿途走来，还是显得举步维艰。就在他前方，他看到一个小女孩，年纪不会超过10岁，背着一个胖嘟嘟的小孩，也正缓慢地向前移动。她气喘得很厉害，也一直在流汗，可她的双手还是紧紧呵护着背上的小孩。

印度教徒经过小女孩身边，很同情地对她说："我的孩子，你一定很疲倦，你背得那么重！"小女孩听了很不高兴地说："你背的是一个重量，但我背的不是一个重量，他是我的弟弟。"

没错，在磅秤上，无论是弟弟还是包袱，都没有差别，都会显示出实际的重量，但就心而言，那小女孩说的一点没错，她背的是弟弟，不是一个重量，包袱才是一个重量。她对弟弟是发自内心的爱。

爱没有重量，不是负担，而是一种喜悦的关怀与无私的付出。

诵读经典 >>>>>
Read classic

The journey was long and the mountain road was hard to walk. So though he carried little baggage, he still walked hard. Just ahead of him, he saw a little girl, less than 10 years old, carrying a chubby boy on her back and also moving on slowly.

路途遥远，山路难行，他虽然携带很少的行李，但沿途走来，还是显得举步维艰。就在他前方，他看到一个小女孩，年纪不会超过 10 岁，背着一个胖嘟嘟的小孩，也正缓慢地向前移动。

妙语连珠 >>>>>
Sparkling discourse

★ Wherever valour true is found, true modesty will there abound.
真正的勇敢，都包含真正的谦虚。

★ To sensible men, every day is a day of reckoning.
对聪明人来说，每一天的时间都精打细算。

The Most Important Is the Shoulders

My mother used to ask me what the most important part of the body was. Through the years I would take a guess at what I thought was the correct answer.

When I was younger, I thought sound was very important to us as humans, so I said, "My ears, Mommy." She said, "No. Many people are deaf. But you keep thinking about it and I will ask you again soon."

Several years passed before she asked me again. Since making my first attempt, I had **contemplated**① the correct answer. So this time I told her, "Mommy, sight is very important to everybody, so it must be our eyes."

She looked at me and told me, "You are learning fast, but the answer is not correct because there are many people who are blind."

Stumped② again, I continued my quest for knowledge and over the years, Mother asked me a couple more times and always her answer was, "No, but you are getting smarter every year, my child."

Then last year, my grandpa died. Everybody was hurt. Everybody was crying. Even my father cried. My mom looked at me when it was our turn to say our final goodbye to Grandpa. She asked me, "Do you know what the most important part of the body is, my dear?"

I was shocked when she asked me this now. I always thought this was a game between her and me. She saw the **confusion**③ on my face and told me, "This question is very

生词有约

① contemplate
vt. 深思

② stump
vt. 难住

③ confusion
n. 混淆；混乱；困惑

important. It shows that you have really lived your life. For every part of the body you gave me in the past, I have told you were wrong and I have given you an example why. But today is the day you need to learn this important lesson."

She looked down at me as only a mother can. I saw her eyes well up with tears. She said, "My dear, the most important part of the body is your shoulder."

I asked, "Is it because it holds up your head?" She replied, "No, it is because it can hold the head of a friend or loved one when they cry. Everybody needs a shoulder to cry on sometimes in life, my dear. I only hope you have enough love and friends you will have a shoulder to cry on when you need it."

最重要的部分是肩膀

母亲过去常问我什么是身体最重要的部分。这些年来，我总猜测着自己认为正确的答案。

我还比较小的时候，我认为声音对我们人非常重要，于是就说："是我的耳朵，妈妈。"她说："不。好多人都是聋子。但你要继续想，我很快就会再问你的。"

几年过去了，她才又问我。因为我做过一次尝试，所以我已经苦思冥想到了正确答案。于是，这次我对她说："妈妈，视力对每个人都很重要，所以一定是我们的眼睛。"

她望着我，对我说："你学得很快，但答案不对，因为有好多人都是瞎子。"

又被难倒后，我继续求知。光阴荏苒，妈妈又问过几次，而她的回答总是："不，但你一年比一年聪明了，我的孩子。"

接着到了去年，爷爷去世了。每个人都很伤心。每个人都在哭泣。甚至父亲也失声痛哭。当轮到我们向爷爷诀别时，妈妈望着我，问道："你知道身体最重要的部分是什么了吗，我的宝贝？"

她现在问我这个问题，我大吃一惊。我总认为这是我和她之间的一个游戏。她看到我脸上的困惑表情，对我说道："这个问题非常重要。它表明你曾真正生活过。过去你对我提到的身体的每个部分，我都曾告诉你是错的，并给你举例说明那是为什么，但今天你需要学习这重要的一课。"

她低头看着我，只有母亲才能这样。我看到她的眼里涌起了泪水。她说："我的宝贝，身体最重要的部分是你的肩膀。"

我问："是因为它支撑着你的头吗？"她回答说："不，是因为它能支撑一位哭泣时的朋友或你爱的人的头。每个人在生命中的某个时候都需要靠着一个肩膀哭泣，我的宝贝。我只希望你有足够的爱和朋友，能在你需要时有一个肩膀哭泣。"

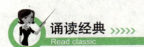

诵读经典 >>>>>
Read classic

She looked down at me as only a mother ca*n*. I saw her eyes well up with tears. She said, "My dear, the most important part of the body is your shoulder."

她低头看着我，只有母亲才能这样。我看到她的眼里涌起了泪水。她说："我的宝贝，身体最重要的部分是你的肩膀。"

妙语连珠 >>>>>
Sparkling discourse

✪　The only limit to our realization of tomorrow will be our doubts of today.

实现明天理想的唯一障碍是今天的疑虑。

✪　We must accept finite disappointment, but we must never lose infinite hope.

我们必须接受失望，因为它是有限的，但千万不可失去希望，因为它是无限的。

The Olive of Life

19 years ago, Iacocca finally became general manager of Ford Company on his own efforts. On July 13, 1978, a little **bloated**①, Iacocca was fired by the big boss Henry Ford. In Ford, Iacocca had worked for 32 years, in which he served as general manager for eight years, but now he was unemployed suddenly. He ate his heart, started drinking, lost confidence in himself, thinking that he would **collapse**② thoroughly.

At this time, Iacocca accepted a new challenge—to apply for general manager of Chrysler close to **bankruptcy**③. With his wisdom, **audacity**④ and charm, Iacocca **drastically**⑤ reorganized and reformed Chrysler and turned to the government for help, argued heated against the congressmen, made a huge loan and revived the enterprise. Under the leadership of Iacocca, Chrysler produced the plan of K-model cars. This plan revived Chrysler successfully, becoming third largest motor company after General Motors and Ford Motor Company.

On July 13, 1983, Iacocca delivered the bank **representative**⑥ an 813-million-dollar check, which he had never seen all his life. Till then, Chrysler paid off all debts. It was on the very day five years ago that Henry Ford fired him.

Afterwards, Iacocca said with a deep feeling, "**Strive**⑦ forward, even if you have a bad time; never despair, even if the sky falls and the earth cracks."

Roman Roland said, "Pain, like a plough, breaks your heart and opens the headspring of life." Pain is like a green

生词有约

① bloated
adj. 傲慢的

② collapse
vi. 倒塌；崩溃

③ bankruptcy
n. 破产

④ audacity
n. 大胆；厚颜

⑤ drastically
adv. 彻底地；激烈地

⑥ representative
n. 代表

⑦ strive
vi. 努力；奋斗；力争

olive; you won't know its sweet taste till you taste it, which
needs courage!

人生的橄榄

19 年前，艾柯卡靠自己的奋斗终于当上了福特公司的总经理。1978 年 7 月 13 日，有点得意忘形的艾柯卡被大老板亨利·福特开除了。在福特工作已 32 年，当了 8 年总经理，艾柯卡突然失业了。他痛不欲生，开始喝酒，对自己失去了信心，认为自己要彻底崩溃了。

就在这时，艾柯卡接受了一个新挑战——应聘到濒临破产的克莱斯勒汽车公司出任总经理。凭着智慧、胆识和魅力，艾柯卡大刀阔斧地对克莱斯勒进了整顿、改革，并向政府求援，舌战国会议员，取得了巨额贷款，重振企业雄风。在艾柯卡的领导下，克莱斯勒公司在最黑暗的日子里推出了 K 型车计划。这个计划的成功令克莱斯勒起死回生，成为仅次于通用汽车公司、福特汽车公司的第三大汽车公司。

1983 年 7 月 13 日，艾柯卡把生平仅见的面额高达 8.13 亿美元的支票交到银行代表手里。至此，克莱斯勒还清了所有债务，而恰恰是 5 年前的这一天亨利·福特开除了他。

事后，艾柯卡深有感触地说："奋力向前，哪怕时运不济；永不绝望，哪怕天崩地裂。"

罗曼·罗兰说："痛苦像一把犁，它一面犁破了你的心，一面掘开了生命的新起源。"痛苦就像一枚青橄榄，品尝后才知其甘甜，这品尝需要勇气！

诵读经典 >>>>>
Read classic

Roman Roland said, "Pain, like a plough, breaks your heart and opens the headspring of life." Pain is like a green olive; you won't know its sweet taste till you taste it, which needs courage!

罗曼·罗兰说："痛苦像一把犁，它一面犁破了你的心，一面掘开了生命的新起源。"痛苦就像一枚青橄榄，品尝后才知其甘甜，这品尝需要勇气！

妙语连珠 >>>>>
Sparkling discourse

✪ Happiness lies not in the mere possession of money; it lies in the joy of achievement, in the thrill of creative effort.

幸福不在于拥有金钱，而在于获得成就时的喜悦以及产生创造力的激情。

✪ Fear not that thy life shall come to an end, but rather fear that it shall never have a beginning.

不要害怕你的生活将要结束，而要担心它永远不会真正开始。

Indeed, when the unemployment swept the country and the people have no way for living, who would not be touched under such care?

确实，在失业席卷全国、人人生计无着无落之际，能得到如此照顾，谁会不感动呢？

画龙点睛

Love and Wisdom

At the beginning of 1933, Harrison Textile Company suffered a crowning **calamity**①—the plant, equipments, stocks and so on turned to ashes.

More than 3,000 employees were **dumbstruck**② in the face of the unexpected disaster. Dejected, they returned home, desperately waiting for the chairman to declare the **bankruptcy**③ and unemployment. But to their surprise, after long waiting, the board posted each person such a letter: pay one month's salary to all the employees of the company.

A month later, when all of them sank in **distress**④ for the life of future, the board's letter came again: pay one month's salary to all the staff of the company.

If the first letter surprised and delighted thousands of employees, this second letter almost moved them to tears. Indeed, when the unemployment swept the country and the people had no way for living, who would not be touched under such care?

Just as the chairman expected, on the day of receiving the second letter, thousands of employees rushed to the company, cleaned up the ruins, tidied up the situation after fire and some of them even took the **initiative**⑤ to contact the interrupted supply of goods.

Three months later, the new Harrison Company sprang up once again.

Today, Harrison Company has become the largest American textile company, whose **subsidiaries**⑥ spread all over 50 countries.

生词有约

① calamity
n. 灾祸；不幸

② dumbstruck
adj. 被吓得目瞪口呆的；吓得发懵的

③ bankruptcy
n. 破产；彻底失败

④ distress
n. 悲痛；忧伤；危难

⑤ initiative
n. 主动性；倡议

⑥ subsidiary
n. 附属物；附属机构；子公司

67

爱与智慧

1933 年初，哈里逊纺织公司遭遇了一场灭顶之灾——大火把厂房、设备、存货等一切都化为灰烬。

3 千余名员工在突如其来的灾难面前目瞪口呆，他们一个个垂头丧气地回到家中，绝望地等待着董事长宣布破产和失业。但让他们意外的是，经过漫长的等待，董事会居然给每个人寄来了一封这样的信：向全公司所有员工继续支付一个月薪水。

一个月后，正当大家再次为以后的生活陷入忧愁时，董事会的信又来了：向全公司所有员工再支付一个月薪水。

如果说接到第一封信让几千名员工感觉意外和惊喜的话，那么这第二封信简直让他们热泪盈眶。确实，在失业席卷全国、人人生计无着无落之际，能得到如此照顾，谁会不感动呢？

结果正如董事长期望的那样，上千名员工在收到第二封信的当天，便纷纷涌向公司，积极清理起废墟，收拾残局，还有人主动联络中断的货源。

3 个月后，新的哈里逊公司重新出现。

如今，哈里逊公司已经成了全美国最大的纺织品公司，分公司遍布 50 个国家。

诵读经典 >>>>>
Read classic

✪ Dejected, they returned home, desperately waiting for the chairman to declare the bankruptcy and unemployment.

他们一个个垂头丧气地回到家中，绝望地等待着董事长宣布破产和失业。

妙语连珠 >>>>>
Sparkling discourse

✪ Great men are rarely isolated mountain-peaks; they are summits of ranges.

伟人很少是突兀的山峰；它们是众山中的最高峰。

✪ A man can succeed at almost anything for which he has unlimited enthusiasm.

只要有无限的热情，一个人几乎就可以在任何事情上取得成功。

A Young Flower in the Desert

There was a young flower in the desert. She was growing by itself enjoying every day and saying to the sun, "When shall I be grown up?"

生词有约

And the sun would say, "Be **patient**① —each time I touch you, you grow a little."

① patient
adj. 有耐心的；能容忍的

She was so pleased because she would have a chance to bring beauty to this corner of sand...And this is all she wanted to do—bring a little bit of beauty to this world.

One day the hunter came by and stepped on her. She was going to die—and she felt so sad. Not because she was dying but because she would not have a chance to bring a little bit of beauty to this corner of the desert.

The Great **Spirit**② saw her, and was listening. Indeed, he said. She should be living...And he reached down and touched her—and gave her life.

② spirit
n. 小精灵；天使

And she grew up to be a beautiful flower. And this corner of the desert became so beautiful because of her.

沙漠之花

沙漠里有一朵小花。她独自生长在那里，享受着每一天，对太阳说道：“我什么时候才能长大？”

太阳总会说：“要耐心。我每次抚摸你，你都会长大一点。”

她非常开心，因为她也有机会为沙漠的这个角落带来美丽……而且这是她唯一想做的事情——为这个世界带来一点美丽。

有一天，一位猎人经过，正好踩在她身上。她快要死了，感到格外伤心。并不是因为她即将死去，而是因为她再也没有机会为沙漠的这个角落带来一点美丽了。

伟大的精灵看到了她，并听到了她的心声。事实上，他说了出来。她应该活着。于是，他俯下身，抚摸着她，给了她生命。

后来，她长成了一朵漂亮的花朵。沙漠的这个角落因她而变得十分美丽。

诵读经典 >>>>>
Read classic

✪　She was growing by itself enjoying every day and saying to the sun, "When shall I be grown up?"

她独自生长在那里，享受着每一天，对太阳说道："我什么时候才能长大？"

✪　Not because she was dying but because she would not have a chance to bring a little bit of beauty to this corner of the desert.

并不是因为她即将死去，而是因为她再也没有机会为沙漠的这个角落带来一点美丽了。

妙语连珠 >>>>>
Sparkling discourse

✪　A happy marriage is the union of two good forgivers.
幸福婚姻是两个宽容者的结合。

✪　Marriage is not a commercial treaty but a free link of two souls.
婚姻不是商业契约，而是心灵的自由结合。

"Sometimes, a hug is all we need. A Free hug is to reach out and hug a stranger to brighten up their lives," said the young man.

有时，我们需要的只是一个拥抱。免费拥抱就是伸出双臂，拥抱陌生人，照亮他们的人生，"年轻人说。

画龙
点睛

A Free Hug

"Do you want a hug?" the young man asked Ginny.

He held a sign in his hand—Free Hugs. I looked around. There were other people with him. They held their handmade signs high. The message was the same on all of them—Free Hugs!

"Sure!" Ginny smiled and walked up to him. She reached out, wrapped her arms around his neck, pulled him down to her level and hugged him with all the love she had in her heart.

"WOW!" he **exclaimed**①. "That is the best hug I've had all day!"

"I'm a hugger," Ginny smiled at him.

He looked at me. "How about a hug?"

"You got it!" I walked into his open arms. We held briefly and parted.

A young lady walked up and hugged Ginny. She turned to me, opened her arms and hugged me, too.

I felt a warmth—a glow—filling my heart. Ginny and I were going through **rough**② times. Money was scarce; bill collectors called on a regular basis. We were **stressed**③ and worried, but on that afternoon, for a brief moment, it was all forgotten.

"Sometimes, a hug is all we need. A Free hug is to reach out and hug a stranger to brighten up their lives," said the young man.

生词有约

① exclaim
v. 大声呼喊；惊叫

② rough
adj. 艰难的
③ stressed
adj. 重压的

免费拥抱

"你想拥抱吗？"年轻人问金妮。

他手里举着一个标牌——免费拥抱。我环顾四周。还有其他人跟他一起。他们都高高地举着自己手做的标牌，上面都传递着同样的信息——免费拥抱！

"当然！"金妮微微一笑走到他跟前。她伸出手，抱住他的脖子，将他拉到和她水平的高度，心里充满爱意地拥抱了他。

"哇！"他高声叫道。"这是我今天得到的最好拥抱！"

"我是一个拥抱族，"金妮对他微笑着说。

他望着我。"拥抱一下如何？"

"你说得对！"我走进他张开的怀抱。我们短暂拥抱了一下，就分开了。

一位年轻女士走过来，拥抱金妮。她转向我，张开怀抱，又拥抱了我。

我感到一阵温暖——一股热流——充满心间。我和金妮的日子正艰难。囊中羞涩，收账人总是定期来要账。我们倍感压力，忧心忡忡，但在那天下午那个短暂的时刻，一切都忘到了脑后。

"有时，我们需要的只是一个拥抱。免费拥抱就是伸出双臂，拥抱陌生人，照亮他们的人生，"年轻人说。

诵读经典 >>>>>
Read classic

I felt a warmth—a glow—filling my heart. Ginny and I were going through rough times. Money was scarce; bill collectors called on a regular basis. We were stressed and worried, but on that afternoon, for a brief moment, it was all forgotten.

我感到一阵温暖——一股热流——充满心间。我和金妮的日子正艰难。囊中羞涩，收账人总是定期来要账。我们倍感压力，忧心忡忡，但在那天下午那个短暂的时刻，一切都忘到了脑后。

妙语连珠 >>>>>
Sparkling discourse

❂ Life is ten percent what you make it and ninety percent how you take it.
生活有百分之十在于你如何塑造它，有百分之九十在于你如何对待它。

❂ Life can only be understood backwards, but it must be lived forwards.
只有向后才能理解生活；但要生活好，则必须向前看。

The Most Difficult

The unlucky little boy lost his left arm in a car accident, but he wanted to learn **judo**[①] that even healthy people are very difficult to do well.

After he pursued studies, finally a judo master took him. But in 3 months after admission, the master only repeatedly taught the little boy one trick. By and by, the little boy could not help but ask, "Master, I have been practicing it for a few months, so should I learn other tricks?"

The master shook his head immediately, "No, it is good enough for you to practice this one." The little boy felt **chagrined**[②], but because he believed the master so much that he obeyed to continue practicing.

3 years later, the master took the boy to attend the match. Seeing the **opponents**[③] tall and strong, the weak and disabled boy was very afraid. The master encouraged him, "Don't be afraid. You will make it because your master has confidence in you." However, the boy was still laden **with**[④] worries.

Surprisingly, the final champion was actually the little boy without left arm and with only one trick, and the result surprised that little boy.

"Why is it, master?" the little boy asked master.

Seeing he was so puzzled, the master explained, "Because first, it is the most difficult one in judo, which you have spent a few years practicing and you have almost completely mastered; second, as far as I know, the only way against this move is to grasp your left arm."

生词有约

① judo
n. 柔道

② chagrined
adj. 懊恼的；苦恼的

③ opponent
n. 对手；反对者

④ be laden with
载满；充满（烦恼）

最难的一招

不幸的小男孩在车祸中失去了左臂，但他很想学连健全人都很难学好的柔道。

他四处求学后，终于有一位柔道大师接纳了他。但在入学后的3个月里，师傅却只肯反复教小男孩一招。终于，小男孩忍不住问道："老师，这招我已经练了几个月了，是不是应该再学其他招数？"

老师马上摇了摇头："不，你只需要把这一招练好就够了。"小男孩感觉很委屈，但因为非常相信师傅，所以他还是听话地继续练了下去。

3年后，师傅带小男孩去参加比赛，看到对手高大强壮，瘦弱残疾的小男孩很是害怕。这时，师傅鼓励他说："不要怕，你一定会成功，师傅对你有信心。"然而，小男孩还是顾虑重重。

令人惊讶的是，最后的冠军竟然真的是这个没有左臂、只会一招的小男孩，这个结果让小男孩自己都很惊讶。

"这是为什么，老师？"小男孩问师傅。

看着他迷惑不解的样子，师傅解释道："因为首先这是柔道中最难的一招，你用了几年时间去练它，几乎已经完全掌握了它的要领；其次，就我所知，对付这一招唯一的办法就是抓住你的左臂。"

诵读经典 >>>>>
Read classic

3 years later, the master took the boy to attend the match. Seeing the opponents tall and strong, the weak and disabled boy was very afraid. The master encouraged him, "Don't be afraid. You will make it because your master has confidence in you." However, the boy was still laden with worries.

3年后，师傅带小男孩去参加比赛，看到对手高大强壮，瘦弱残疾的小男孩很是害怕。这时，师傅鼓励他说："不要怕，你一定会成功，师傅对你有信心。"然而，小男孩还是顾虑重重。

妙语连珠 >>>>>
Sparkling discourse

✪ Life is measured by thought and action, not by time.
衡量生命的尺度是思想和行为，而不是时间。

✪ The great use of life is to spend it for something that overlasts it.
生命的一大用处是将它用于能比生命更长久的事物上。

The great "magician with bows" and genius who could "display the fiery soul on the violin" spent his short life in distress.

这位伟大的"操琴弓的魔术师"、能"在琴上展示火一样的灵魂"的天才，就这样在痛苦中度过了短暂的一生。

画龙点睛

Hold the Handle or the Blade

He who knows anything about music must know the talented violinist Paganini's name, which often goes with the words such as "great", "super" and "top".

At the age of 12, Paganini held the first solo concert, conquering all the people present with his music. For a time, his name echoed throughout Italy. In the **ensuing**① decades, he continued creating the astonishing sound of nature, and the most famous six *Violin Concerto* even more spread his name to every corner of the world.

But others only saw Paganini's achievements while nobody knew his pain. At the age of 4, he got the measles and **mandatory syncope syndrome**②. At the age of 7, he had a severe **pneumonia**③... At the age of 46, due to dental **suppuration**④, the dentist had to pull out all his teeth. At the age of 47, he got the eye disease. After the age of 50, arthritis, intestinal **inflammation**⑤ and **laryngeal tuberculosis**⑥ and so on continued attacking him, so he almost lost the ability to speak. At the age of 58, severe **pulmonary tuberculosis**⑦ finally took his life, and at the time of his death, only 14-year-old son Arqile accompanied him.

The great "magician with bows" and genius who could "display the fiery soul on the violin" spent his short life in distress. Before dying, God let him suffer the taste of loneliness.

生词有约

① ensuing
adj.（只用于名词前）接着发生的；接踵而至的

② mandatory syncope syndrome
强制性昏厥综合征

③ pneumonia
n. 肺炎

④ suppuration
n. 脓；化脓

⑤ inflammation
n. 炎症；发炎

⑥ laryngeal tuberculosis
喉结核

⑦ pulmonary tuberculosis
肺结核

握住刀刃还是刀柄

凡是对音乐稍有了解的人，就不会不知道天才小提琴家帕格尼尼的名字。他的名字常常与"伟大"、"超级"、"顶尖"等字眼并列在一起。

12 岁那年，帕格尼尼便举办了首场个人音乐会，用他的琴声征服了在场的所有人。一时间，他的名字响彻了整个意大利。在随后的几十年中，他不断创作出震惊世人的天籁之音，最有名的 6 部《小提琴协奏曲》更是让他的名字传播到了世界的各个角落。

但是，外人看到的只是帕格尼尼的成就，无人知晓他的痛苦。4 岁那年，他得了麻疹和强制性昏厥症。7 岁那年，他又患上了严重肺炎……46 岁时，由于牙齿化脓，牙医不得不拔掉他所有的牙齿。47 岁，他得了眼疾。50 岁后，关节炎、肠道炎、喉结核等不断向他袭来，最后他几乎丧失了说话能力。58 岁时，严重的肺结核终于要了他的命，临终时只有 14 岁的儿子阿奇勒陪伴着他。

这位伟大的"操琴弓的魔术师"、能"在琴上展示火一样的灵魂"的天才，就这样在痛苦中度过了短暂的一生。临终前，上苍还让他饱尝了孤独的滋味。

诵读经典 >>>>>
Read classic

For a time, his name echoed throughout Italy. In the ensuing decades, he continued creating the astonishing sound of nature, and the most famous six *Violin Concerto* even more spread his name to every corner of the world.

一时间，他的名字响彻了整个意大利。在随后的几十年中，他不断创作出震惊世人的天籁之音，最有名的 6 部《小提琴协奏曲》更是让他的名字传播到了世界的各个角落。

妙语连珠 >>>>>
Sparkling discourse

★ Before everything else, getting ready is the secret of success.
做好准备是成功的首要秘诀。

★ Only the person who has faith in himself is able to be faithful to others.
只有对自己有信心的人才会对别人忠诚。

The Disaster Naturally Has Its Value

One day in 1912, when he was in the studio trial-producing nickeliron battery for silent film, Edison **triggered**① a fire for his carelessness. The flaming fire soon lost control, so the laboratory was burnt to a pile of rubble. Although a loss of $2,000,000 was nothing, but Edison's all the information and samples of sound film were burnt to ashes, and almost a lifetime of **painstaking**② efforts were on fire.

Edison's son Charles was terribly worried for his father rescuing those valuable research results in the lab. After many times' search there were still no results, but Charles accidentally heard his father's call. He was standing in the **smother**③ and ruins, saying in a most calm tone, "Charles, get your mother to come. Such a fire once in a lifetime, what a pity if we don't take a look."

After seeing the **messy**④ spot, Edison's wife cried sadly. Unexpectedly, at that moment Edison still said very calmly, "The disaster naturally has its value, for all my mistakes and faults have been burnt completely." Then he raised his hands and declared, "I can start again."

The very next day, he summoned the employees and declared, "We will rebuild!"

The new laboratory was soon built up.

The **conflagration**⑤ apparently inspired Edison's more **exuberant**⑥ fighting spirit.

Three months later, he launched the first **phonograph**⑦ in the history of mankind.

生词有约

① trigger
vt. 扣……的扳机；引发；触发

② painstaking
adj. 辛苦的；煞费苦心的；苦干的

③ smother
n. 浓烟；浓雾

④ messy
adj. 凌乱的；肮脏的

⑤ conflagration
n. 大火（灾）

⑥ exuberant
adj. 生气勃勃的；充沛的；茂盛的

⑦ phonograph
n. 留声机

灾难自有灾难的价值

1912年的一天，爱迪生正在工作室里为无声电影试制镍铁电池，一不小心，引发了火灾。熊熊大火很快就无法控制，实验室渐渐地被烧成了一片瓦砾。虽然200万美元的损失算不得什么，但爱迪生研究有声电影的所有资料和样板也被烧成了灰烬，几乎一生的心血都因此付之一炬。

爱迪生的儿子查尔斯为自己的父亲在实验室里抢救那些宝贵的研究成果非常担心。当一次次寻找后仍没什么结果时，查尔斯却意外地听到了父亲的呼唤。只见他站在浓烟和废墟里，声调极其平静地说道："查尔斯，快把你的母亲找来，这样的大火，百年难得一见，不看一看太可惜了。"

看到现场的狼藉后，爱迪生的老伴难过地哭了起来。没想到这时候爱迪生依然非常平静地说道："灾难自有灾难的价值，我所有的谬误和过失都被大火烧得一干二净了。"然后，他高高地举起双手宣言道："我又可以重新开始了。"

第二天，他就召集职工们宣布："我们重建！"

新的实验室很快就建起来了。

而这场大火显然激发了爱迪生更旺盛的斗志。

3个月后，他就推出了人类历史上的第一部留声机。

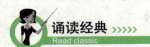

诵读经典 >>>>>
Read classic

After many times' search there were still no results, but Charles accidentally heard his father's call. He was standing in the smother and ruins, saying in a most calm tone, "Charles, get your mother to come. Such a fire once in a lifetime, what a pity if we don't take a look."

当一次次寻找后仍没什么结果时，查尔斯却意外地听到了父亲的呼唤。只见他站在浓烟和废墟里，声调极其平静地说道："查尔斯，快把你的母亲找来，这样的大火，百年难得一见，不看一看太可惜了。"

妙语连珠 >>>>>
Sparkling discourse

❂ A bold attempt is half success.
勇敢的尝试是成功的一半。

❂ It has been my philosophy of life that difficulties vanish when faced boldly.
如果勇敢地正视困难，困难就会消失，这一直是我的人生哲学。

Wait and see. Sooner or later, I will run a greater and more luxurious hotel than yours. Remember what I'm saying now!

等着瞧，早晚有一天，我会开一家比你们饭店更大、更豪华的酒店，记住我现在说的话！

Excellence Is the Greatest Revenge

As an orphan, Hilton met with the most serious economic crisis in the history of the United States, so he was forced to wander and live by begging.

Once, Hilton wandered to a city. For a few nights, he slept in the corner of the entrance hall of a hotel. But one midnight, he was suddenly wakened by a **pang**①. When he opened his eyes, he found the hotel doorman was kicking him hard with disdain. As soon as he resisted, the muscular big boy lifted him, threw him on the snow 10 meters away from the hotel and shouted abused at him, "Early tomorrow morning, our boss of hotel group will come to inspect the work. How can you dirty and **paltry**② beggar sleep here? It is humiliating us! People like you should sleep in the dustbin, even never dreaming of such a high-class place!"

Hearing this, Hilton was so extremely indignant that he **gnashed**③ his teeth, clenched his fists and really wanted to beat the doorman. But "a wise man does not fight when the odds are against him." He apparently needn't invite trouble for himself, so he pointed at the man shouting, "Wait and see. Sooner or later, I will run a greater and more luxurious hotel than yours. Remember what I'm saying now!"

After that night, he underwent all kinds of hardships, worked hard and saved up every penny he had earned. Years later, Hilton had finally broken out, founded the first "Hilton Hotel", and expanded rapidly into one of the largest hotel groups—Hilton Hotel Group in the world.

生词有约

① pang
n. 剧痛；苦闷

② paltry
adj. 微小的；不重要的；可鄙的

③ gnash
vt. 咬（牙）；上下叩击

优秀是最大的报复

希尔顿是个孤儿，年幼时又正遇到美国历史上最严重的经济危机，只好四处流浪，靠乞讨为生。

一次，小希尔顿流浪到了一座城市，接连几个晚上，都躲在一间大饭店门廊的角落里过夜。但一天半夜时分，他突然被一阵疼痛弄醒了，睁开眼睛一看，原来是饭店的门童正带着满脸的不屑使劲踢他。他刚一反抗，那个身体健壮的大男孩便把他拎起来扔到了距离饭店10米外的雪地上，对他破口大骂："明天一大早，我们饭店集团的老板要来视察工作，你这个肮脏下贱的乞丐怎么可以呆在这里过夜，简直就是给我们丢人！像你这种人应该钻进垃圾筒里去睡觉，这种高级地方你做梦都不配梦到！"

听到这话，希尔顿异常愤怒，咬牙握拳，真想冲上去揍那个门童一顿。但是，"好汉不吃眼前亏"。他显然没必要再给自己找麻烦，于是指着对方大声说道："等着瞧，早晚有一天，我会开一家比你们饭店更大、更豪华的酒店，记住我现在说的话！"

那夜之后，他历尽艰难，拼命工作，并存下自己赚的每一分钱。数年后，希尔顿终于破茧而出，创立了第一家"希尔顿大饭店"，并迅速扩充成全世界最大的饭店集团之———希尔顿饭店集团。

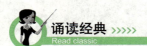

诵读经典 >>>>>
Read classic

✪ Hearing this, Hilton was so extremely indignant that he gnashed his teeth, clenched his fists and really wanted to beat the doorman. But "a wise man does not fight when the odds are against him."

听到这话，希尔顿异常愤怒，咬牙握拳，真想冲上去揍那个门童一顿。但是，"好汉不吃眼前亏"。

✪ …he underwent all kinds of hardships, worked hard and saved up every penny he had earned. Years later, Hilton had finally broken out…

……他历尽艰难，拼命工作，并存下自己所赚的每一分钱。数年后，希尔顿终于破茧而出……

妙语连珠 >>>>>
Sparkling discourse

✪ Energy and persistence conquer all things.
能量和毅力征服一切。

✪ Strength alone knows conflict, weakness is below even defeat, and is born vanquished.
只有强者才懂得斗争；弱者甚至失败都不够资格，而是生来就是被征服的。

Wind, Frost, Thunder and Storm

Once upon a time there was a farmer who had a farm. Because the farmland was so poor that his annual harvest was not very good, he often complained, "If God lets me control the weather, everything will get better, for I'm a farmer, who knows better how to grow crops than God, and what kind of weather the crops will need."

His words happened to be heard by God who was just passing by here, so he said to him, "From now on, I give one year to you. You will be **in command of**① wind, rain, thunder and lightning, and finally we'll see what your crops will grow like."

On hearing this, the farmer was delighted and immediately tried shouting, "Sunny." Suddenly the cloud parted and the fog dispersed. He was pleased and shouted again, "Rain." The sky was overcast with dark clouds right away, and after a while, the heavy rain poured down.

Thus, in the following year, his command always switched between sunny and rainy.

Watching the seeds growing larger and larger and becoming crops, the farmers felt much exulted in his heart. Then, he saw the large leaves that he had never seen, and the unbelievable **aquamarine**② . Then, the harvest season came.

The farmer carried his basket and sickle to the field to reap his crops, but his heart suddenly sank to the bottom when he found the vigorous-looking crops even hadn't grown a grain at all.

生词有约

① in command of
指挥；统率

② aquamarine
n. 碧绿色；海蓝宝石

Confused, the farmer burst into tears sadly, which attracted God.

"How about your crops?" God asked.

The farmer pointed to the **infertile**③ crops, without a word.

③ infertile
adj. 不结果实的；贫瘠的

"Don't you have your wish to control the weather?" God asked again.

"Yes. This is why I'm confused about. I got the sunshine and rain I wanted, but the crops didn't have any harvest," said the farmer finally.

"That's because you never asked for wind, rainstorm, snow and ice and anything that could purify air and harden the roots with more resistance; without enough developed roots, the crops won't, of course, grow any fruit," God **snapped**④.

④ snap
v. 呵斥

It turned out that only through the challenges would he have the fruit of life. After he understood this truth, the farmer begged God to take back the weather he controlled.

Thereafter, despite constantly with wind, frost, thunder and storm, the crops could bear fruit after all.

风霜雷雨也有功

从前有一位农夫，他有一块农田。因为农田十分贫瘠，他每年的收成都不是很好，所以他经常抱怨："如果神让我来掌控天气，一切事情都将会变得更好，因为我自己是农夫，我比神更懂得怎么种庄稼，更懂得庄稼需要什么样的天气。"

他的这些话刚好被路过此地的上帝听到了，于是上帝便对他说道："从现在开始，我把一年的时间送给你，由你来指挥风雨雷电，最后看看你的庄稼会长成什么样吧。"

农夫一听大喜，马上试探着喊道："晴天。"顿时云开雾散。他欣喜不已，又喊道："下雨。"空中立刻阴云四起，不一会儿，瓢泼大雨就下来了。

就这样，在接下来的一年中，他的命令总是在晴天和下雨之间转换着。

眼看着种子越长越大，长成庄稼，农夫心里得意极了。然后，他就看到了从来不曾见过的大叶子，还有令人难以置信的碧绿色。再然后，收获的季节到了。

农夫背上筐子，带上镰刀，去地里收割他的庄稼，但他的心一下子沉到了谷底，那看上去苗壮无比的庄稼上面居然一粒粮食也没长。

农夫不解，伤心地大哭起来，他的哭声引来了上帝。

"你的农作物怎么样了？"上帝问道。

农夫指指颗粒无收的庄稼，一句话也说不出来。

"你不是如愿以偿地控制了天气吗？"上帝又问道。

"是的。这正是我困惑的地方。我得到了我想要的阳光和雨水，可庄稼居然没有收成。"农夫终于开口说道。

"那是因为你从来没有要求过风、暴雨、冰雪以及任何一件能净化空气和让根更坚硬、更有抵抗力的东西，没有足够发达的根，庄稼当然长不出什么果实。"上帝厉声说道。

原来，只有经历挑战才可能有生命的果实。农夫明白了这个道理后，乞求神收回了自己控制的天气。

此后，虽然风霜雷雨不断，但毕竟庄稼又可以结果了。

诵读经典 >>>>>
Read classic

That's because you never asked for wind, rainstorm, snow and ice and anything that could purify air and harden the roots with more resistance; without enough developed roots, the crops won't, of course, grow any fruit.

那是因为你从来没有要求过风、暴雨、冰雪以及任何一件能净化空气和让根更坚硬、更有抵抗力的东西，没有足够发达的根，庄稼当然长不出什么果实。

妙语连珠 >>>>>
Sparkling discourse

❂ Humility is the foundation of glory.
谦卑是荣誉的基础。

❂ Choose a life of action, not one of ostentation.
选择行动的一生，而不是炫耀的一生。

Every cloud has a silver lining. Even if God closes all the doors, it will also leave you a window.

天无绝人之路，即便上帝关闭了所有的门，也会给你留下一扇打开的窗。

画龙点睛

Every Cloud Has a Silver Lining

Paul was a wealthy young man. When his father died, he left Paul a lifelong endless wealth—a beautiful forest **manor**①. But unfortunately, before the forest was replaced by money, a fire caused by thunderbolt had destroyed it **mercilessly**②. Watching the luxuriantly green trees turned into black coke overnight, Paul was heartbroken.

In order to restore the forest manor to its original beauty, Paul applied to the bank for a huge loan, but the bank refused him, for he could not submit any **guarantee**③. Extremely gloomy, Paul neither ate nor drank, hid in his room and would not go out for a few days. His wife was afraid he would be sick and persuaded him to relax outside.

Paul came to the street. When he just turned the first corner, his eyes were attracted by a store with a huge crowd. It turned out that the housewives were lining up to buy charcoal used for **barbecue**④ and winter heating.

Paul's eyes suddenly lit up, so he immediately ran home, employed some **deft**⑤ charcoal workers to process the burnt trees of the manor into high-quality charcoal. As soon as a large quantity of good charcoal came into the market, it was warmly welcomed by the townspeople. Pretty soon, more than 1,000 boxes of charcoal was **snapped up**⑥. In the spring of the second year, he used the money to purchase a large number of **seedlings**⑦. After a few years, the forest manor everyone thought it had disappeared came to life again.

Every cloud has a silver lining. Even if God closes all the doors, it will also leave you a window.

生词有约

① manor
n. 庄园；领地

② mercilessly
adv. 无慈悲地；残忍地

③ guarantee
n. 担保；抵押品

④ barbecue
n. 烤肉；烧烤野餐

⑤ deft
adj. 灵巧的；熟练的

⑥ snap up
抢购

⑦ seedling
n. 幼苗；树苗

天无绝人之路

保罗是一个年轻富有的小伙子，父亲去世时，给他留下了一笔终生享用不尽的财富——一座美丽的森林庄园。但不幸的是，还没等这片森林被置换成金钱，一场由雷电引发的大火便无情地摧毁了它。看着郁郁葱葱的树木一夜之间都变成了黑乎乎的焦炭，保罗伤心欲绝。

为了让森林庄园恢复到最初的美丽模样，保罗向银行申请了巨额贷款，但银行却以他不能提交任何担保拒绝了他。郁闷透顶的保罗茶饭不思，躲进自己的房间里，一连几天都不肯出门。妻子怕他闷出病来，就劝他出去散散心。

保罗来到大街上，刚拐过大街的第一个弯，目光便被一家人山人海的商店吸引住了。原来这些家庭主妇们正在排队购买用于烤肉和冬季取暖用的木炭。

保罗的眼睛猛地一亮，他立刻跑回家里，雇了几个手脚麻利的炭工，让他们把庄园里烧焦的树木加工成优质木炭。这一大批上好的木炭刚一上市，便受到了市民们的热烈欢迎。没过多久，千余箱木炭便被抢购一空。第二年春天，他用这笔钱购进了大量树苗。又过了几年，人人都以为消失的森林庄园再次焕发生机。

天无绝人之路，即便上帝关闭了所有的门，也会给你留下一扇打开的窗。

诵读经典 >>>>>
Read classic

❂ Watching the luxuriantly green trees turned into black coke overnight, Paul was heartbroken.

看着郁郁葱葱的树木一夜之间都变成了黑乎乎的焦炭，保罗伤心欲绝。

❂ Pretty soon, more than 1,000 boxes of charcoal was snapped up. In the spring of the second year, he used the money to purchase a large number of seedlings. After a few years, the forest manor everyone thought it had disappeared came to life again.

没过多久，千余箱木炭便被抢购一空。第二年春天，他用这笔钱购进了大量树苗。又过了几年，人人都以为消失的森林庄园再次焕发生机。

妙语连珠 >>>>>
Sparkling discourse

❂ Man can only be free through mastery of himself.
只有通过掌握自己，才能使自己得到解放。

❂ A man can fail many times, but he isn't a failure until he begins to blame somebody else.
一个人可以失败许多次，但只要他没有开始责怪别人，他就不是一个失败者。

A Surprise Move

Hans was a manager of a **canning**① company in the United States. At the beginning, Hans's name was little known, so he tried his best to make himself known.

In 1957, a national **exposition**② was held in Chicago. In order to promote his products and expand his fame, Hans also applied to the exposition for a stall. Because most goods participating in the exposition were well known in the United States, the principal of the exposition had to arrange Hans' exhibits in the most **inconspicuous**③ small attic.

After the exposition began, visitors were in an endless stream. However, few visitors **patronized**④ Hans' stall. Hans was very worried about it. The first day passed, and the very next day, Hans got a good idea. So he well prepared the same night.

The third day, on the floor suddenly appeared a lot of small bronze plates. On the back of each was **engraved**⑤ with the words, "Whoever picks up the small bronze plate can go to Hans Food Company stall in the exhibition hall attic for a Hans' **souvenir**⑥." Just as Hans predicted, the small attic no one had patronized was soon crowded.

"Hans's Little Bronze Plate" was widely praised, and the reporters swarmed to report it. Therefore, Hans's products rose to fame quickly.

生词有约

① canning
n. 罐头制造
② exposition
n. 博览会；展览会

③ inconspicuous
adj. 不显著的；不引人注目的
④ patronize
vt. 惠顾

⑤ engrave
vt. 雕刻；印刷

⑥ souvenir
n. 纪念品；礼物

出奇制胜

汉斯是美国一家罐头公司的经理。开始时，汉斯的名字并没有多少人知道，因此汉斯要想办法使别人认识自己。

1957年，芝加哥市举办了一个全国博览会。汉斯为了推销自己的产品，扩大知名度，也向博览会申请了一个摊位。因为参加博览会的大多数商品在美国的名气都非常大，所以博览会的负责人只好把毫无名气的汉斯的展品安排在一个展厅中最不引人注意的小阁楼上。

博览会开始后，参观的人络绎不绝。然而，光顾汉斯台前的人却少得可怜。为此，汉斯很是苦恼。第一天过去了，到了第二天，汉斯想出了一条妙计。于是，他连夜做好了准备工作。

第三天，会场的地面上突然出现了许多小铜牌，小铜牌的背面刻着一行字："谁拾到这块小铜牌，谁就可以到展厅阁楼上的汉斯食品公司处取一件汉斯纪念品。"正如汉斯预测的那样，本来无人光顾的小阁楼不久便水泄不通了。

"汉斯的小铜牌"被人们到处传诵着，记者们纷纷前来报道。因此，汉斯的产品很快就名声大振。

诵读经典 >>>>>
Read classic

After the exposition began, visitors were in an endless stream. However, few visitors patronized Hans' stall. Hans was very worried about it. The first day passed, and the very next day, Hans got a good idea. So he well prepared the same night.

博览会开始后，参观的人络绎不绝。然而，光顾汉斯台前的人却少得可怜。为此，汉斯很是苦恼。第一天过去了，到了第二天，汉斯想出了一条妙计。于是，他连夜做好了准备工作。

妙语连珠 >>>>>
Sparkling discourse

✪ A wise man never loses anything if he has himself.
聪明的人只要能掌握自己，便什么也不会失去。

✪ It is while you are patiently toiling at the little tasks of life that the meaning and shape of great whole of life dawn on you.
在你耐心地操劳于生活琐事的过程中，你才能领悟整个生活的伟大意义和形象。

If I Have One Million Dollars

A young man pursued studies at the University. One day he proposed to the president some suggestions about how to improve the university education system **malpractice**①. His opinion was not accepted by the president. So he decided to run a university independently and **eliminate** ② these drawbacks.

To run the school would require at least one million dollars. Where would he find so much money? Every day he was in the bedroom thinking hard how to get one million dollars. His classmates thought he was crazy, dreaming the money would fall from the sky. But the young man didn't think so, firmly believing that he could raise the money.

Finally, one day he thought out a way. He called the newspaper that tomorrow he would hold a lecture titled "If I Have One Million Dollars." The next day the speech attracted many business people. **In the presence of** ③ the audience and many successful people, he spoke out his idea. At last, after the speech, a businessman called Philip Armer stood up and said, "Young man, you spoke so well. I decide to invest one million dollars as you said." Thus, with the money the young man ran Armer Polytechnic Institute, which is now the **predecessor** ④ of famous Illinois Polytechnic Institute.

This young man was the philosopher and educator Gunsaulus widely loved and **esteemed** ⑤ later.

生词有约

① malpractice
n. 营私舞弊；胡作非为
② eliminate
vt. 排除；消除

③ in the presence of
在……面前

④ predecessor
n. 前任；前身
⑤ esteem
vt. 尊敬；尊重

如果我有100万美元

一位年轻人在大学读书，有一天他向校长提出了改进大学教育制度弊端的若干建议。他的意见没被校长接受。于是，他决定自己办一所大学，来消除这些弊端。

办学校至少需要100万美元。上哪儿去找这么多钱呢？他每天都在寝室内苦思冥想如何能有100万美元。同学们都认为他有神经病，梦想天上掉钱来。但是，年轻人不以为然，坚信自己可以筹到这笔钱。

终于有一天，他想到了一个办法。他打电话到报社说，他准备明天举行一个演讲会，题目叫《如果我有100万美元》。第二天的演讲吸引了许多商界人士。面对台下诸多成功人士，他在台上全心全意发自内心地说出了自己的构想。最后演讲完毕，一个叫菲利普·亚默的商人站了起来，说："小伙子，你讲得非常好。我决定投资100万，就照你说的办。"就这样，年轻人用这笔钱办了亚默理工学院，也就是现在著名的伊利诺理工学院的前身。

这个年轻人就是后来备受人们爱戴的哲学家、教育家冈索勒斯。

诵读经典 >>>>>
Read classic

He called the newspaper that tomorrow he would hold a lecture titled "If I Have One Million Dollars." The next day the speech attracted many business people. In presence of the audience and many successful people, he spoke out his idea.

他打电话到报社说，他准备明天举行一个演讲会，题目叫《如果我有100万美元》。第二天的演讲吸引了许多商界人士。面对台下诸多成功人士，他在台上全心全意发自内心地说出了自己的构想。

妙语连珠 >>>>>
Sparkling discourse

❂ Most of the trouble in the world is caused by people wanting to be important.
世界上大部分的麻烦都是要想成为伟大人物的人搞出来的。

❂ In education we are striving not to teach youth to make a living, but to make a life.
教育不是为了教会青年人谋生，而是教会他们创造生活。

Little Snail cried, "We are so poor that neither the sky nor the earth will protect us."

小蜗牛哭了起来："我们好可怜，天空不保护，大地也不保护"

画龙点睛

Depend on Ourselves

Little Snail asked her mother, "Why do we bear this hard and heavy shell as soon as we were born?"

Mother said, "Because our bodies don't have bones to support and we have to climb, no so fast, we need this shell to protect!"

生词有约

Little Snail said, "Sister **Caterpillar**① has no bones and doesn't climb fast, why she doesn't bear this hard and heavy shell?"

① caterpillar
n. 毛虫

Mother said, "Because she can turn into a **butterfly**②, the sky will protect her."

② butterfly
n. 蝴蝶

Little Snail said, "But Brother **Earthworm**③ has no bones and doesn't climb fast either, no will he become a butterfly, why doesn't he bear the hard and heavy shell?"

③ earthworm
n. 蚯蚓

Mother replied, "Because he can dig into the earth, the earth will protect him."

Little Snail cried, "We are so poor that neither the sky nor the earth will protect us."

Mother comforted him, "So we have the shells! We neither rely on the sky nor the earth, but we rely on ourselves."

我们靠自己

小蜗牛问妈妈："为什么我们从生下来，就要背负这个又硬又重的壳呢？"

妈妈说："因为我们的身体没有骨骼的支撑，只能爬，又爬不快，所以要这个壳的保护！"

小蜗牛说："毛虫姐姐没有骨头，也爬不快，为什么她却不用背这个又硬又重的壳呢？"

妈妈说："因为她能变成蝴蝶，天空会保护她。"

小蜗牛说："可是，蚯蚓弟弟也没骨头爬不快，也不会变成蝴蝶，为什么他也不背这个又硬又重的壳呢？"

妈妈说："因为蚯蚓弟弟会钻土，大地会保护他。"

小蜗牛哭了起来："我们好可怜，天空不保护，大地也不保护。"

蜗牛妈妈安慰他说："所以我们有壳啊！我们不靠天，也不靠地，我们靠自己。"

诵读经典 >>>>>
Read classic

Mother comforted him, "So we have the shells! We neither rely on the sky nor the earth, but we rely on ourselves."

蜗牛妈妈安慰他说："所以我们有壳啊！我们不靠天，也不靠地，我们靠自己。"

妙语连珠 >>>>>
Sparkling discourse

❂ It is impossible to defeat an ignorant man in argument.

在争论中是无法击败无知者的。

❂ Every person has two educations, one which he receives from others, and one, more important, which he gives himself.

每个人都接受两种教育，一种来自别人，另一种更重要的来自自己。

画龙
点睛

I Want to Be for the Rest of My Life

There was once a **placid** ① and beautiful town in which there were a couple of lovers who would often stay together on the top of the mountain enjoying the sunrise and by the sea watching the sunset. Everyone who knew them could not help envying them and praying for their happy love.

But one day, the man was severely injured and lying in bed in hospital for several days without any consciousness. The woman guarded him by the bed in the daytime, calling his name **relentlessly** ② while at night she would go to the church and pray to God until her tears ran up.

A week passed by and the man was still sleeping. The woman **pined away** ③ drastically, but she still persisted. One day, the God was finally moved by her love and persistence and would like to do her a special favor.

The God asked her, "Do you really want to exchange your beloved's life with yours?"

The woman answered without the least hesitation, "Yes."

The God said, "Alright. I can help your lover recover quickly on condition that you should promise to be a butterfly for three years. Do you agree with the deal?"

She said excitedly and firmly, "Yes, I do!"

The next day, the woman became a beautiful butterfly and said goodbye to God, flying hurriedly to the hospital. It turned out that the man came to his consciousness and woke up, talking with a doctor. She could not hear what they were

生词有约

① placid
adj. 宁静的；温和的

② relentlessly
adv. 不懈地；不屈不挠地

③ pine away
消瘦；憔悴

talking about because she could not fly into the house. What she could do was watch her beloved through the windows helplessly.

Another spring came in a **blink**④ and the butterfly was in a hurry to fly back to see the man, only to realize that there was a pretty lady standing by him. At that moment, she was so shocked that she almost fell down from the sky. She could barely believe what she saw and other people's discussion about it.

④ blink

n. 眨眼；转眼间；一瞬间

People were talking about that the man was seriously ill during Christmas and that the pretty and **cute**⑤ female doctor took good care of him and that finally they fell in sweet love. The man seemed to be as happy as before…

⑤ cute

adj. 漂亮的；娇小可爱的

The butterfly felt heart-stricken. In the following days, she often saw the man take the woman to the top of the mountain and enjoy the sunrise with her. Also the man would take the woman to the seaside and watched the sunset together. The butterfly knew that all these should have belonged to her, but now they belonged to another woman. She could do nothing but rest on the man's shoulder off and on.

On the last day of the third year when the **deal**⑥ between the God and the butterfly was almost over, the man held a wedding with his girlfriend. The church was crowded with people. The butterfly flew into the church quietly and rested on the shoulder of God, listening to the man's **oath**⑦ to the bride and seeing him put a ring on her finger and kiss her sweetly. The butterfly could not help shedding her tears sadly.

⑥ deal

n. 交易；（尤指秘密的）协议

⑦ oath

n. 誓言；誓约

God also felt sad and sighed to the butterfly, "Do you regret for what you have done?"

The butterfly cleaned her tears on the face and said, "No."

God felt a bit relieved and said, "Tomorrow you can become human again."

But she shook her head and said, "No, I want to be a butterfly for the rest of my life…"

我要做一辈子

从前有一座平静美丽的小镇，小镇里有一对恋人，他们常常一起守在山顶欣赏日出，坐在海边眺望落日。每个认识他们的人都不禁羡慕他们，为他们幸福的爱情祈祷。

但是，有一天，男人受了重伤，躺在医院的病床上好几天都昏迷不醒。白天，女人守在床边不停低呼唤他，夜里常常教堂里向上帝祈祷，直到哭干了眼泪。

一周过去了，男人仍然昏睡着。女人彻底憔悴，但她仍然坚持。有一天，上帝终于被她的爱和执著感动了，就想特别帮助她。

上帝问她："你真的想用自己的生命交换爱人的生命吗？"

女人毫不犹豫地答道："想。"

上帝说："好吧。我可以帮助你的爱人康复，条件是你要答应做3年蝴蝶。你同意这个交易吗？"

她激动而坚定地说："是的，我同意！"

第二天，女人变成了一只美丽的蝴蝶，告别上帝，匆匆飞到医院。男人果真恢复了意识，醒了过来，正在跟一名医生聊天。她听不到他们在聊什么，因为她飞不进那个房子。她只能无助地隔着窗户望着心爱的人。

转眼间就到了第二年春天，蝴蝶匆匆飞回去见爱人，只见一位漂亮女人正站在他身边。此时此刻，她大为震惊，差点儿从空中坠落下来。她简直难以相信自己看到的情景和别人谈论的事儿。

人们正在谈论着圣诞节时男人病重，漂亮可爱的女医生对他精心照顾，最后他们堕入了甜蜜的爱河。男人似乎像以前一样快乐……

蝴蝶悲痛欲绝。接下来的几天，她常常会看到男人带着那个女人到山顶去欣赏日出。他还带着那个女人到海边一起看日落。蝴蝶知道本来所有这一切应该属于自己，但现在却属于了另一个女人。她只能断断续续落在男人的肩上。

在上帝和蝴蝶约定的3年就要结束的最后一天，男人和他的女友举行了婚礼。教堂里坐满了人。蝴蝶悄悄地飞进了教堂，落在上帝的肩上，听着男人对新娘，看到他把戒指戴到她的手指上，甜蜜地吻她。蝴蝶禁不住流下了伤心的眼泪。

上帝也感到伤心，对蝴蝶叹息说："你为自己所做的一切后悔吗？"

蝴蝶擦干了脸上的眼泪，说道："不后悔。"

上帝稍微感到放心，说道："明天你就又能变成人了。"

但是，蝴蝶摇了摇头说："不，我要做一辈子蝴蝶……"

诵读经典 >>>>>
Read classic

The church was crowded with people. The butterfly flew into the church quietly and rested on the shoulder of God, listening to the man's oath to the bride and seeing him put a ring on her finger and kiss her sweetly. The butterfly could not help shedding her tears sadly.

教堂里坐满了人。蝴蝶悄悄地飞进了教堂，落在上帝的肩上，听着男人对新娘，看到他把戒指戴到她的手指上，甜蜜地吻她。蝴蝶禁不住流下了伤心的眼泪。

妙语连珠 >>>>>
Sparkling discourse

✪ Patience is bitter, but its fruit is sweet.
忍耐是痛苦的，但它的果实是甜蜜的。

✪ Learning is an ornament in prosperity, a refuge in adversity, and a provision in old age.
学问在成功时是装饰品，在失意时是庇护所，在年老时是供应品。

Hurry on Shouldering the Boat

A young man with a large parcel on his back came from afar for Master Wuji. He said, "Master, I'm so lonely and so painful that the long trek makes me tired out, my shoes **worn-out** [1], my feet cut by the thorns, my hands also injured and bleeding and my voice **hoarse** [2] due to the long shouting...why can't I find the sun in the heart?"

The master asked, "What do you put in your large parcel?"

The young man said, "It is very important to me, inside it including the suffering each time I fall, the weeping each time I'm hurt, the trouble each time I feel lonely...relying on it, I can come to you here."

So Master Wuji took the young man to the river, where they crossed in a boat. Ashore, the master said, "Hurry on your journey **shouldering** [3] the boat!"

"What, shouldering the boat?" the young man was surprised, "it is so heavy. How can I shoulder it?"

"Yes, my son, you can't carry it," the master just smiled and said, "when you cross the river, the boat is useful. But after crossing it, you will put down the boat and hurry on. **Otherwise** [4], it will become a burden. Suffering, loneliness and tears—all these are useful to life. They can **sublimate** [5] life, but if you don't forget them all the time, they will become the burden in life. Put it down! My son, life can't bear a heavy burden."

The young man put down his parcel and hurried on. He felt his pace was easy and merry, and much faster than before.

生词有约

① worn-out
adj. 筋疲力竭的；耗尽的
② hoarse
adj. 嘶哑的

③ shoulder
vt. 肩负；肩扛

④ otherwise
adv. 否则；另外
⑤ sublimate
vt. 使升华；使高尚

扛船赶路

一个青年背着一个大包裹千里迢迢跑来找无际大师，他说："大师，我是那样的孤独和痛苦，长期的跋涉使我疲倦到了极点；我的鞋子破了，荆棘割破双脚；手也受伤了，流血不止；嗓子因为长久的呼喊而暗哑……为什么我还不能找到心中的阳光？"

大师问："你的大包裹里装的什么？"

青年说："它对我非常重要。里面是我每次跌倒时的痛苦，每次受伤后的哭泣，每次孤寂时的烦恼……靠它，我才能走到您这里来。"

于是，无际大师带青年来到河边，他们坐船过了河。上岸后，大师说："你扛着船赶路吧！"

"什么，扛着船赶路？"青年吃了一惊，"它那么沉，我扛得动吗？"

"是的，孩子，你扛不动它。"大师微微一笑说，"过河时，船是有用的。但过了河，就要放下船赶路，否则它会成为包袱。痛苦、孤独、眼泪，这些对人生都是有用的。它们能使生命得到升华，但须臾不忘，就成了人生的包袱。放下它吧！孩子，生命不能太负重。"

青年放下包袱，继续赶路，他发觉自己的步子轻松而愉悦，比以前快得多。

诵读经典 >>>>>
Read classic

When you cross the river, the boat is useful. But after crossing it, you will put down the boat and hurry on. Otherwise, it will become a burden. Suffering, loneliness and tears—all these are useful to life. They can sublimate life, but if you don't forget them all the time, they will become the burden in life.

过河时，船是有用的。但过了河，就要放下船赶路，否则它会成为包袱。痛苦、孤独、眼泪，这些对人生都是有用的。它们能使生命得到升华，但须臾不忘，就成了人生的包袱。

妙语连珠 >>>>>
Sparkling discourse

✪ He who seize the right moment, is the right man.

谁把握机遇，谁就心想事成。

✪ Loveliness, needs not the foreign aid of ornament, but is when unadorned, adorned the most.

可爱，并不需要外来的装饰，天然的可爱远比雕饰的更可爱。

> **Accidentally, a lily seed dropped in the wheat field. The seed budded, shot out the slender stems and leaves, grew the buds and burst into the pure white flowers.**
>
> 一粒百合花籽意外地落在麦田里。花籽发芽了，抽出了修长的茎和叶，又孕育出了花蕾，开出了洁白的花。

画龙点睛

The Lily in the Wheat Field

Accidentally①, a lily seed dropped in the wheat field. The seed budded, shot out the slender stems and leaves, grew the buds and burst into the pure white flowers. Looking at the uniform wheat **seedlings**② surrounding it, the lily was so proud, "Look, you're all ordinary wheat seedlings and your value is to **yield**③ several **ears**④ of wheat and become the food of mankind. As for me, I'm the noble lily, who is the symbol of purity, so you can't compare with me..."

The lily was so pleased with itself while the wheat seedlings remained silent. At this moment, a farmer went over. He took no interest in flowers. He only had the crops in his eyes, so the beautiful lily was only a weed. He pulled out the lily right away and threw it off on the ridge of the field.

The lily was **insolated**⑤ by the **scorching**⑥ sun and gradually **withered**⑦.

I believe you are so excellent and the people around you are not as good as you. Perhaps you are a lily, but are you wrong to grow in the wheat field? The lily growing in the wheat field is a weed. You'd better consider in earnest where your proper position is.

生词有约

① accidentally
adv. 意外地；偶然地

② seedling
n. 幼苗；秧苗

③ yield
vt. 生长出（作物）；结出（果实）

④ ear
n. 穗

⑤ insolate
vt. 使暴晒

⑥ scorching
adj. 灼热的；激烈的

⑦ wither
vi. 枯萎；凋谢

麦田里的百合

一粒百合花籽意外地落在麦田里。花籽发芽了，抽出了修长的茎和叶，又孕育出了花蕾，开出了洁白的花。看看周围都是青一色的麦苗，百合非常骄傲："看看你们，都是凡俗

98

的麦苗，你们的价值也就是结出几穗麦子，成为人类的食物。而我呢，是高贵的百合，是纯洁的象征，你们谁都不能跟我相提并论……"

百合扬扬自得，麦苗却一言不发。这时，一个农夫走了过来。他对花卉没有兴趣，眼里只有他的庄稼，美丽的百合对于他不过是一株杂草。他随手拔掉百合，扔到田埂上了。

百合被烈日暴晒着，渐渐枯萎。

我相信你很优秀，你周围的人都比不上你。也许你是一株百合，但你是不是错长在了麦田里？长在麦田里的百合，就是杂草。还是认真想一下，适合自己的位置在哪里吧。

诵读经典 >>>>>
Read classic

Look, you're all ordinary wheat seedlings and your value is to yield several ears of wheat and become the food of mankind. As for me, I'm the noble lily, who is the symbol of purity, so you can't compare with me...

看看你们，都是凡俗的麦苗，你们的价值也就是结出几穗麦子，成为人类的食物。而我呢，是高贵的百合，是纯洁的象征，你们谁都不能跟我相提并论……

妙语连珠 >>>>>
Sparkling discourse

✪ Character is the first and last word in the success
品德是成功的决定因素。

✪ The man who has made up his mind to win will never say "Impossible."
凡是决心取得胜利的人从来不说"不可能"。

Seize the Chance

After death, John went to see God. God looked through his **curriculum vitae**①, feeling very unhappy, "You've lived in this world for 60 years. Why haven't you gotten any result at all?"

John argued, "My God, you didn't give me any chance. If you let that magic apple hit on my head, the man who found the law of **gravity**② should be me."

God said, "OK, we might as well try again." God waved his hand and the time turned back to the apple orchard a few hundred years ago. God shook the apple tree, when a red apple fell and happened to drop on John's head. John picked up the apple, wiped it and ate it up as soon as possible.

God allowed a bigger apple drop on John's head and John ate it up once again.

God sighed and shook the apple tree again, when a much bigger apple fell on John's head.

John flew into a rage, picked up the apple and **mercilessly**③ threw it out, "The damned apple disturbed my sweet dream!"

The apple flew out and happened to fall on Newton's head. Newton awoke and picked up the apple when he was suddenly **enlightened**④ and discovered the law of **gravitation**⑤.

The time returned once again now. God said to John, "You're now **convinced**⑥!"

John **implored**⑦, "My God, please give me another chance…"

生词有约

① curriculum vitae
n.（拉）简历

② gravity
n. 重力；地心引力

③ mercilessly
adv. 残酷无情地；残忍地

④ enlighten
vt. 启发；启蒙；开导

⑤ gravitation
n. 重力；万有引力

⑥ convince
vt. 使信服；说服

⑦ implore
vi. 恳求；乞求

God shook his head and said, "No. The chance that the apple drops on the head of everyone is the same, but each person's ability to seize the chance is different."

把握机会

约翰死后去见上帝，上帝查看了一遍他的履历，很不高兴："你在人间活了60年，怎么一点成绩也没有？"

约翰辩解说："主啊，是你没给我机会。如果你让那个神奇的苹果砸在我头上，那个发现万有引力定律的人就应该是我。"

上帝说："好吧，我们不妨再试验一次。"上帝把手一挥，时光倒流回到了几百年前的那个苹果园。上帝摇动苹果树，一只红苹果落下来，正好掉在约翰的头上。约翰捡起苹果，擦了擦，很快就把苹果吃了。

上帝让一只大点的苹果落在约翰头上，约翰又把那只苹果吃了。

上帝叹了口气，再次摇动苹果树，一只更大的苹果落在了约翰的头上。

约翰勃然大怒，捡起苹果狠狠地扔出去："该死的苹果，搅了我的好梦！"

苹果飞出去，正好落在睡觉的牛顿头上。牛顿醒了，捡起苹果，豁然开朗，就发现了万有引力定律。

时光重新回到现在，上帝对约翰说："你现在该口服心服了吧！"

约翰哀求道："主啊，请你再给我一次机会吧……"

上帝摇了摇头说："不用了。苹果砸在每个人头上的机会都是相同的，只是每个人把握机会的能力有所不同。"

诵读经典 >>>>>
Read classic

God waved his hand and the time turned back to the apple orchard a few hundred years ago. God shook the apple tree, when a red apple fell and happened to drop on John's head. John picked up the apple, wiped it and ate it up as soon as possible.

上帝把手一挥，时光倒流回到了几百年前的那个苹果园。上帝摇动苹果树，一只红苹果落下来，正好掉在约翰的头上。约翰捡起苹果，擦了擦，很快就把苹果吃了。

妙语连珠 »»»»»
Sparkling discourse

❂ Don't waste life in doubts and fears.

不要把生命浪费在怀疑与恐惧之中。

❂ Something attempted, something done.

有所尝试，就等于有所作为。

To Win Time

Andre's grandmother died. Andre who was in primary school was very sad because his grandma was very fond of him. He ran around and around the school playground every day till he was too tired to fall on the ground and throw himself down the lawn to cry his eyes out.

The mourning days lasted for a long time **intermittently**①. Mom and dad didn't know how to comfort him. They knew that to tell the truth rather than to cheat his son she fell asleep: Grandma would never come back. "What does it mean 'never come back?'" Andre asked.

"All the things in the time never come back; once yesterday is gone, it will become yesterday forever, so you cannot go back to yesterday. Dad used to be like you, and now can't go back to your so little boyhood; one day you'll grow up, you will be old like the grandma; one day when you spend all your time, you can never come back," his father said.

After that, back home from school every day, Andre would be in the home garden watching the sun sink below the horizon slowly. He knew the day had gone. There was a new sun, but it would never be today's sun any more.

Time flew. Anxiety and sorrow mixed in the Andre's young heart. One day, he came home from school, saw the sun go down, made up his mind and said, "I will go home faster than the sun." He ran back like mad. When he stood in the front courtyard and **gasped**②, he saw the sun still exposing half of its face. He was excited to jump up. He felt he outran the sun that day. Later he would often do the game, sometimes

生词有约

① **intermittently**
adv. 断断续续地；间歇地

② **gasp**
vi. 喘气；喘息

race against the sun or the wind; sometimes the homework would take him one summer vacation, but he finished it only in ten days. He was in Grade Three that time, but he would often do the homework of Grade Five in **advance** ③.

Every time he won Time, Andre was **overwhelmed** ④ with joy.

In his growing days, he **benefited** ⑤ from **racing** ⑥ against Time. Though he knew that people can't run faster than Time, they can be faster compared to their original time, if running fast, they sometimes can be faster several steps, which may seem small, but their effect is great.

③ in advance
adv. 预先；提前
④ overwhelm
vt. 压倒；淹没
⑤ benefit
vi. 受益，得益
⑥ race
vi. 比速度；参加竞赛

胜过时间

安德烈的祖母去世了。读小学的安德烈心里难过极了，因为祖母生前非常疼爱他。他每天在学校操场上一圈又一圈地跑着，跑得累倒在地，扑在草坪上痛哭。

哀痛的日子断断续续维持了很久。爸爸妈妈也不知道如何安慰他。他们知道与其骗儿子说祖母睡着了，还不如说实话：祖母永远不会回来了。"什么是永远不会回来呢？"安德烈问道。

"所有时间里的事物都永远不会回来，昨天一旦过去，它就永远变成昨天，你不能再回到昨天。爸爸以前也和你一样小，现在也不能回到你这么小的童年了；有一天，你会长大，你会像祖母一样老；有一天你度过了你的时间，就永远不能回来了。"爸爸说。

以后，每天放学回家，安德烈就在家里的庭院里面看着太阳慢慢地沉到地平线以下，就知道一天真的过完了。尽管明天还会有新的太阳，但永远不会再有今天的太阳。

时间过得飞快，在安德烈幼小的心里不只是着急，还有悲伤。有一天，他放学回家，看到太阳快落山了，就下决心说："我要比太阳更快回家。"他狂奔回去，站在庭院前喘气时，看到太阳还露着半边脸，就高兴地跳跃起来，那一天他觉得自己跑赢了太阳。以后他就时常做那样的游戏，有时和太阳赛跑，有时和风比快，有时一个暑假才能完成的作业，他十天就做完了。那时他三年级，常常把五年级的作业拿来做。

每次比赛胜过时间，安德烈就乐不可支。

在他渐渐长大的日子里，和时间赛跑让他受益无穷。尽管他知道人永远跑不过时间，但人可以比自己原有的时间跑快一步；如果跑得快，有时可以快好几步。那几步看起来也许很小，但用途很大。

诵读经典 >>>>
Read classic

After that, back home from school every day, Andre would be in the home garden watching the sun sink below the horizon slowly. He knew the day had gone. There was a new sun, but it would never be today's sun any more.

以后，每天放学回家，安德烈就在家里的庭院里面看着太阳慢慢地沉到地平线以下，就知道一天真的过完了。尽管明天还会有新的太阳，但永远不会再有今天的太阳。

妙语连珠 >>>>
Sparkling discourse

✪ What is the man's first duty? The answer is brief: to be himself.
一个人的首要职责是什么？答案很简单：做自己。

✪ Fame usually comes to those who are thinking something else.
通常是没想到成名的人反而成了名。

The Wall of Indians

The climate in the desert is very special. In the daytime, after the gravel's **reflection**① and the **accumulation**② of heat, the fiery red sun can bake people to death; at night, the wilderness and desolation spreading with nothing covered can freeze people to death.

Although the desert climate is so terrible, American Indians still can live in there quite comfortably because their buildings have the function of turning ill luck in good.

In the desert, the wall of Indians is specially designed, its thickness just right—the heat of the sun cannot pass through the wall during the day, and when it's time for passing, the night has fallen. So in the night, while it is bitter cold in the outside, that hot wall slowly gives out the heat gained in the daytime, making the room warm.

If the wall is thin, the room will become an oven in the daytime, and even at night, it will not send out enough heat. But if the wall is thick, thought not hot in the day night, it will become cold at night because the heat can't pass thought it.

All the secret lies in the wall neither thick nor thin.

Whether or not living in the desert, each of us has such a wall—**reserve**③ people's praise for the **frustrated**④ time, get the arrows shot from the enemy as our weapon at the shortage of arms, turn the attacking words from the others into useful suggestions, leave the surplus money that can only cause crime to the possible poverty in future, just as the Indians leave the **scorching**⑤ sunlight to the cold night.

生词有约

① reflection

n. 反射

② accumulation

n. 累积；积聚

③ reserve

vt. 保留；储备

④ frustrated

adv. 失意的；挫败的

⑤ scorching

adj. 灼热的；激烈的

印第安人的墙

沙漠的气候非常特殊。白天，经过沙石的反射和热量的累积，火红的太阳能把人活活烤死；夜晚，旷野和荒寒在一无遮掩的情况下泛滥，又能把人冻僵。

尽管沙漠气候如此可怕，但美国印第安人却能安适地住在那里，因为他们的建筑有逢凶化吉的功用。

在沙漠里，印第安人的墙是经过特别设计的，它的厚度恰到好处——白天炽热的艳阳晒不透向阳的墙壁，正将热透时，夜晚就已经降临。于是，在外面酷寒难耐的夜里，晒热的土墙正慢慢散发出白天储存的热量，使室内变得温暖。

如果墙壁薄，白天室内就会变成烤箱，夜晚也不能散发足够的热力。如果墙壁厚，白天固然不至于炎热，夜晚却因透不过热力而变得寒冷。

这一切的奥妙就在于那不厚不薄的墙。

无论是否住在沙漠，我们每个人都要有这么一堵墙——把得意时别人的赞美留给失意时用；把敌人射来的箭接下，作为我们兵器短缺时的武器；把别人攻讦的言语化为有用的建议；把只能造成罪恶的多余钱财留给日后可能的贫困，就像印第安人将灼人的阳光留给寒冷的夜晚。

诵读经典 >>>>>
Read classic

In the desert, the wall of Indians is specially designed, its thickness just right—the heat of the sun cannot pass through the wall during the day, and when it's time for passing, the night has fallen. So in the night, while it is bitter cold in the outside, that hot wall slowly gives out the heat gained in the daytime, making the room warm.

在沙漠里，印第安人的墙是经过特别设计的，它的厚度恰到好处——白天炽热的艳阳晒不透向阳的墙壁，正将热透时，夜晚就已经降临。于是，在外面酷寒难耐的夜里，晒热的土墙正慢慢散发出白天储存的热量，使室内变得温暖。

妙语连珠 >>>>>
Sparkling discourse

✪ Patience! The windmill never strays in search of the wind.
耐心等待！风车从不跑去找风。

✪ If you would go up high, then use your own legs! Do not let yourselves carried aloft; do not seat yourselves on other people's backs and heads.
如果你想走到高处，就要使用自己的两条腿！不要让别人把你抬到高处；不要坐在别人的背上和头上。

The Biggest Winner

In some **affiliated**① bookstores of Germany Goldman Press, a large number of books were missing every year and this made the bookstore staff quite **annoyed**②. Usually, at the end of each year, the names and quantities of these lost books would be registered in a form and the form would be hung in the bookstore so as to alert the staff.

One day, an executive of the press **occasionally**③ found the form when he was making an inspection in the bookstores. He was even inspired. After he returned to the press, **designedly**④, he began publishing those books that were stolen most frequently.

In Frankfurt, a worldwide book fair is held annually. At the fair, every participating publisher will resort to various means of **propaganda**⑤ to **promote**⑥ the sale of their own books.

But the publicity of Goldman Press had a unique style— they showed a list of "the ten greatest German books that were stolen most frequently." **In consequence**⑦, the list attracted a large number of booksellers coming to order books and this made Goldman Press the biggest winner on the book fair.

The booksellers might not believe what the publishing houses advertised, but they were only convinced of the fact that the books that were stolen most frequently are usually readers' favorite ones and certainly they would become the most popular books.

生词有约

① affiliated
adj. 附属的；有关连的
② annoyed
adj. 恼怒的；烦恼的
③ occasionally
adv. 偶尔；间或

④ designedly
adv. 有计划地；故意地

⑤ propaganda
n. 宣传；宣传活动
⑥ promote
vt. 促进；提升；推销
⑦ in consequence
adv. 因此；结果

最大的赢家

德国戈尔德曼出版社下属的一些书店每年都有大量的图书丢失，这让书店的工作人员十分苦恼。通常，每年年终这些丢失图书的名称和数量都要被登记在一个表格上。这个表格将被悬挂在书店里，对员工起到一个提醒作用。

一天，出版社的一位负责人在巡视书店时偶然看到了这张表格，竟然被激发了灵感，他回到出版社后，开始有计划地出版那些被偷次数最多的图书。

法兰克福每年都要举行一次世界性书展。书展上，每个参展的出版社都要使出各种宣传手段推销自己的图书。

但是，戈尔德曼出版社的宣传却别具一格。他们展示了一份"被偷窃次数最多的十大德文书籍"名单。结果，这份名单一下子吸引了大量书商前来订货，这使戈尔德曼出版社成为书展上最大的赢家。

书商们可能不相信出版社的广告，但他们只相信一个事实：被偷次数最多的图书通常是读者最喜欢的图书，它们也必然会成为最畅销的书。

诵读经典 >>>>>
Read classic

But the publicity of Goldman Press had a unique style—they showed a list of "the ten greatest German books that were stolen most frequently." In consequence, the list attracted a large number of booksellers coming to order books and this made Goldman Press the biggest winner on the book fair.

但是，戈尔德曼出版社的宣传却别具一格。他们展示了一份"被偷窃次数最多的十大德文书籍"名单。结果，这份名单一下子吸引了大量书商前来订货，这使戈尔德曼出版社成为书展上最大的赢家。

妙语连珠 >>>>>
Sparkling discourse

✪ The three foundations of learning: seeing much, suffering much, and studying much.
求学的三个基本条件是：多观察，多吃苦，多研究。

✪ As long as the world shall last there will be wrongs, and if no man rebelled, those wrongs would last forever.
只要世界还存在，就会有错误，如果没有人反叛，这些错误将永远存在下去。

The Distance between Hearts

The master asked his disciples, "Why shall we shout out when we get angry? Why shall we yell at each other when we are vexed?"

One **disciple**[①] said, "We are not **self-composed**[②] enough, so we yell at each other."

"But why do you still choose to shout when the other person is right next to you? Can't you speak to them in a soft voice?" The master continued.

The master explained, "When two people are both angry, one heart will become far from another. In order to fill up this distance, they must shout so that one can hear another. The angrier they get, the greater the distance between the two hearts will be, so they will have to shout more loudly, and only in this way can they hear."

The master asked again, "When two **adore**[③] each other, what will happen? They don't need to yell at each other but only talk quietly, because the distance between two hearts is shortened. When they love each other more dearly, what will happen then? When the two fall in love, their hearts get closer. They even don't need to speak. Only looking at each other, that will be enough."

生词有约

① disciple
n. 弟子；门徒
② self-composed
adj. 镇定的；沉着的

③ adore
vt. 崇拜；爱慕

心与心的距离

大师问他的弟子："为什么在愤怒时，我们会大声喊叫？为什么在烦恼时，我们要彼此喊叫？"

一名弟子说："因为我们不够镇定，所以彼此喊叫。"

"但是，为什么当另一个人就在你旁边，你还是选择喊叫呢？难道不能以柔和的语气跟对方说吗？"大师继续问道。

大师解释道："当两个人带着愤怒情绪时，他们的心和心距离很远。为了填补这段距离，他们必须喊叫，这样彼此才能听到。他们越是愤怒，心和心的距离就越远，他们只能更大声地喊叫，那样他们才能听到。"

大师再次问道："当两个人相互爱慕，会发生什么呢？他们不需要彼此喊叫，只要轻声交谈，那是因为心与心的距离变近了。当他们彼此爱得更深，又会发生什么呢？两个人相爱时，他们的心靠得更近，他们甚至不需要说话，只需看着对方，就够了。"

诵读经典 >>>>>
Read classic

When two people are both angry, one heart will become far from another. In order to fill up this distance, they must shout so that one can hear another. The angrier they get, the greater the distance between the two hearts will be, so they will have to shout more loudly, and only in this way can they hear.

当两个人带着愤怒情绪时，他们的心和心距离很远。为了填补这段距离，他们必须喊叫，这样彼此才能听到。他们越是愤怒，心和心的距离就越远，他们只能更大声地喊叫，那样他们才能听到。

妙语连珠 >>>>>
Sparkling discourse

✪ Always bear in mind that your own resolution to succeed is more important than any one thing.

永远记住：你自己的取得成功的决心比什么都重要。

✪ The profoundest thought or passion sleeps as in a mine until an equal mind and heart finds and publishes it.

最深的思想或感情就如同深睡的矿藏，在等待着同样深沉的头脑与心灵去发现和开采。

There Is No Giant

Once, Einstein gave a lecture in a university, where the large classroom was full of teachers and students who respected him. After his speech, the audience on the scene started to ask questions.

A girl got up and asked, "You're known as a giant of science. Do you think you're a giant?"

Einstein said with a smile, "A giant isn't a person who is tall in height. You see I'm so small, how can I have an image of a giant? Maybe I see a bit farther, only because I stand higher!"

Then a boy asked, "You mentioned you stand higher than others, it reminds me that you had a long talk with a lady on the peak of the Alps. I don't want to ask what you talked, but I want to know whether you realized you have been a peak in the history of science when you stood on the peak."

Looking at the boy carefully, Einstein asked, "Do you think I'm like a peak? Anyhow, my height cannot become a peak. And what's more, there is no peak that no one can conquer, so we don't want to be a peak, but we want to be a person to climb the **summit**[1]!"

Then, he took up a piece of chalk and wrote on the blackboard, "Standing on the peak, you are not tall, but even smaller!"

He then turned to the audience and said, "Although I stand tall, in the eyes of the world I'm still small! Finally, I can

生词有约

① summit

n. 顶点；最高阶层

tell you a sentence, which was the last one I told the lady on the peak of the Alps: 'Any peak can be conquered, for there is no giant in the world but the one who stands higher!'"

A storm of **applause**② sounded. The lady who listened to Einstein's **instruction**③ on the Alps that year was no other than Madam Curie!

② applause

n. 喝彩；鼓掌欢迎

③ instruction

n. 指示；教导

从来没有巨人

有一次，爱因斯坦在一所大学演讲，大教室里坐满了对他充满崇敬之情的师生。演讲完毕，由现场人员开始自由提问。

一位女生站起来问："您被誉为科学界的巨人，您认为自己是巨人吗？"

爱因斯坦微笑着说："巨人并不是长得高大的人。大家看我如此瘦小，怎么能有巨人的形象呢？也许我看得远一些，那也只是因为我站得高一些而已！"

一个男生接着问："您提到比别人站得高一些，我想起了不久前您在阿尔卑斯山的高峰之巅曾和一位女士长谈过一次。我不想问您谈话的内容，只想知道站在山顶的那一刻，您是否意识到在科学史上自己也已站成一座山峰。"

爱因斯坦仔细地看了看发问的人，问道："你看我像一座山峰吗？我这个身高不管怎么站都成不了山峰。而且，没有一座高峰不是被人征服的，我们不要做高峰，而要做登上山顶的人！"

说着，他拿起粉笔在黑板上写下一行字："站在山顶，你并不高大，反而更加渺小！"

随后，他转过身，对台下的人说："虽然我站得高，但在世人的眼中依然是渺小的！最后，我可以告诉大家一句话，这句话也是我在阿尔卑斯山绝顶之上对那位女士讲的最后一句：'任何一座高峰都是可以征服的，世上从来没有巨人，只有站得更高的人！'"

台下掌声一片。当年在阿尔卑斯山上聆听爱因斯坦教诲的那位女士正是居里夫人！

诵读经典 >>>>>
Read classic

Although I stand tall, in the eyes of the world I'm still small! Finally, I can tell you a sentence, which was the last one I told the lady on the peak of the Alps: "Any peak can be conquered, for there is no giant in the world but the one who stands higher!"

虽然我站得高，但在世人的眼中依然是渺小的！最后，我可以告诉大家一句话，这句话也是我在阿尔卑斯山绝顶之上对那位女士讲的最后一句："任何一座高峰都是可以征服的，世上从来没有巨人，只有站得更高的人！"

妙语连珠 >>>>>
Sparkling discourse

✪ Laziness is like a lock, which bolts you out of the storehouse of information and makes you an intellectual starveling.

懒惰就像一把锁，锁住了知识的仓库，使你的智力变得匮乏。

✪ The people who get on in this world are the people who get up and look for circumstances they want, and if they cannot find them, they make them.

在这个世界上，取得成功的人是那些努力寻找他们想要机会的人，如果找不到机会，他们就去创造机会。

What You Want to Look for Is What You Will Find

A young man called Cindy came to an oasis, where he met an old man.

Cindy asked, "What about here?"

The old man asked, "What about your hometown?"

Cindy replied, "It's horrible! I **loathe**① it."

The old man went on, "Well, hurry away. It's as horrible as your hometown."

Later came a young man called Rockery. He asked the same question and the old man also **countered**② with the same question.

Rockery replied, "My hometown is so good. I miss its people, flowers and things..."

The old man said, "It's equally good here."

The listener was so surprised that he asked the old man why his answer was different from the first one.

The old man said, "What you want to look for is what you will find!"

If you're **enterprising**③, you will live in the oasis. If you reach for what's beyond your grasp and reap without **sowing**④, the oasis of life will become the desert.

生词有约

① loathe
vt. 讨厌；厌恶

② counter
vi. 还击；反驳

③ enterprising
adj. 有事业心的；有进取心的

④ sow
vi. 播种

你要寻找什么，就会找到什么

一个名叫辛迪的青年来到一片绿洲。他碰到一位老人。

辛迪问："这里如何？"

老人反问说："你的家乡如何？"

辛迪回答："糟透了！我很讨厌。"

老人接着说："那你快走，这里同你家乡一样糟。"

后来又来了一个名叫罗加瑞的青年问同样的问题，老人家也是同样的反问。

罗加瑞回答说："我的家乡很好，我很想念家乡的人、鲜花和事物……"

老人便说："这里也是同样的好。"

旁听者觉得诧异，问老人为什么前后说法不一致。

老人说："你要寻找什么，就会找到什么！"

如果有进取心，生活则处处是绿洲。如果好高骛远、不劳而获，生活中的绿洲就会变成沙漠。

诵读经典 >>>>>
Read classic

If you're enterprising, you will live in the oasis. If you reach for what's beyond your grasp and reap without sowing, the oasis of life will become the desert.

如果有进取心，生活则处处是绿洲。如果好高骛远、不劳而获，生活中的绿洲就会变成沙漠。

妙语连珠 >>>>>
Sparkling discourse

❂ Work is the grand cure of all the maladies and miseries that ever beset mankind.

工作是医治人间一切病痛和疾苦的万应良药。

❂ Diligence is the mother of good luck; plough deep while shuggards sleep, you will have corn to sell and to keep.

勤奋是幸运之母；如果懒汉睡觉的时候你深耕土地，你就会有谷物出售和储存。

Courage Is Strength

A father was worried about his son, who was sixteen years old but had no courage at all. So the father decided to call on a **Buddhist** ① monk to train his boy.

The Buddhist monk said to the boy's father, "You should leave your son alone here. I'll make him into a real man within three months. However, you can't come to see him during this period."

Three months later, the boy's father returned. The Buddhist monk arranged a **boxing match** ② between the boy and an experienced boxer. Each time the fighter struck the boy, he fell down, but at once the boy stood up; and each time a **punch** ③ knocked him down, the boy stood up again. Several times later, the Buddhist monk asked, "What do you think of your child?"

"What a shame!" the boy's father said. "I never thought he would be so easily knocked down. I needn't have him left here any longer."

"I'm sorry that that's all you see. Don't you see that each time he falls down, he stands up again instead of crying? That's the kind of courage you wanted him to have."

生词有约

① Buddhist
adj. 佛教的

② boxing match
n. 拳赛

③ punch
n. 一拳，一击

勇气就是力量

一位父亲为儿子担心。儿子16岁了，却没有一点勇气。于是，父亲决定去拜访一位禅师，请他训练儿子。

禅师对男孩的父亲说："你应该让他单独留在这里。不出 3 个月，我要让他成为一个真正的男子汉。不过，在这段时间，你不能来见他。"

3 个月后，男孩的父亲又来见禅师。禅师安排这个男孩和一位经验丰富的拳师进行拳击比赛。拳师每次一出手，男孩就倒在地上，但男孩又马上站起来；每次将他击倒，他就又站起来。几个回合后，禅师问道："你认为自己的孩子怎么样？"

"真丢人！"男孩的父亲说，"我决没想到他这样不堪一击。我不需要他再留在这里了。"

"很遗憾，你只看到这一点。难道你没看到他每次倒下后并没有哭泣，而是重新站起来了吗？这才是你想要他拥有的那种勇气。"

诵读经典 >>>>>
Read classic

I'm sorry that that's all you see. Don't you see that each time he falls down, he stands up again instead of crying? That's the kind of courage you wanted him to have.

很遗憾，你只看到这一点。难道你没看到他每次倒下后并没有哭泣，而是重新站起来了吗？这才是你想要他拥有的那种勇气。

妙语连珠 >>>>>
Sparkling discourse

❀ Do not, for one repulse, forgo the purpose that you resolved to effort.
不要只因一次挫败，就放弃你原来决心想达到的目的。

❀ We must accept finite disappointment, but we must never lose infinite hope.
我们必须接受失望，因为它是有限的，但千万不可失去希望，因为它是无限的。

After hearing this, the officer, as if electrified, jumped from the velvet chair right off and ordered his troops, "Retreat!"

军官听后，像触了电似的，一下从天鹅绒椅子上跳了下来，向他的部队下令道：“撤退！”

画龙点睛

The Blue Force and the Red Army

After a captive from the Blue Force was released by the Red Army, the Blue Force officer asked this released solider what he had seen in the Red Army's **barracks**① in order to master the conditions. The solider answered, "I saw they drinking water."

"Drinking water?" the officer said, "Are you too thirsty to see anything else? For example, how many guns, how many troops, and how many **fortifications**② do they have? What's the use of drinking water?"

"Drinking water is not worth seeing," the soldier threw a piece of chocolate into his mouth, "But it was really funny that their soldiers drank water."

"Funny to drink water? Adventure! Tell us how they drank water." With this, the officer leaned against the velvet **lounge**③.

"Hey! So ridiculous," said the soldier, "All their soldiers were so thirsty that their lips **parched**④, but there was only one kettle of water left. The kettle was passed on in their hands. When all the soldiers finished drinking, guess what? More than a half of the water was left! At last I drank the last half."

After hearing this, the officer, as if **electrified**⑤, jumped from the velvet chair right off and ordered his troops, "Retreat!"

"Why?" asked his soldiers.

"Seeing how you **scramble for**⑥ tins and food like hell, I know it will be in vain to defeat such a united and **companionate**⑦ troop!"

生词有约

① barracks
n. 兵营；营房

② fortifications
n. 防御工事

③ lounge
n. 躺椅
④ parch
vi. 焦干；烤干

⑤ electrify
vt. 使充电；使触电
⑥ scramble for
争夺；勉强拼凑
⑦ companionate
adj. 友好的；有爱的；同伴的

蓝军与红军

一个蓝军的俘虏被红军释放回来后，蓝军军官问这个被红军放回来的士兵，被俘后在红军的兵营里见到了什么，以便能掌握一些情况。

士兵答道："我见到他们的士兵喝水。"

"喝水？"蓝军军官说，"你是不是渴坏了，别的看不见？比如他们有多少炮，有多少兵力，筑了多少工事？喝点水有什么好看的？"

"本来喝水是没有什么好看的，"这个士兵把一块巧克力扔进嘴里，"只是他们的士兵喝水实在好笑。"

"喝水都好笑？新鲜！告诉我们，他们是怎么喝法。"说完，蓝军军官靠在天鹅绒躺椅上。

"嘿！真好笑。"士兵说，"他们所有的士兵嘴唇都渴得干裂了，但只剩下一壶水。他们传着喝水壶里的水，所有的士兵都传完了，你猜怎么样？水还没喝去半壶！最后半壶被我喝了。"

军官听后，像触了电似的，一下从天鹅绒椅子上跳了下来，向他的部队下令道："撤退！"

"为什么？"士兵不解地问。

"看你们见到罐头、食物就不要命争抢的劲头，我就知道我们要战胜这样一支团结友爱的部队，简直是妄想！"

诵读经典 >>>>>
Read classic

All their soldiers were so thirsty that their lips parched, but there was only one kettle of water left. The kettle was passed on in their hands. When all the soldiers finished drinking, guess what? More than a half of the water was left!

他们所有的士兵嘴唇都渴得干裂了，但只剩下一壶水。他们传着喝水壶里的水，所有的士兵都传完了，你猜怎么样？水还没喝去半壶！

妙语连珠 >>>>>
Sparkling discourse

❂ When I was young, I admired clever people. Now that I am old, I admire kind people.

少时喜欢聪明人，老来喜欢仁厚人。

❂ Dare and the world always yields. If it beats you sometimes, dare it again and again and it will succumb.

你勇敢，世界就会让步。如果有时它战胜你，你要不断地勇敢再勇敢，它就会屈服。

The Best Nourishment

Life is like a garden and you reap what you sow in it. Anything is within your own control.

We can plant the positive seeds, or negative ones, in this garden. Positive seeds can give us strength and lead us to the other shore of success. Negative seeds, however, eventually will grow to be a kind of crop **devouring**① our **potential**② ability to success and result in negative action, with which we can't win success.

Just like the fact that weed will grow in the gardens, all people have shortcomings. People's shortcomings are like the weed in the gardens, which can still grow without **cultivating**③. So, if not being cleared in time, they will soon seize the whole garden.

Seeds need water to sow and **irrigate**④. To sow the seed in the garden of life, the water of minds is needed. The seed sowed and irrigated with the water of mind will never die back, and will help us grow into **towering**⑤ trees.

Crops need fertilizers to thrive. If you want to grow a wish in the garden of your life, you are expected to mix up your desire and passion, because passion is the best fertilizer to ensure the rapid growth of your desire.

The garden of life is not a wide field and it can't accept all things in the world. Therefore, you must be selective when planting. We must concentrate on what we want, but not on the things we don't. Only in this way can we **maximize**⑥ the good use of our small garden.

Will you make your garden of life full of beautiful

生词有约

① devour
vt. 吞噬；毁灭
② potential
adj. 潜在的；可能的

③ cultivate
vt. 栽培；种植；培育
④ irrigate
vi. 灌溉；冲洗

⑤ towering
adj. 高耸的；卓越的

⑥ maximize
vt. 取……最大价值；对……极为重视

flowers or full of weeds?

Make your decision and choice right away because a person's garden of life is not **eternal**⑦.

⑦ eternal
adj. 永恒的；不朽的

最佳养料

人生如同花园，你在里面种瓜得瓜，种豆得豆，一切全都在于你自己的把握之中。

我们可以在这个花园里播种积极的种子，也可以播种消极的种子。积极的种子能给我们力量，让我们到达成功的彼岸。消极的种子最终长成的将会是一种吞噬我们成功潜能的消极行动作物，让我们无法获得成功。

花园会长杂草，人会有缺点。人的缺点如同花园里的杂草，杂草不需培植照样生长。所以，如不及时清除，它们很快就会占领整个花园。

种子需用水来播种和浇灌。在人生花园里播种的种子，就要使用心灵之水。用心灵之水播种和浇灌的种子是不会枯死的，它将会有助我们长成参天大树。

作物需要肥料才能茁壮成长。如果你想在人生花园中种植一个愿望，那就请你将这个愿望与热情混合起来，因为热情是确保这个愿望快速成长的最佳肥料。

人生花园不是广阔的田野，它无法接纳世上所有的东西。因此，必须要有所选择地种植。我们必须专注于我们想要的东西，而不是关注我们不想要的东西。这样，我们才能最大限度地用好这片小花园。

是让你的人生花园姹紫嫣红呢，还是让它杂草丛生？

赶快作出决定和选择吧，因为一个人的人生花园并不是永恒的。

诵读经典 >>>>>
Read classic

The garden of life is not a wide field and it can't accept all things in the world. Therefore, you must be selective when planting. We must concentrate on what we want, but not on the things we don't. Only in this way can we maximize the good use of our small garden.

人生花园不是广阔的田野，它无法接纳世上所有的东西。因此，必须要有所选择地种植。我们必须专注于我们想要的东西，而不是关注我们不想要的东西。这样，我们才能最大限度地用好这片小花园。

妙语连珠 >>>>>
Sparkling discourse

★ Try not to become a man of success but rather try to become a man of value.

不要为成功而努力，要为作一个有价值的人而努力。

★ The reasonable man adapts himself to the world; the unreasonable one persists in trying to adapt the world to himself.

明白事理的人使自己适应世界；不明事理的人想使世界适应自己。

So, what magic prompted the supernormal development of the steel company?

那么，是什么魔力促使了伯利恒钢铁公司超常规的发展呢？

画龙
点睛

Do Important Things Every Day

Bethlehem Steel Company in the USA, once a little-known small plant, became the world's largest independent steel works after just five years.

So, what magic **prompted**① the **supernormal**② development of the steel company? It totally benefited from one gold idea of Elvialy. He told Suwap, the company's president, "Write down the most important thing you are going to do on a piece of paper, then use the number to mark the order of importance of everything to you and your company. The next morning, the first thing you should do is to take out that piece of paper, try your best to do the most important thing; don't do any other until it has been done. Then set about the second important by the same **approach**③, and the third, until you come off work. If you only finish the first thing, it doesn't matter, because you're always doing the most important thing!"

Bethlehem Steel Company developed and **thrived**④ because it was always doing important things every day.

When you **haggle over**⑤ every ounce and are swayed by considerations of gain and loss, shouldn't you remind yourself to do important things every day? For a man's time and energy is limited, and care about small things too much will waste the great ones and your whole life.

生词有约

① prompt
vt. 促进；激起
② supernormal
adj. 非凡的；异于寻常的

③ approach
n. 方法；途径

④ thrive
vi. 繁荣；兴旺；茁壮成长
⑤ haggle over
斤斤计较

每天都做重要的事

美国伯利恒钢铁公司曾经只是一个鲜为人知的小钢铁厂，短短 5 年的时间，便一跃成为世界上最大的独立钢铁厂。

那么，是什么魔力促使了伯利恒钢铁公司超常规的发展呢？这全得益于美国效益专家艾维·利的一个金点子，他对公司总裁舒瓦普说："在一张纸片上写下你明天要做的最重要的事，然后用数字标明每件事对你和你公司重要性的次序。第二天早上，你首先要做的，就是把纸片拿出来，做第一项最重要的事，不要做其他的，全力办第一件事，直至办完为止。然后用同样的方法对待第二项，第三项，直至你下班为止。如果只做完第一件事，那不要紧，因为你总是在做最重要的事！"

伯利恒钢铁公司的发展壮大，就是因为每天都在做重要的事。

当你还在为小事斤斤计较、患得患失、烦恼不已时，是不是该提醒提醒自己：每天都做重要的事。因为人的时间和精力是有限的，过分在小事上劳心费神，就会荒废大事，荒废整个人生。

诵读经典 >>>>>
Read classic

When you haggle over every ounce and are swayed by considerations of gain and loss, shouldn't you remind yourself to do important things every day? For a man's time and energy is limited, and care about small things too much will waste the great ones and your whole life.

当你还在为小事斤斤计较、患得患失、烦恼不已时，是不是该提醒提醒自己：每天都做重要的事。因为人的时间和精力是有限的，过分在小事上劳心费神，就会荒废大事，荒废整个人生。

妙语连珠 >>>>>
Sparkling discourse

★ If you do not learn to think when you are young, you may never learn.

如果你年轻时不学会思考，那就永远不会。

★ Do not know how high the sky is until one climbs up the tops of mountains, and do not know how thick the earth is until one comes to the deep river.

不登高山，不知天之高也；不临深溪，不知天之厚也。

He walked to the corner almost in despair, but accidentally discovered a water pump.

他几近绝望地走到屋角，却意外地发现了一台抽水机。

画龙
点睛

Re-fill It with Water

A man walked in the desert for two days. He encountered sand storm en route. After a **gust**① of sand storm, he couldn't identify the right direction. While unable to hold fast, he suddenly found an abandoned cabin. He dragged his exhausted body into the room. This was a small airless cabin, **stacked**② with some **decaying**③ wood. He walked to the corner almost in despair, but accidentally discovered a water pump.

Excitedly, he went forward to draw water, but he couldn't pump water no matter how hard he tried. He sat on the ground **dejected**④ when he saw a small bottle with a cork plugging the mouth; on the bottle was posted a yellowed note, which read: You must pour the water into the pump before you can draw water! Don't forget, before you leave, re-fill it with water! He **unplugged**⑤ the stopper and found the bottle was really filled with water!

At this moment he thought: if I'm a little selfish, as long as I drink the water in the bottle, I can go out of this room alive! If I do as the note told to pour the only water into the pump, in case the water can't come back, I will be thirsty to death. Will I take the risk or not?

Finally, he decided to pour the only water into the worn-out pump and began to draw water with his trembling hands. **Sure enough**⑥, the water really **gushed**⑦ out richly!

After he drank enough water, he filled the bottle with water, enveloped it with the cork and added his words after the note: Believe me, it's really useful. Before you get it, you should first learn to pay out.

生词有约

① gust

n. 一阵狂风

② stack

vt. 堆积；堆叠

③ decay

vi. 腐烂；衰退

④ dejected

adj. 沮丧的；灰心的

⑤ unplug

vt. 拔去……的塞子或插头

⑥ sure enough

果真；果然

⑦ gush

vi. 涌出；迸出

126

请再装满水

一个人在沙漠行走了两天。途中遇到暴风沙。一阵狂沙过后，他已认不得正确的方向。正当快撑不住时，他突然发现了一幢废弃的小屋。他拖着疲惫的身子走进了屋内。这是一间不通风的小屋子，里面堆了一些枯朽的木材。他几近绝望地走到屋角，却意外地发现了一台抽水机。

他兴奋地上前汲水，却任凭他怎么抽水，也抽不出半滴来。他颓然坐地，却看见抽水机旁有一个用软木塞堵住瓶口的小瓶子，瓶上贴了一张泛黄的纸条，纸条上写着：你必须用水灌入抽水机才能引水！别忘了，你离开前，请再装满水！他拔开瓶塞，发现瓶子里果然装满了水！

此时，他心里想：如果自私点，只要将瓶子里的水喝掉，我就不会渴死，就能活着走出这间屋子！如果照纸条做，把瓶子里唯一的水倒入抽水机内，万一水一去不回，我就会渴死在这地方了。到底要不要冒险？

最后，他决定把瓶子里唯一的水全部灌入看起来破旧不堪的抽水机里，以颤抖的手汲水，水真的大量涌了出来！

他将水喝足后，把瓶子装满水，用软木塞封好，然后在原来那张纸条后面再加他自己的话：相信我，真的有用。在取得之前，要先学会付出。

诵读经典 ❯❯❯❯❯
Read classic

After he drank enough water, he filled the bottle with water, enveloped it with the cork and added his words after the note: Believe me, it's really useful. Before you get it, you should first learn to pay out.

他将水喝足后，把瓶子装满水，用软木塞封好，然后在原来那张纸条后面再加他自己的话：相信我，真的有用。在取得之前，要先学会付出。

妙语连珠 ❯❯❯❯❯
Sparkling discourse

✪ We must accept finite disappointment, but we must never lose infinite hope.
我们必须接受失望，因为它是有限的，但千万不可失去希望，因为它是无穷的。

✪ Great nations write their autobiographies in three manuscripts—the book of their deeds, the book of their words and the book of their art.
伟大的民族用三种手稿写他们的自传——行为之书、言语之书和艺术之书。

There's only one rule: It must be a story which I cannot believe; if I can believe it, I won't give away the bag of gold.

只有一条规定：它必须是一个我不相信的故事；如果我相信这个故事，我就不会送这袋金子。

画龙点睛

The Old Man and the King

In Spain there once lived a king and he was very fond of jokes. "I'll give a bag full of gold," he said, "to the person who can tell me the best story. There's only one rule: It must be a story which I cannot believe; if I can believe it, I won't give away the bag of gold."

People came to the king from all parts of the country. They brought strange and wonderful stories. The king sat in his palace and listened to all the stories. He enjoyed them very much, but to each person be said, "I can believe that story. It could happen and it may be true. So I won't give you the bag of gold."

As last a poor old man came to the palace. He was carrying a huge stone jar. The old man went into the king's room and said, "Oh, King, your good father was once a poor man and my father was rich. They were very good friends. My father gave your father a large **jar**①, like this one, and it was full of gold. Your father promised to give back the gold when he became rich. But he didn't give it back. Now I am poor and you are rich. And I want the gold."

The king said, "I don't believe that story. The jar is very big. There isn't enough gold in all my country to fill that jar. My father didn't tell me anything about a large jar full of gold."

"All right," the old man said. "**Never mind**②. If you don't believe the story, give me the bag of gold, please."

The king remembered the rule, and he gave the old man a bag of gold.

生词有约

① jar
n. 罐；广口瓶

② never mind
没关系

老人和国王

从前，西班牙有一位国王，他非常喜欢笑话。他说："谁能给我讲最好的故事，我就送给他满满一袋金子。只有一条规定：它必须是一个我不相信的故事；如果我相信这个故事，我就不会送这袋金子。"

人们从全国四面八方来到国王身边，带来了各种稀奇古怪的故事。国王坐在王宫里听着所有的故事。他非常喜欢这些故事。但是，他对每个人说："我相信这个故事。它可能会发生，也许是真的。所以，我不会送这袋金子。"

最后，一个穷困的老人来到了王宫。他扛着一个大石罐。老人走进国王的房间说："噢，国王，你的好父亲曾经是一个穷人，而我的父亲却十分富有。他们曾经是非常要好的朋友。我的父亲送给你的父亲一只像这样的大罐子，罐子里装满了金子。你的父亲答应在他富裕之后还回金子。但是，他没有还。现在我穷、你富，所以我想要那袋金子。"

国王说："我不相信那个故事。那个罐子很大。我的国家没有足够的金子放满那个罐子。我的父亲从来没有告诉过我任何一大罐金子的事儿。"

"好吧，"老人说。"没关系。如果你不相信这个故事，请把那袋金子给我吧。"

国王想起了那个规定，就送给了老人一袋金子。

诵读经典 >>>>>
Read classic

❂ People came to the king from all parts of the country. They brought strange and wonderful stories.

人们从全国四面八方来到国王身边，带来了各种稀奇古怪的故事。

❂ The king said, "I don't believe that story. The jar is very big. There isn't enough gold in all my country to fill that jar. My father didn't tell me anything about a large jar full of gold."

国王说："我不相信那个故事。那个罐子很大。我的国家没有足够的金子放满那个罐子。我的父亲从来没有告诉过我任何一大罐金子的事儿。"

妙语连珠 >>>>>
Sparkling discourse

❂ A man is not old as long as he is seeking something. A man is not old until regrets take the place of dreams.

只要一个人还有追求，他就没有老。直到后悔取代了梦想，一个人才算老。

❂ One's real value first lies in to what degree and what sense he set himself.

一个人的真正价值首先决定于他在什么程度上和在什么意义上从自我解放出来。

He looked all round. Now he was alone. He put the bag on the ground and opened it. How disappointing! There was no gold in the bag— only beans.

他看了看四周，四周只有他一个人。他将小袋子放在地上，打开来。他是多么失望！袋子里没有金子，只有蚕豆。

The Best Gift

One day two travelers met at the foot of the Golden Mountains.

"Hello, young man. Where are you going?" asked the old one.

"To the mountains," replied the young traveler.

"Be careful! There are dangerous men in those mountains. They don't like strangers."

"Don't worry," said the young man. "I've got a gun."

"That's not necessary," said the old man. "You don't need any gun. I went there yesterday. Just take a present. If you take a present, everything will be all right. I went there yesterday. I just took a small bag of beans and gave them to the chief. He was very pleased with them. He had never seen beans before. He was so pleased that he gave me a small bag of gold."

The young traveler was very excited. "Oh, gold! Wonderful!" he said excitedly.

The next morning he prepared his things and walked up the mountain. He took a present for the chief①—a small bag of peas. Soon he met the dangerous men and their chief. The young traveler smiled nervously② and gave him the bag of beans. The chief was pleased with the peas. He laughed and showed them to his men. Then he invited the young man to eat with them. After the meal the chief smiled and gave the young traveler a small brown bag. The young man took the bag and went quickly down the road. After about a kilometer he stopped—he was impatient③ to count the gold.

生词有约

① chief
n. 首领；酋长

② nervously
adv. 焦急地；提心吊胆地

③ impatient
adj. 不耐心的；焦躁的

He looked all round. Now he was alone. He put the bag on the ground and opened it. How disappointing! There was no gold in the bag—only beans.

最好的礼物

有一天，两个旅行者在金山脚下相遇。

"你好，年轻人，你要到什么地方去呀？"年龄大的那个问道。

"到山里去，"年轻的旅行者回答说。

"小心！那些山里有危险的人。他们不喜欢陌生人。

"别担心，"年轻人说。"我带有枪。"

"那倒不必，"年纪大的那个人说。"你不需要枪。我昨天去了那里。请带一份礼物就行了。如果你带一份礼物，一切都会平安无事。我昨天去过那里，只带了一小包蚕豆，并将它们送给了首领。他对此非常高兴。他以前从来没有见过蚕豆。他一高兴就送给了我一小袋金子。"

年轻人听了非常激动。"噢，金子！太棒了！"他兴奋地说。

第二天早上，他准备了东西，就上山了。他为首领带了一份礼物——是一小袋蚕豆。他马上就碰到那帮危险的人和他们的首领。年轻人忐忑不安地微笑着将那包蚕豆送给了首领。首领看到那些蚕豆，非常高兴。他哈哈大笑，又让那帮人看那些蚕豆。随后，首领邀请年轻人跟他们一块吃饭。饭后，首领微微一笑，送给年轻人一个棕色小袋子。年轻人接住袋子，沿路飞快地下了山。走了大约一公里后，他停住脚步，迫不及待地想数那些金子。

他看了看四周，四周只有他一个人。他将小袋子放在地上，打开来。他是多么失望！袋子里没有金子，只有蚕豆。

诵读经典 >>>>>
Read classic

After the meal the chief smiled and gave the young traveler a small brown bag. The young man took the bzag and went quickly down the road. After about a kilometer he stopped—he was impatient to count the gold.

饭后，首领微微一笑，送给年轻人一个棕色小袋子。年轻人接住袋子，沿路飞快地下了山。走了大约一公里后，他停住脚步，迫不及待地想数那些金子。

妙语连珠 〉〉〉〉〉
Sparkling discourse

✪ Books are the advisor in hand anytime.

书是随时在近旁的顾问。

✪ In a happy marriage it is the wife who provides the climate, the husband the landscape.

幸福婚姻在于妻子提供好天气，丈夫提供好风景。

At last, they agreed that the first crow would fill his sack with cotton and the second crow would fill his with salt.

最后，它们同意第一只乌鸦的袋子里装满棉花，第二只乌鸦的袋子里装满盐。

画龙
点睛

Who Can Fly Higher?

There were once two crows who were **fierce**① rivals.

One day, one of the crows said to the other, "You realize, of course, that I can fly much higher than you can."

"Don't be **ridiculous**②," the other crow said. "Everyone knows that I can fly much higher than you."

"No, you can't," the first crow said.

"Yes, I can," the second crow replied, and the argument went on and on.

At last, they decided to have a contest to **settle**③ the **issue**④.

"We will **compete**⑤ to find out who can fly higher while carrying a sack," the first crow said.

They argued for some time over the size of the sack, but finally came to an agreement.

Then there was further argument about what each sack would contain.

At last, they agreed that the first crow would fill his sack with cotton and the second crow would fill his with salt.

The first crow thought he was being very clever to agree to this because salt is much heavier than cotton.

In the end, they were ready for the contest, and holding their sacks in their beaks, they flew up into the sky.

They had not been flying for long, however, when it began to rain—as the second crow had expected it would.

As the cotton got wetter and wetter, it became heavier and heavier.

However, the salt just **dissolved**⑥ in the rain, so the second crow was easily able to fly higher than the first.

生词有约

① fierce
adj. 凶猛的；暴烈的

② ridiculous
adj. 可笑的；荒谬的

③ settle
vt. 解决；安排

④ issue
n. 问题

⑤ compete
vi. 竞争；对抗

⑥ dissolve
vi. 溶解；消失

谁会飞得更高?

从前有两只乌鸦,它们是死对头。

有一天,一只乌鸦对另一只说:"你当然知道我能飞得比你高得多。"

"别荒唐了,"另一只乌鸦说。"大家都知道我能比你飞得高得多。"

"不,你不能,"第一只乌鸦说。

"能,我能,"第二只乌鸦答道。随后,争论就没完没了。

最后,它们决定进行一场比赛,来解决争端。

"我们比一比看谁能带上一袋子东西飞得更高,"第一只乌鸦说。

它们就袋子的大小又争论了一阵子。但是,终于达成了协议。

接下来,它们又为每只袋子里装什么东西进一步争论起来。

最后,它们同意第一只乌鸦的袋子里装满棉花,第二只乌鸦的袋子里装满盐。

第一只乌鸦心想,同意这样做,自己真聪明,因为盐比棉花重得多。

最终,它们准备进行这场比赛,它们嘴里衔着袋子,飞上了天空。

然而,它们没有飞多久,天就开始下起雨来,就像第二只乌鸦预料的那样。

随着棉花越来越湿,袋子变得越来越重。

然而,盐却溶化在了雨水里。于是,第二只乌鸦轻而易举就比第一只乌鸦飞得高了。

诵读经典 >>>>>
Read classic

✪ The first crow thought he was being very clever to agree to this because salt is much heavier than cotton.

✪ In the end, they were ready for the contest, and holding their sacks in their beaks, they flew up into the sky.

第一只乌鸦心想,同意这样做,自己真聪明,因为盐比棉花重得多。

最终,它们准备进行这场比赛,它们嘴里衔着袋子,飞上了天空。

妙语连珠 >>>>>
Sparkling discourse

✪ The soul of the past times hides in the books.

书籍里藏着过去时代的灵魂。

✪ Books are a kind of calm and reliable friends.

书籍是一种冷静可靠的朋友。

Kant's Virtue

In 1779, Kant wanted to go to a small town to visit Mr. William, so he wrote him a letter saying that he would arrive there before 11 a.m. on March 5th. William wrote back expressing his warm welcome.

He hastened to the town on March 4th. In order to arrive at the appointed time, he rented a carriage hurrying to Mr. William's house early the next morning. Mr. William lived on a farm ten miles away from the small town. The town and the farm were separated by a river, so Kant needed to go across the bridge. But when the carriage came to the river, the wheeler stopped and said to Kant, "Sorry, sir, we couldn't cross the river now. The bridge was broken. It would be very dangerous to go any further."

Thereupon①, Kant jumped off the carriage, and found the bridge indeed broke in the middle. Kant looked at his watch. It was over 10 o'clock already. He asked vexedly②, "Aren't there any other bridges nearby?"

The wheeler said, "Yes, sir. There's a bridge in the upstream of the river, about six miles from here."

Kant said, "If we go across that bridge, how much will it take to arrive at the farm at a usual speed?"

"Forty minutes soonest," the wheeler answered.

Kant thought for a while, and then ran to a close-by old cottage and said to the owner, "Excuse me, sir, would you like to sell this cottage to me?"

The farmer was surprised at his words, "Sir, my cottage was shabby and old. What will you buy it for?"

生词有约

① thereupon
adv. 于是；立刻
② vexedly
adv. 焦急地

Kant said, "Don't mind what I will do. Just tell me whether you would like to sell it."

The farmer said, "Of course. 100 D-marks will be enough."

Kant paid the farmer 100 D-marks right away. He said to the farmer, "If you can **detach**③ some wood from the cottage and get the bridge repaired in twenty minutes, I will give the cottage back to you."

③ detach
vt. 拆卸

The farmer was astonished, but he still **dismantled**④ some wood and put the bridge right in time.

④ dismantle
vt. 从（房子、船等）拆除

Finally, the carriage crossed the bridge in safety. At 10:50, Kant appeared in front of Mr. William's door. William saw Kant, stepped forward, gave him a hug and said with a smile, "My dear friend, you are still so **punctual**⑤."

⑤ punctual
adj. 准时的

Kant had a happy time on the farm with his old friend but never mentioned the process of his arrival on time. Later William knew everything from the farmer. He specially wrote a letter to Kant, "My dear friend, it's unnecessary to be so **elaborate**⑥ for a date between friends. It's also excusable even if you arrived a bit late."

⑥ elaborate
adj. 煞费苦心的

Kant answered in a letter, "Whether to strangers or old friends, punctuality is the **utmost**⑦ respect to others."

⑦ utmost
adj. 最大的

康德的美德

1779 年，康德想去一座小镇拜访威廉先生。于是，他给威廉写了一封信，说他会在 3 月 5 日上午 11 点前到达那里。威廉回信表示热烈欢迎。

3 月 4 日，他就赶到了小镇。为了在约定时间到达，他第二天一早就租了一辆马车赶往威廉先生家。威廉先生住在距离小镇 10 英里的农场上。小镇和农场被一条河隔断，所以康德需要穿桥过去。但当马车来到河边时，车夫停下来，对康德说："先生，对不起，我们现在过不了河。桥坏了，再向前走会非常危险。"

于是，康德从马车上跳下来，发现桥的确从中间断开了。康德看看手表，已经 10 点多了。他焦急地说："附近没有别的桥了吗？"

车夫说："有，先生。河岸上游有一座桥，离这里大约有 6 英里。"

康德说："如果我们从那座桥上过去，以平常的速度需要多久到达农场？"

车夫回答："最快 40 分钟。"

康德想了一会儿，然后跑到附近的一个旧茅屋，对主人说："先生，请问，你愿意将这个茅屋卖给我吗？"

农夫对他的话非常吃惊："先生，我的房子又破又旧。你买它干什么？"

康德说："别管我干什么。请告诉我说你愿不愿卖给我。"

农夫说："当然愿意。100 马克就够了。"

康德立刻付给了农夫 100 马克。他对农夫说："如果你能从房子上拆一些木头，20 分钟内修好这座桥，我就把房子还给你。"

农夫大为惊讶，但他还是拆下了一些木头，及时修好了那座桥。

最后，马车平安过桥。10 点 50 分，康德出现在了威廉先生的门前。威廉看到康德，走上前拥抱他，笑着说道："我亲爱的朋友，你还是那么准时。"

康德和老朋友在农场度过了一段快乐时光，但对他为了准时到达的过程从未提起。后来，威廉从农夫那里得知了所有的一切。他专门给康德写了一封信："我亲爱的朋友，朋友间的约会不必这么费心，即使晚点儿也有情可原。"

康德在回信中说："无论是对陌生人还是对老朋友，守时都是对别人最大的尊重。"

诵读经典 >>>>>
Read classic

Kant had a happy time on the farm with his old friend but never mentioned the process of his arrival on time. Later William knew everything from the farmer. He specially wrote a letter to Kant, "My dear friend, it's unnecessary to be so elaborate for a date between friends. It's also excusable even if you arrived a bit late."

康德和老朋友在农场度过了一段快乐时光，但对他为了准时到达的过程从未提起。后来，威廉从农夫那里得知了所有的一切。他专门给康德写了一封信："我亲爱的朋友，朋友间的约会不必这么费心，即使晚点儿也有情可原。"

妙语连珠 >>>>>
Sparkling discourse

✪ Reading is an opportunity and a privilege to meet people you've never seen in places you've never been to before.

阅读就是一种在你从未去过的地方结识从未见过的人的机会和特权。

✪ In science, read, by preference, the newest books; in literature, the oldest.

在科学中，最好读最新的书；在文学中，最好看最老的书。

From then on, he also had two treasures of life: sunny attitude and firm faith.

从此，他也拥有了人生的两件宝贝东西：良好的心态和坚定的信念。

画龙点睛

An Old Man's Mirror

A young man was **diagnosed**[①] with **leukemia**[②] at the peak of life. His heart was **shrouded**[③] in infinite despair right off. He felt life was meaningless and refused any medical treatment.

On a late autumn afternoon, he escaped from the hospital, wandering aimlessly along the streets. Suddenly, a piece of melody which was faintly **hoarse**[④] but **singular**[⑤] heroic attracted him. Not far off, a blind old man was **fiddling**[⑥] with a polished instrument, playing sentimentally to a few **pedestrians**[⑦]. And also what caught people's eye was that a mirror hung in the blind man's arms.

The young man came up curiously and asked after the blind person finished playing a song, "Excuse me, is this your mirror?"

"Yes. My instrument and my mirror are two treasures of mine! Music is the finest thing in the world. I often amuse myself with it and can feel how beautiful the life is..."

"But what does this mirror mean to you?" the young man couldn't wait to ask.

The blind smiled faintly and said, "I hope a miracle will appear one day and I believe that someday I can see my face in this mirror. So wherever I may go, no matter what time it is, I will take it with myself."

The leukemia patient's heart was shocked. A blind person could even love life so much, but I... Suddenly, he got a thorough understanding and calmly returned to the hospital for treatment.

From then on, he also had two treasures of life: sunny attitude and firm faith.

生词有约

① diagnose
vt. 诊断
② leukemia
n. 白血病
③ shroud
vt. 笼罩
④ hoarse
adj. 嘶哑的
⑤ singular
adj. 奇异的
⑥ fiddle
vt. 盲目摆弄
⑦ pedestrian
n. 行人

盲人的镜子

一个年轻人正在人生的顶峰时却被诊断出患了白血病。他的心立刻笼罩在无边无际的绝望之中。他感到人生没有意义,拒绝接受任何治疗。

一个深秋的下午,他从医院里逃出来,漫无目的地走在街上。突然,一首略微嘶哑却又非常豪壮的乐曲吸引住了他。不远处,一位双目失明的老人正在摆弄一件锃亮的乐器,向几个行人富有情感地弹奏着。同样引人注目的还有盲人的怀里挂着一面镜子。

年轻人好奇地走上前,等盲人弹奏完一曲时问道:"请问,这镜子是你的吗?"

"是的。我的乐器和镜子是我的两件宝贝!音乐是世界上最美好的东西。我常常靠这个自得其乐,可以感到人生是多么美好……"

"可这镜子对你有什么意义?"年轻人迫不及待地问道。

盲人微微一笑,说:"我希望有一天奇迹会出现,也相信有朝一日我能用这镜子看见自己的脸。所以,无论去哪里,无论什么时候,我都带着它。"

白血病患者的心受到了震撼。一个盲人甚至都能这样热爱生活,但我……他突然大彻大悟,便平静地返回医院接受治疗。

从此,他也拥有了人生的两件宝贝东西:良好的心态和坚定的信念。

诵读经典 >>>>>
Read classic

On a late autumn afternoon, he escaped from the hospital, wandering aimlessly along the streets. Suddenly, a piece of melody which was faintly hoarse but singular heroic attracted him. Not far off, a blind old man was fiddling with a polished instrument, playing sentimentally to a few pedestrians.

一个深秋的下午,他从医院里逃出来,漫无目的地走在街上。突然,一首略微嘶哑却又非常豪壮的乐曲吸引住了他。不远处,一位双目失明的老人正在摆弄一件锃亮的乐器,向几个行人富有情感地弹奏着。

妙语连珠 >>>>>
Sparkling discourse

❂ A good book is the purest essence of a human soul.
一本好书是人类灵魂最纯洁的精髓。

❂ From your parents you learn love and laughter and how to put one foot before the other. But when books are opened you will discover that you have wings.
你从父母亲那里学会爱、学会笑、学会走路。但一打开书本,你就会发现自己有了翅膀。

The Smile of a Photographer

After the "Pearl Harbor Incident", Churchill made a speech in the House of Representatives at the invitation of Prime Minister of Canada. When he saw Churchill sipping brandy in the lounge and smoking a cigar after his speech, Yusuf Karsh, who was an **outstanding**① Canadian portrait photographer, hurriedly came up to him and said, " Mr. Prime Minister, I hope I can be lucky to take a photo for you as a souvenir on such a historic **occasion**②."

Churchill agreed **readily**③.

Karsh adjusted the focus ready to take pictures but found Churchill on camera gentle and **cultivated**④ nothing to do with an earthshaking heroic figure at all. He then had an idea. All of a sudden, he walked **briskly**⑤ toward Churchill and pulled out the cigar in his mouth with a rush.

Seeing this, Churchill was wide-eyed, left hand on the small of back, and seemed to lose his temper.

Karsh pressed the shutter. After that, he stepped forward with a smile, bowed to apologize to Churchill, and handed the cigar with both hands.

Churchill took the cigarette, saying with a smile, "Sir, you are amazing. You **incredibly**⑥ **subdued**⑦ a roaring lion!"

This photograph was not only published in many newspapers or magazines but also printed on stamps and well known all over the world.

生词有约

① outstanding
adj. 杰出的

② occasion
n. 时刻；时机；场合

③ readily
adv. 欣然

④ cultivate
vt. 培养

⑤ briskly
adv. 轻快地

⑥ incredibly
adv. 难以置信地

⑦ subdue
vt. 征服

摄影家的微笑

"珍珠港事件"后，应加拿大总理的邀请，丘吉尔在众议院演讲。加拿大杰出肖像摄影家尤素福·卡什看到丘吉尔演讲完后正在休息室一边呷着白兰地，一边抽着雪茄烟，赶忙走上前说道："首相先生，我希望能有幸在这历史的一刻为你拍一张照片留念。"

丘吉尔欣然同意。

卡什调好焦距准备拍照时，却发现镜头里的丘吉尔温文尔雅，根本不像叱咤风云的英雄人物。于是，他灵机一动，计上心来。突然，他快步走向丘吉尔，猛地拽掉了他嘴里叼着的雪茄。

见此情景，丘吉尔两眼圆睁，左手叉腰，像要发火。

卡什按下了快门。之后，他走上前，微笑着向丘吉尔鞠躬道歉，双手递过雪茄。

丘吉尔接过雪茄，微笑着说："先生，你真了不起！你居然制服了一头怒吼的狮子！"

这张照片不仅被刊登在许多报纸杂志上，而且被印成了邮票，举世闻名。

诵读经典 >>>>>
Read classic

Karsh adjusted the focus ready to take pictures but found Churchill on camera gentle and cultivated nothing to do with an earthshaking heroic figure at all. He then had an idea. All of a sudden, he walked briskly toward Churchill and pulled out the cigar in his mouth with a rush.

卡什调好焦距准备拍照时，却发现镜头里的丘吉尔温文尔雅，根本不像叱咤风云的英雄人物。于是，他灵机一动，计上心来。突然，他快步走向丘吉尔，猛地拽掉了他嘴里叼着的雪茄。

妙语连珠 >>>>>
Sparkling discourse

❂ Books are a flight of stairs for the human progress.
书籍是人类进步的阶梯。

❂ The best refuge of spirit is a book. It will neither forget you nor cheat you.
精神上最好的避难所是书，它既不会忘你也不会骗你。

After hearing this, the father didn't comfort her but looked at her with a smile, and suddenly he said, "I'm able to reach our ceiling."

听完这话后，她的父亲没有安慰她，而是面带微笑看着她，突然说道："我能够到我们的天花板。"

画龙点睛

I'm Able to Reach Our Ceiling

Sonia Smits, a well-known American actress, spent her childhood on a **cattle farm**[1] on the outskirts of **Ottawa**[2], Canada.

At that time, she studied in a primary school near the farm. One day she came home full of **grievance**[3] and wept. Her father asked her why she was crying. She choked with sobs, "A girl in our class said I was ugly, and so was my running **posture**[4]."

After hearing this, the father didn't comfort her but looked at her with a smile, and suddenly he said, "I'm able to reach our ceiling."

Sonia was weeping at that time. She was surprised by her father's words and wasn't sure what her father meant, so she asked in return, "What did you say?"

Her father repeated, "I'm able to reach our ceiling."

Sonia stopped weeping, looking upwards at the ceiling which was nearly four meter's high. Could father reach it? Although she was small at that time, she didn't believe what her father said.

Seeing a look of disbelief on her face, father said to her, "You don't believe it? Then you shouldn't believe what that girl said either, because some people just didn't tell the truth."

生词有约

① cattle farm
n. 奶牛场
② Ottawa
n. 渥太华（加拿大首都）
③ grievance
n. 冤情；不满
④ posture
n. 姿势；仪态

我能够得到天花板

美国著名女演员索尼娅·斯密茨在加拿大渥太华郊外的一个奶牛场度过了她的童年。

当时，她在奶牛场附近的一所小学学习。一天，她满怀委屈地回到家里，泪流不止。她的父亲问她为什么哭。她哽咽着说："我们班的一个女生说我很丑，还说我跑步的姿势难看。"

听完这话后，她的父亲没有安慰她，而是面带微笑看着她，突然说道："我能够到我们的天花板。"

索尼娅当时正在哭泣。她对父亲的话非常吃惊，拿不准父亲是什么意思，所以就反问道："你说什么？"

她的父亲重复道："我能够得到我们的天花板。"

索尼娅停止了哭泣，抬头看着天花板，差不多有 4 米高。父亲能够得着吗？尽管她当时还小，但她不相信父亲的话。

看到她将信将疑的脸色，她的父亲对她说："你不相信吧？那你也不应该相信那个女孩子的话，因为有些人说的本来就不是实话。"

诵读经典 >>>>>
Read classic

✪ At that time, she studied in a primary school near the farm. One day she came home full of grievance and wept.

当时，她在奶牛场附近的一所小学学习。一天，她满怀委屈地回到家里，泪流不止。

✪ Seeing a look of disbelief on her face, father said to her, "You don't believe it? Then you shouldn't believe what that girl said either, because some people just didn't tell the truth."

看到她将信将疑的脸色，她的父亲对她说："你不相信吧？那你也不应该相信那个女孩子的话，因为有些人说的本来就不是实话。"

妙语连珠 >>>>>
Sparkling discourse

✪ A book is life with visible characters. Men of passion can deeply understand it.
书是有字的生活，感情丰富的人才能深刻领会。

✪ Books and friends should be few but good.
书和朋友不在多而在好。

In a flash, he was middle-aged. He still hadn't accomplished anything. Even his wife left him for his poverty, taking their daughter with her.

转眼间，他到了中年。他还是一事无成。就连妻子也因他的贫困而带着女儿离去。

画龙点睛

The Unexpected Success

His father died when he was less than five years old. At the age of fourteen, he left school due to poor **academic performance**①. At that time, his family had a large farm in Indiana. Being a teenager, he worked on the farm all days, **invariably**② with full sadness in his eyes. At seventeen, he opened a **blacksmith**③ shop but soon closed. After eighteen, he lived a **vagrant**④ life, working on the dock as a coolie, selling insurance policies, marketing steamships and so on, but all failed **without exception**⑤.

In a flash, he was middleaged. He still hadn't accomplished anything. Even his wife left him for his poverty, taking their daughter with her. After the divorce, even to meet his daughter would be an **extravagant**⑥ hope. He reached the age of retirement drifting in this way.

In the first year after retirement, he received 105 dollars of social welfare payments. Holding the money, he struggled inward—his life was not over yet, why not do something?

So he **went for broke**⑦, opening a fast-food restaurant with that small amount of payment. Unexpectedly, the business was booming. With the money he earned, he began to open chain stores all over the United States. Later, his fast-food restaurants are well known all over the world. He was Harlan Sanders, founder of the KFC.

绝处逢生

他不到 5 岁，父亲就撒手而去。14 岁那年，他因学习成绩差而辍学。那时，他的家人在印第安纳州有一个大农场。他年少时整天在农场干活，眼里总是充满忧伤。17 岁那年，他开了一家铁匠铺，但很快就倒闭了。18 岁后，他过起了漂泊的生活，在码头当过苦力，卖过保险，推销过轮船等，但毫无例外地纷纷失败。

转眼间，他到了中年。他还是一事无成。就连妻子也因他的贫困而带着女儿离去。离婚后，他甚至见女儿一眼都会是一种奢望。他就这样一直挨到了退休年龄。

退休后的第一年，他收到了 105 美元的社会福利。他拿着那笔钱，内心开始斗争——他的生命还没有结束，何不做点什么呢？

于是，他全力以赴，用那笔区区福利金开了一家快餐店。生意居然非常火爆。赚钱后，他开始在全国开起了连锁店。后来，他的快餐店享誉全球。他就是肯德基的创始人哈兰·桑德斯。

诵读经典 >>>>>
Read classic

So he went for broke, opening a fast-food restaurant with that small amount of payment. Unexpectedly, the business was booming. With the money he earned, he began to open chain stores all over the United States. Later, his fast-food restaurants are well known all over the world.

于是，他全力以赴，用那笔区区福利金开了一家快餐店。生意居然非常火爆。赚钱后，他开始在全国开起了连锁店。后来，他的快餐店享誉全球。

妙语连珠 >>>>>
Sparkling discourse

✪ One person with a belief is a social power equal to 99 who have only interests.
一个有信仰的人和九十九个只有兴趣的人一样都是一股社会力量。

✪ Society is a masked ball, where every one hides his real character, and reveals it by hiding.
社会是一个假面舞会，那里的每个人都掩盖着自己的真实本性，而且正是因为掩盖才暴露无遗。

> **Just for today I will be unafraid, especially I will not be afraid to be happy, to enjoy what is beautiful, to love, and to believe that those I love, love me.**
>
> 只为今天，我要毫不畏惧，尤其要不害怕快乐，要去欣赏美的东西，去爱和相信那些我爱和爱我的人。

Just for Today

Just for today I will be happy. This **assumes**① that what Abraham Lincoln said is true, that "most folks are about as happy as they make up their minds to be." Happiness is from within; it is not a matter of externals.

Just for today I will try to adjust myself to what is, and not try to adjust everything to my own desires. I will take my family, my business, and my luck as they come and fit myself to them.

Just for today I will take care of my body. I will exercise it, care for it, **nourish**② it, not abuse it nor neglect it, so that it will be a perfect machine for my **bidding**③.

Just for today I will try to strengthen my mind. I will learn something useful. I will not be a mental **loafer**④. I will read something that requires effort, thought and concentration.

Just for today I will exercise my soul in three ways: I will do somebody a good turn and not get found out. I will do at least two things I don't want to do, as William James suggests, just for exercise.

Just for today I will be agreeable. I will look as well as I can, dress as becomingly as possible, talk low, act **courteously**⑤, be liberal with praise, criticize not at all, nor find fault with anything and not try to regulate nor improve anyone.

Just for today I will try to live through this day only, not to tackle my whole life problem at once. I can do things for twelve hours that would **appall**⑥ me if I had to keep them up

生词有约

① assume
vt. 表明

② nourish
vt. 滋养；怀有
③ bidding
n. 命令；投标
④ loafer
n. 游手好闲的人；流浪者

⑤ courteously
adv. 有礼貌地；亲切地

⑥ appall
vt. 使胆寒；使惊骇

for a lifetime.

Just for today I will have a program. I will write down what I expect to do every hour. I may not follow it exactly, but I will have it. It will eliminate two pests, hurry and indecision.

Just for today I will have a quiet half-hour all by myself and relax. In this half-hour sometimes I will think of God, so as to get a little more **perspective**⑦ into my life.

Just for today I will be unafraid, especially I will not be afraid to be happy, to enjoy what is beautiful, to love, and to believe that those I love, love me.

⑦ perspective
n. 远景；观点

只为今天

只为今天，我就会快乐。这表明，亚伯拉罕·林肯说的"大多数人只要下定决心，就能快乐"是正确的。快乐来自内心，并不是身外之物。

只为今天，我要设法让自己适应一切，而不是让一切来适应自己的欲望。我要接受家庭、事业和运气，让自己适应它们。

只为今天，我要照顾自己的身体。我要锻炼、关心、滋养自己的身体，既不虐待也不忽视自己的身体，从而使它成为听我召唤的完美机器。

只为今天，我要设法加强自己的思想。我要学有用的东西，不做思想的流浪者。我要读一些需要努力、思考和专心的东西。

只为今天，我要在三个方面塑造自己的灵魂：我要为别人做一件好事，不让人发现。我要像威廉·詹姆斯建议的那样做两件自己不想做的事情，只是为了锻炼。

只为今天，我要和蔼可亲。我要尽可能外表适当，尽可能衣着得体，低声说话，举止有礼，慷慨赞扬，绝不责难，既不对一切都吹毛求疵，也不干涉他人，更不管制和改良任何人。

只为今天，我要努力过好今天，而不要马上解决自己全部的人生问题。尽管我可以连续工作 12 个小时，但我如果一生都得这样做，那一定会让我胆寒。

只为今天，我要有一个计划。我要写下每小时希望做什么。我不可能完全遵照执行，但我一定要有这个计划。这样会消除两个弊端——仓促行事和优柔寡断。

只为今天，我要给自己留半小时安静时间放松。在这半小时里，我有时要想起上帝，以便使自己的生活多一点前景。

只为今天，我要毫不畏惧，尤其要不害怕快乐，要去欣赏美的东西，去爱和相信那些我爱和爱我的人。

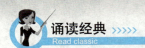

与**青春**有关的日子 砥砺派

诵读经典 >>>>>
Read classic

Just for today I will be agreeable. I will look as well as I can, dress as becomingly as possible, talk low, act courteously, be liberal with praise, criticize not at all, nor find fault with anything and not try to regulate nor improve anyone.

只为今天，我要和蔼可亲。我要尽可能外表适当，尽可能衣着得体，低声说话，举止有礼，慷慨赞扬，绝不责难，既不对一切都吹毛求疵，也不干涉他人，也不管制和改良任何人。

妙语连珠 >>>>>
Sparkling discourse

✪ Kindness is the golden link by which society is bound together.

善良是将社会联系在一起的金色链条。

✪ Interpersonal relations are a kind of social capital. If you keep them long, you must economize them.

人际关系是一种社会资本，想长久拥有，就得节约使用。

Where the Happiness Was

A group of young people were looking for happiness everywhere, but **encountered**① many troubles, sorrows and pains. They went to ask the ancient Greek philosopher Socrates where the happiness was.

Socrates said, "Help me build a boat first!"

Those young people put aside the matter of seeking happiness and fetched the tools for shipbuilding. They spent forty-nine days cutting down a big tree which was tall and thick, hollowed out the pith and built a canoe.

The canoe was **launched**②. They invited Socrates to get on the boat, **paddling**③ and singing.

"Children, are you happy?" asked Socrates.

They all chorused, "So happy!"

Socrates summed up, "This is happiness. It often pays you a sudden visit when you are too busy with a definite **purpose**④."

生词有约

① encounter
vt. 遭遇

② launch
vt. 发动；使……下水

③ paddle
vi. 划桨；戏水

④ purpose
n. 目的；意图

快乐在哪里

一群年轻人到处寻找快乐，却遇到许多烦恼、忧愁和痛苦。他们去向古希腊哲学家苏格拉底请教快乐在哪里。

苏格拉底说："你们还是先帮我造一条船吧！"

年轻人把寻找快乐的事儿放在一边，找来造船的工具，用49天锯倒了一棵又高又粗的大树，挖空树心，造出了一条独木舟。

独木舟下水了。他们把苏格拉底请上船，一边荡桨，一边唱歌。

苏格拉底问："孩子们，你们快乐吗？"

大家不约而同地高呼："快乐极了！"

苏格拉底概括道："快乐就是这样，它常常在你为一个明确目的忙得不可开交时突然来访。"

诵读经典 >>>>>
Read classic

Those young people put aside the matter of seeking happiness and fetched the tools for shipbuilding. They spent forty-nine days cutting down a big tree which was tall and thick, hollowed out the pith and built a canoe.

年轻人把寻找快乐的事儿放在一边，找来造船的工具，用 49 天锯倒了一棵又高又粗的大树，挖空树心，造出了一条独木舟。

妙语连珠 >>>>>
Sparkling discourse

★ The society is a ship, on which everyone must be ready for steering.

社会就像一条船，每个人都要有掌舵的准备。

★ The society won't treat someone with generosity unless he proves himself to the society that he is worthy of being treated in this way.

社会不会厚待一个人，除非他自己向社会证明他值得社会厚待。

画龙点睛

Sweetness with a Little Bitterness

In a harvest season, a beekeeper tried making honey. He had no knowledge of skills, so he **consulted**[①] his father.

The retired, old beekeeper told his son, "It's okay to make it in the common method. However, on the point of completing it, remember to drop a little bitter medicine into the honey."

He **retorted**[②], "Why so? It is simply to ruin the **precious**[③] honey."

His father just smiled without reply.

Upon this, he made honey as he liked. Until the honey was done, he took a bit to taste. But his honey was not as sweet as his father's.

He was so **confused**[④] that he had to ask his father.

"Why did you ask me to add bitter medicine to the done honey? Won't it ruin the taste of the honey?"

"It is the little bitterness in the honey that excites your tongue and makes the honey sweet."

生词有约

① consult
vt. 向……请教

② retort
vt. 反驳

③ precious
adj. 宝贵的；珍贵的

④ confused
adj. 困惑的；混乱的

有点苦，才会甜

在一次收获季节，养蜂人想尝试酿蜜。他并不懂得其中的技巧，就请教他的父亲。

年老退休的养蜂人告诉儿子说："你照着一般的方法做就行了。不过，在即将完成前，记住在蜂蜜里滴一点苦药。"

他反问道："为什么要这么做呢？这样简直是糟蹋宝贵的蜂蜜。"

他的父亲只是笑笑，并不回答。

于是，他按照自己的意思来酿蜜。等到蜂蜜熟成后，取出一点来尝。但是，他酿成的蜂蜜却不如父亲的甜。

他百思不解，最后只好问父亲。

"为什么您告诉我要在酿好的蜂蜜里加苦药呢？这样不会破坏蜂蜜的味道吗？"

"正是因为里边有点苦味，刺激人的舌头，才能显出蜂蜜的香甜。"

诵读经典 >>>>>
Read classic

The retired, old beekeeper told his son, "It's okay to make it in the common method. However, on the point of completing it, remember to drop a little bitter medicine into the honey."

年老退休的养蜂人告诉儿子说："你照着一般的方法做就行了。不过，在即将完成前，记住在蜂蜜里滴一点苦药。"

妙语连珠 >>>>>
Sparkling discourse

✪ Marriage is a covered dish.

婚姻是一道盖着的佳肴。

✪ Shy and unready men are great betrayers of secrets; for there are few wants more urgent for the moment than the want of something to say.

脑膜和迟钝的人是最容易泄密的人，因为在一定场合找点话说比其他任何事情都更急迫。

Jerry said, "My father is blind, so he has never watched my match. Now, he has gone to the paradise and finally can watch my match. As soon as I think of my father watching me, I have everything…"

杰利说：“我的父亲是个盲人，从来没有看过我的比赛。现在，他到了天堂，终于能看到我比赛了。一想到父亲在看着我，我就有了一切……”

画龙
点睛

Love Can Drive Everything

There was a player named Jerry in the rugby team, his father died. Returning from the funeral, an important match was going to begin. He found the coach at once and asked to attend the match. He was not good at the skill, so the coach should not allow him to attend the match. But now, as he **relented**① and agreed. He was ready to ask to play for three minutes. When the time was up, he would be changed by others.

On the court, Jerry turned very **agilely**② with his deft skill. He broke through the opposition line **valiantly**③. Three minutes passed. The coach made Jerry keep staying on the court. Jerry continued his **outstanding**④ performance and led the team to win the match.

The coach hugged excitedly and said, "Kid, you have never been so fast, so strong and so skilled. What happened on earth?"

Jerry said, "My father is blind, so he has never watched my match. Now, he has gone to the paradise and finally can watch my match. As soon as I think of my father watching me, I have everything…"

The coach understood: love can drive everything.

生词有约

① relent
vi. 变温和；变宽厚

② agilely
adv. 敏捷地；头脑灵活地

③ valiantly
adv. 英勇地；勇敢地

④ outstanding
adj. 杰出的；显著的

爱能推动一切

橄榄球队有个叫杰利的队员，他的父亲去世了。他奔丧回来时，一场重要的比赛正要开始。他马上找到教练，请求参加比赛。杰利水平不高，教练本来不想让他参赛，但这时心一软，就同意了，准备让杰利上场3分钟，时间一到，马上把他换下来。

到了球场上，杰利突然变得非常敏捷、技巧纯熟，一次次勇猛地突破对方防线。3分钟过去了，教练让杰利继续留在场上。杰利继续出色发挥，率领球队赢得了比赛。

教练激动地抱住杰利，说："孩子，你从来没有这样快，这样强，这样熟。到底发生了什么事儿？"

杰利说："我的父亲是个盲人，从来没有看过我的比赛。现在，他到了天堂，终于能看到我比赛了。一想到父亲在看着我，我就有了一切……"

教练明白：爱能推动一切。

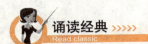 **诵读经典** >>>>>
Read classic

On the court, Jerry turned very agilely with his deft skill. He broke through the opposition line valiantly. Three minutes passed. The coach made Jerry keep staying on the court. Jerry continued his outstanding performance and led the team to win the match.

到了球场上，杰利突然变得非常敏捷、技巧纯熟，一次次勇猛地突破对方防线。3分钟过去了，教练让杰利继续留在场上。杰利继续出色发挥，率领球队赢得了比赛。

 妙语连珠 >>>>>
Sparkling discourse

★ Saddle your dreams afore you ride them.

在驾乘梦想之前，给它们装一副鞍座。

★ When I give a man an office, I watch him carefully to see whether he is swelling or growing.

我任用一个人时，会仔细观察，看他是自我膨胀还是茁壮成长。

After a long silence, an archangel suddenly said, "I know. Put it into everyone's heart. As long as he's willing to seek for it, anyone can find it."

沉默许久，一个天使长突然说道："我知道了。把它放在每个人的心里。只要肯努力寻找，谁都可以找到它。"

画龙点睛

The Secret of Life

God fell across a puzzle when he created the world. Thinking over and over, he decided to listen to the **archangels**[1]' views. After the **summoned**[2] archangels arrived, God asked them, "Tell me, where should I put the secret of life?"

"Bury it in the ground," an archangel replied.

"Put it at the bottom of sea," another said.

"Hide it on the high mountain," the third suggested.

God shook his head and said, "If I do as you suggest, there will be a small group of people who can find it. But my **original**[3] purpose is to let everyone find the secret of life!"

After a long silence, an archangel suddenly said, "I know. Put it into everyone's heart. As long as he's willing to seek for it, anyone can find it."

"Yes!" God said in delight, "Put it in everyone's heart."

Then the secret of life lies in everyone's heart.

生词有约

① archangel
n. 大天使；天使长
② summon
vt. 召唤；召集

③ original
adj. 最初的；原始的

生命的秘密

上帝在创造世界时遇到了一个难题。思考再三，他决定听听天使长们的意见。被召唤的天使长们到齐后，上帝问道："你们说，我应该把生命的秘密放在哪里呢？"

"把它埋在地下。"一个天使长答道。

"把它放到海底。"另一个天使长说道。

"把它藏在高山上。"又一个天使长建议。

上帝摇摇头，说："如果我照你们说的建议去做的话，这个世界上只有一小部分人能找到它，但我的初衷是每个人都能找到生命的秘密！"

沉默许久，一个天使长突然说道："我知道了。把它放在每个人的心里。只要肯努力寻找，谁都可以找到它。"

"对啊！"上帝欣喜地说道，"放在每个人的心里。"

于是，生命的秘密就在我们每个人的心里。

诵读经典 >>>>>
Read classic

God shook his head and said, "If I do as you suggest, there will be a small group of people who can find it. But my original purpose is to let everyone find the secret of life!"

上帝摇摇头，说："如果我照你们说的建议去做的话，这个世界上只有一小部分人能找到它，但我的初衷是每个人都能找到生命的秘密！"

妙语连珠 >>>>>
Sparkling discourse

❂ The most solid stone in the structure is the lowest one in the foundation.
建筑物中最坚硬的石头是地基里最底下的那块。

❂ You cannot stop the birds of sorrow from flying over your head, but you can prevent them from building their nest in your hair.
你无法阻止悲痛之鸟在头顶盘旋，但你可以阻止它们在头发里筑巢。

The last son disagreed with all of them, saying that it was overhung with fruits, full of life and content.

小儿子不同意他们三个的说法，他说树上结满了果子，充满了生气和满足。

画龙点睛

The Scenery of Four Seasons

There was a man who had four sons.

He hoped that his sons could learn not to judge things too quickly.

So he gave his four sons a question in turn asking them to go to see a pear tree at a distance **respectively**①.

The first son set out in the winter, the second in the spring, the third in the summer, and the youngest in the autumn.

When all of them returned home, he called them together to describe what they had seen.

The first son said the tree was ugly, bent and **distorted**②.

The second son said it was not like that, but the tree was covered with green buds and full of hope.

The third son disagreed, saying that it **was laden with**③ blossoms which smelled so sweet and looked so beautiful. And he had never seen such beautiful scenery.

The last son disagreed with all of them, saying that it was overhung with fruits, full of life and **content**④.

The man told his four sons that you were all correct because you only saw the scenery of the tree in one season; you could not judge a tree only by one season, and it could only be measured when all the seasons were over.

生词有约

① respectively
adv. 分别地；各自地

② distorted
adj. 歪曲的；受到曲解的

③ was laden with
满载……；充满着……

④ content
n. 满足

四季的风景

有一个人，他有四个儿子。

他希望他的儿子能够学会不要太快对事情下结论。

所以，他依次给四个孩子一个问题，要他们分别去远方看一棵梨树。

大儿子在冬天前往，二儿子在春天，三儿子在夏天，小儿子则是在秋天前往。

当他们都回家后，他把他们一起叫到跟前，让他们形容自己看到的情景。

大儿子说，那棵树很丑，枯槁、扭曲。

二儿子说，不是这样子，这棵树被青青的嫩芽覆盖，充满了希望。

三儿子不同意，他说树上花朵绽放、充满香气，看起来十分美丽，这美景是他从来不曾见到过的。

小儿子不同意他们三个的说法。他说树上结满了果子，充满了生机和满足。

这个人对四个儿子说，你们都对，因为每个人都只看这棵树一个季节的风景，你们不能用一季的风景来评判一棵树，只有在经历过所有季节之后，才能衡量。

诵读经典 >>>>>
Read classic

The man told his four sons that you were all correct because you only saw the scenery of the tree in one season; you could not judge a tree only by one season, and it could only be measured when all the seasons were over.

这个人对四个儿子说，你们都对，因为每个人都只看这棵树一个季节的风景，你们不能用一季的风景来评判一棵树，只有在经历过所有季节之后，才能衡量。

妙语连珠 >>>>>
Sparkling discourse

★　God gives the milk, but not the pail.

上帝赐牛奶，桶要自己买。

★　A mill cannot grind with the water that is past.

磨轮不能利用流走的水来转动。

Magnifier and Telescope

There was a famous public relations master who cited an example when he talked about building good interpersonal relationships. He said that no matter how beautiful a young lady was, but if the **beautician**[①] took a magnifier of 500 times to see her pretty face, what he saw must be a face full of bumps and hollows. It was a very disappointing result. But when we look at the green hills with a telescope, what come into view is all **picturesque**[②] scenery and charming mountains, and these make us refreshing.

This suggests that if you always look at others with a **magnifier**[③], this will definitely betray them and make them without a single virtue. This can also make you not trust others and have no friends. On the contrary, if using a telescope, we will always be able to enjoy the beauty of others.

In the meantime, it tells us that if we focus the magnifier on ourselves but not on others, if we can consult others with an open mind, in this way, magnifier and telescope can **simultaneously**[④] display the biggest **effectiveness**[⑤].

Be strict with ourselves and **lenient**[⑥] towards others—it is the best **interpretation**[⑦] for magnifier and telescope.

生词有约

① beautician
n. 美容师

② picturesque
adj. 图画般的；生动的

③ magnifier
n. 放大镜；放大器

④ simultaneously
adv. 同时地

⑤ effectiveness
n. 效力；作用

⑥ lenient
adj. 宽大的；仁慈的

⑦ interpretation
n. 解释；翻译

放大镜与望远镜

有一位公关名家谈到建立良好人际关系时，举了一个例子。他说，无论多么漂亮的小姐，如果美容师以 500 倍的放大镜看她美丽的脸庞，看到的一定是坑坑洼洼、凹凸不平的脸，使人大失所望。而当我们拿望远镜看青山时，映入眼帘的尽是如画的风景、迷人的山色，令人心旷神怡。

这说明，如果你永远拿着放大镜看别人，必定使对方原形毕露，显得一无是处，也使自己无法信任他人，交到朋友。相反，如果拿着望远镜，就始终能欣赏到别人美好的一面。

同时也告诉我们，如果放大镜的焦点对准自己，而不是别人，如果能虚心请求他人，这样放大镜和望远镜便能同时发挥最大的效用。

严以律己与宽以待人正是放大镜与望远镜的最好诠释。

诵读经典 >>>>>
Read classic

This suggests that if you always look at others with a magnifier, this will definitely betray them and make them without a single virtue. This can also make you not trust others and have no friends. On the contrary, if using a telescope, we will always be able to enjoy the beauty of others.

这说明，如果你永远拿着放大镜看别人，必定使对方原形毕露，显得一无是处，也使自己无法信任他人，交到朋友。相反，如果拿着望远镜，就始终能欣赏到别人美好的一面。

妙语连珠 >>>>>
Sparkling discourse

★ The flower sheds all its petals and finds the fruit.

花掉落了所有花瓣，就会找到果实。

★ You can discover what your enemy fears most by observing the means he uses to frighten you.

通过观察你的敌人用来恐吓人的方法，你就可以发现他最害怕的东西。

"My friend, no need to have lunch! Aren't you the same with now after two hours?" Voltaire said.

"我的朋友，吃什么午饭呀！两小时后，你不也和现在一样吗？"伏尔泰说。

画龙
点睛

Serve the Valet with the Same Sauce

Voltaire had a **valet**[①], who was so lazy.

One day Voltaire said to him, "Bring my shoes here quickly."

The valet brought his shoes very quickly.

Startled, Voltaire saw the shoes were covered with dust.

He asked, "Why did you forget **polishing**[②] them?"

"No need, sir," the valet answered calmly, "The road is full of dust, so two hours later aren't your shoes as dirty as now?"

Voltaire wore the shoes with a smile and went out of the door without a word.

The servant ran behind and to catch up with him, "Sir, don't go yet! Where is the key?"

"Key?"

"Yes. The key to the kitchen. I need to have lunch."

"My friend, no need to have lunch! Aren't you the same with now after two hours?" Voltaire said.

生词有约

① valet
n. 贴身男仆

② polish
vt. 磨光，擦亮

以其人之道还治其人之身

伏尔泰有一个随身佣人，但这个人很懒。

一天，伏尔泰对他说："快把我的鞋子拿来。"

仆人很快把鞋子拿来了。

伏尔泰一看惊呆了：鞋上布满了尘土。

他问："你怎么忘了把它擦擦？"

"用不着，先生，"仆人平静地答道，"路上尽是灰尘，两小时后，您的鞋子不是又和现在一样脏了吗？"

伏尔泰微笑着穿上鞋，没有吭声，走出门去。

佣人在他身后跑步追上来："先生，慢走！钥匙呢？"

"钥匙？"

"对。食橱上的钥匙。我还要吃午饭呢。"

"我的朋友，吃什么午饭呀！两小时后，你不也和现在一样吗？"伏尔泰说。

诵读经典 >>>>>
Read classic

"No need, sir," the valet answered calmly, "The road is full of dust, so two hours later aren't your shoes as dirty as now?"

"用不着，先生，"仆人平静地答道，"路上尽是灰尘，两小时后，您的鞋子不是又和现在一样脏了吗？"

妙语连珠 >>>>>
Sparkling discourse

❂ When you go in search of honey, you must expect to be stung by bees.
寻找蜂蜜时，你必须想到会被蜜蜂蜇咬。

❂ He that boasts of his knowledge proclaims his ignorance.
吹嘘自己博识，等于宣扬自己无知。

The disciple couldn't believe, how could a palm cover the whole sky?

弟子无法相信，一只手掌怎么可能遮住整个天空呢？

画龙
点睛

The Root of Suffering

For a period of time, the **disciple**① felt his life was so painful that he was very **annoyed**②.

The master led the disciple to an open field and asked, "Look up, what can you see?"

"The sky," the disciple answered.

"The sky is big enough, isn't it?" said the master, "But I can cover the whole sky with a palm."

The disciple couldn't believe, how could a palm cover the whole sky?

Then the master covered the disciple's eyes with a palm and asked, "Can you see the sky now? Isn't it very easy to cover the whole sky with a palm?" Then, the master changed the topic and said, "In life, some little pains, little troubles or **setbacks**③ are also like this little palm. Though they look small, but if you can't put them down, always pull them close to watch, put them before your eyes and lay them in your mind, they will be like the palm, covering the whole sky of your life, and then you will miss the sun of the life, miss the blue sky, the white clouds and the beauty of the rosy clouds."

The disciple finally understood the root of his suffering.

生词有约

① disciple
n. 门徒；弟子
② annoyed
adj. 烦闷的；恼怒的

③ setback
n. 挫折；退步

痛苦的根源

一段时间，弟子感到活得痛苦，非常烦恼。

师父把弟子带到一片空旷地带，问："你抬头看看，看到了什么？"

"天空。"弟子答。

"天空够大的吧。"师父说，"但我可以用一只手掌遮住整个天空。"

弟子无法相信，一只手掌怎么可能遮住整个天空呢？

只见师父用一只手掌盖住了弟子的双眼，问："你现在看见天空了吗？我不是很容易用一只手掌遮住了整个天空吗?"继而,师父把话题一转,说:"生活中,一些小痛苦,一些小烦恼,一些小挫折,也像这一只小小的手掌,看上去虽然很小,但如果放不下,总是拉近来看,放在眼前,放在心头,就会像这只手掌一样,遮住你人生的整个晴空。于是,你将错失人生的太阳,错失蓝天、白云和美丽的彩霞。"

弟子终于明白了自己痛苦的根源。

诵读经典 >>>>>
Read classic

In life, some little pains, little troubles or setbacks are also like this little palm. Though they look small, but if you can't put them down, always pull them close to watch, put them before your eyes and lay them in your mind, they will be like the palm, covering the whole sky of your life, and then you will miss the sun of the life, miss the blue sky, the white clouds and the beauty of the rosy clouds.

生活中,一些小痛苦,一些小烦恼,一些小挫折,也像这一只小小的手掌,看上去虽然很小,但如果放不下,总是拉近来看,放在眼前,放在心头,就会像这只手掌一样,遮住你人生的整个晴空。于是,你将错失人生的太阳,错失蓝天、白云和美丽的彩霞。

妙语连珠 >>>>>
Sparkling discourse

✪ Quietude is the crown of life.
平静是生命的王冠。

✪ When a man says he approves of something in principle, it means he hasn't the slightest intention of putting it into practice.
当一个人说他原则上赞成某事时,那就是说他根本不想把那件事付诸实践。

"Get on my back," said the elephant proudly. "I shall carry you. I am big and strong, and I am not afraid to swim across a rapid river."

"骑在我的背上，"大象自豪地说，"我背你过去。我高大强壮，不怕游过水流湍急的河流。"

画龙点睛

The Advantage Is Complementary

Once upon a time an elephant and a monkey had a quarrel. The elephant was proud because he was so strong. "Look, how big and strong I am!" he said. "I can pull a tree down, can you?"

Now the monkey was proud because he was so quick. "Look, how fast I can run and climb!" he said. "Can you climb a tree?"

At last they went to a wise old owl. "We cannot agree," they said. "Tell us what you think about it. Which is better—to be strong or to be quick?"

The owl said to them, "Do just as I tell you, and then I shall find out which is better. Go and pick the fruit and bring it to me."

So the elephant and the monkey went to the river, but the water was swift and the monkey was afraid.

"Get on my back," said the elephant proudly. "I shall carry you. I am big and strong, and I am not afraid to swim across a **rapd** ① river."

Soon they got to the other bank. There stood the tree. It was so tall that the fruit hung above them.

The elephant tried to break the tree down, but it was too strong. He tried to reach the fruit with his **trunk** ②, but it was too high.

"Wait a minute, I can climb," said the monkey proudly. He ran quickly up the tree, and threw the rich and ripe fruit to the ground. The elephant put it into his mouth.

Then they crossed the river again, and gave the owl some

生词有约

① rapid
adj. 湍急的

② trunk
n. 象鼻

165

of the fruit they had picked. "Now tell us," they said, "which is better—to be strong or to be quick?"

"Can anyone tell which is better?" asked the owl. "Neither of you could get the fruit alone. It took both the elephant's strength and the monkey's quickness to get it."

优势互补

从前，一头大象和一只猴子发生了争吵。大象非常傲慢，因为它非常强壮。"瞧，我是多么高大强壮！"它说。"我可以把一棵树拉倒，你能吗？"

猴子也妄自尊大，因为它反应非常快。"瞧，我能跑得快，爬得也快！"它说。"你能爬树吗？"

最后，它们来到了一个聪明的老猫头鹰面前。"我们意见不一致，"它们说。"告诉我们你对这个问题有什么看法。哪一个更好，是身体强壮还是反应敏捷？"

猫头鹰对它们说："请按我对你们说的去做，然后我就会发现哪一个更好。去摘那些水果，给我送来。"

于是，大象和猴子来到了河边。但是，水流太急，猴子非常害怕。

"骑在我的背上，"大象自豪地说。"我背你过去。我高大强壮，不怕游过水流湍急的河流。"

不一会儿，它们就到了对岸。树耸立在那里。树非常高，果子挂在它们上方。

大象想设法把树推倒，但树太坚固了。它想尽力用鼻子去够水果，但树又太高了。

"等一下，我会爬树，"猴子骄傲地说。它飞快地爬上树，将熟透的鲜果扔到了地上。大象将果子放进了自己的嘴里。

随后，它们又穿过河去，将它们摘的一些果子送给了猫头鹰。"现在告诉我们，"它们说。"哪一个更好，是身体强壮还是反应敏捷？"

"谁能告诉哪一个更好？"猫头鹰问。"你们谁也不能单独摘到果子。它需要大象的力量和猴子的敏捷才能得到。"

诵读经典 >>>>>
Read classic

"Can anyone tell which is better?" asked the owl. "Neither of you could get the fruit alone. It took both the elephant's strength and the monkey's quickness to get it."

"谁能告诉哪一个更好？"猫头鹰问。"你们谁也不能单独摘到果子。它需要大象的力量和猴子的敏捷才能得到。"

妙语连珠 >>>>>
Sparkling discourse

✪ Some birds have never realized the value of wings.

有些鸟从来认识不到翅膀的价值。

✪ Gold is the soul of all civil life that can resolve all things into itself and turn itself into all things.

黄金是所有文明生活的灵魂，它既可以把一切归结为它自己，又可以将自己转变成一切。

"Wait a moment," Grandpa Hodge stroked his beard and cut him short, "Have you sifted the news you will tell me with three sieves?"

"等一下，"霍奇爷爷摸了摸胡子，打断了他的话，"你要告诉我的消息，用三个筛子筛过了吗？"

画龙点睛

Grandpa Wisdom

Grandpa Hodge was the most popular **sage**① in the village because he was so **philosophic**② in speaking and doing things that everyone revered him as "Grandpa Wisdom."

One day, a man hurried to Grandpa Wisdom and said, "Grandpa, I have a piece of news to tell you..."

"Wait a moment," Grandpa Hodge stroked his beard and cut him short, "Have you sifted the news you will tell me with three sieves?"

"Three sieves? Which three sieves?" the man asked with **puzzlement**③.

"The first sieve is Truth. Is the news you will tell me is true?" Grandpa Hodge asked, narrowing his eyes.

"I don't know because I overheard it from the street."

"Now let's check it with the second sieve," Grandpa Hodge went on, "If the new you will tell me is not true, it should be friendly."

The man hesitantly answered, "No, just the other way round..."

Grandpa Hodge once again **interrupted**④ him, "So let's use the third sieve. Can you tell me if the news that is exciting you is very important?"

"It is not so important," the man answered with embarrassment.

Grandpa Hodge patted the shoulder of the man and said **significantly**⑤, "Now that the news you will tell me is not true, friendly or important, please don't tell me. Then it won't trouble you and me."

生词有约

① sage
n. 圣人；贤人；哲人
② philosophic
adj. 哲学的；贤明的

③ puzzlement
n. 迷惑；费解

④ interrupt
vt. 中断；打断

⑤ significantly
adv. 意味深长地；值得注意地

The man took a tumble and never spread the overheard news ever since.

智慧爷爷

霍奇爷爷是村里最受欢迎的长者，因为他说话做事都很有哲理，大家都尊称他为"智慧爷爷"。

有一天，一个人匆匆跑到智慧爷爷那里说："爷爷，我有一个消息要告诉你……"

"等一下，"霍奇爷爷摸了摸胡子，打断了他的话，"你要告诉我的消息，用三个筛子筛过了吗？"

"三个筛子？哪三个筛子？"那人不解地问道。

"第一个筛子叫真实。你要告诉我的消息确实是真的吗？"霍奇爷爷眯着眼问道。

"不知道，我是从街上听来的。"

"现在再用第二个筛子来审查吧，"霍奇爷爷接着说。"你要告诉我的这个消息就算不是真实的，也应该是善意的吧。"

那人迟疑地回答说："不，刚好相反……"

霍奇爷爷再次打断他的话："那我们再用第三个筛子。你能告诉我，让你如此激动的消息非常重要吗？"

"并不怎么重要，"那人尴尬地回答说。

霍奇爷爷拍了拍那人的肩膀，意味深长地说："既然你要告诉我的事儿，既不真实，也非善意，更不重要，那就请别说了。这样，它就不会打扰你和我了。"

那人恍然大悟，从此再也不道听途说了。

诵读经典 >>>>>
Read classic

Grandpa Hodge patted the shoulder of the man and said significantly, "Now that the news you will tell me is not true, friendly or important, please don't tell me. Then it won't trouble you and me."

霍奇爷爷拍了拍那人的肩膀，意味深长地说："既然你要告诉我的事儿，既不真实，也非善意，更不重要，那就请别说了。这样，它就不会打扰你和我了。"

妙语连珠 >>>>>
Sparkling discourse

★ Economy is the poor man's mint, and extravagance the rich man's pitfall.
节约是穷人的造币厂，浪费是富人的陷阱。

✪　Mishaps are like knives that either serve us or cut us as we grasp them by the handle or blade.

灾祸就像刀子，握住刀柄便可为我们服务，抓住刀刃则会割破手。

画龙
点睛

The Sunny Mind

David once booked a room in a hotel of San Francisco. The day's work made him tired. At the general **reception**[①] he met a servant.

The servant said to him, "Good morning! Good morning! Good morning!" How strange! He said "Good morning!" for three times, but David was not fed up with him at all. Instead, he felt the servant was so sincere.

"How **enthusiastic**[②] you are!" David greeted him.

"It should be like this!" the servant said with a smile, "I have a good job and live in such a nice country. Ah, sir, would I pour you a cup of coffee?"

"OK," David answered.

"It's **exceptionally**[③] fine today," said the servant bringing the coffee.

"But the weather forecast tells it will rain."

"It will be nice even if it rains, for after the rain the earth will be more **vital**[④]. **In addition**[⑤], flowers and trees also need rain water."

The servant made a good impression on David, which made him rich in his mind. Now he knows how to face his work.

生词有约

① reception

n. 接待

② enthusiastic

adj. 热情的；热心的

③ exceptionally

adv. 异常地；例外地

④ vital

adj. 生机勃勃的；充满生命力的

⑤ in addition

另外；此外

阳光心态

有一次，戴维在旧金山的一家旅馆预订了一个房间。那天的工作使他感到疲倦。在总台，他遇见了一个服务生。

服务生对他说："早安！早安！早安！"好奇怪啊！说了3次早安，但戴维一点也不厌烦。相反，他觉得服务生很诚恳。

"你真热情啊！"戴维对他招呼道。

"就应该这样！"服务生笑着说道，"我有好工作，又生活在这样好的国家。啊，先生，我为您倒杯咖啡，好吗？"

"好。"戴维回答。

"今天天气格外好，"服务生端来咖啡说。

"可天气预报说会下雨。"

"即使下雨，雨后大地也会更加生机勃勃。再说，花草树木也需要雨水。"

服务生给戴维留下了美好印象，这使他心里充实。他现在知道要如何面对自己的工作了。

诵读经典 >>>>>
Read classic

The servant made a good impression on David, which made him rich in his mind. Now he knows how to face his work.

服务生给戴维留下了美好印象，这使他心里充实。他现在知道要如何面对自己的工作了。

妙语连珠 >>>>>
Sparkling discourse

✪ When you need salt, sugar won't do.
当你需要盐时，糖是没有用的。

✪ Applause is a receipt, not a bill.
掌声是收据，不是账单。

Approach the Destination

Dwight Morrow was a famous banker and **diplomat**① of America in the 20th century.

Once, Morrow travelled in Rugby, England. During this period, he left the station, strolled nearby. While walking on and on, he got lost.

So he asked a local boy of the way.

The boy told him, "Turn right from here until a grocery store, and then turn left from there. Go straight on and you will find a place with a four-street **intersection**②..."

With that, the boy thought for a while and went on saying, "When you get there, you are not far away from the station. Then you'd better ask someone else. Even if I tell you now, you may not remember."

According to the boy's guide, Morrow got to the four street intersections pretty soon, and then asked a passerby there and quickly turned back to the station in no time.

This was a minor matter, but it had a tremendous **impact**③ on Morrow.

Morrow realized that each person's ability is limited and many problems cannot be solved in one day.

Thus, we must act step by step and approach the **destination**④ gradually.

生词有约

① diplomat
n. 外交家；外交官

② intersection
n. 交叉点；十字路口

③ impact
n. 冲击；影响；效果

④ destination
n. 目的地；终点

走近目的地

德怀特·莫罗是 20 世纪美国著名的银行家和外交家。

有一次，莫罗在英国的拉格比市旅行。在这期间，他离开车站，到附近逛街，走着走着竟然迷路了。

于是，莫罗向当地一个少年问路。

那个少年告诉他："从这里往右走，一直到有个杂货店的地方，然后从那里往左拐，一直走下去，你会看到有个地方是四条街交会……"

说到这里，少年想了想继续说："你走到那里时，距离车站就不远了，然后你最好再向其他人打听一下。我现在告诉你走法，你也记不住。"

根据这位少年的指引，莫罗很快就到了四条街交会的地方，然后他再向那边的路人打听，很快就回到了车站。

这是一件小事，但对莫罗产生了巨大影响。

莫罗意识到，我们每个人的能力都是有限的，许多问题不可能一朝一夕就获得解决。

因此，我们必须一步一步行动，逐渐走近目的地。

诵读经典 >>>>>
Read classic

According to the boy's guide, Morrow got to the four street intersections pretty soon, and then asked a passerby there and quickly turned back to the station in no time.

根据这位少年的指引，莫罗很快就到了四条街交会的地方，然后他再向那边的路人打听，很快就回到了车站。

妙语连珠 >>>>>
Sparkling discourse

★ If you get too much, even sunshine will burn.

如果你接受太多照射，即使阳光也会造成灼伤。

★ I wept because I had no shoes, until I saw a man who had no feet.

我之所以哭，是因为我没有鞋，直到我看到一个没有脚的人。

画龙
点睛

The Buddhist Monk and a Thief

One night, a Buddhist monk who **cultivated**① himself in the mountain walked from the woods path in the bright moonlight and went back to his cottage, when he happened to run into a thief there. He was afraid to startle the thief, so he kept waiting at the door.

The thief couldn't find any valuable thing. When he turned to leave, he saw the monk. He was in a **panic**②, but the monk said, "Since you came from afar to visit me, after all I can't let you back empty-handed!" With that, he undressed his **cloak**③. "It's chilly in the night, so you can go with this cloak."

Then, the monk **draped**④ the clothes over the thief. Out of his wits, the thief slipped away with his head bowed.

Seeing off the thief, the monk said with emotion, "Poor man, I wish I could send you a moon!"

The next day the warm sun shone. The monk opened his eyes and saw the cloak he had draped over the thief the previous night was neatly folded on the doorstep. The monk was very pleased and said, "I finally sent him a moon..."

生词有约

① cultivate
vt. 培养；陶冶

② panic
n. 恐慌，惊慌

③ cloak
n. 宽大外衣；斗篷

④ drape
vt. 披在……上；覆盖

禅师与小偷

一天夜里，一位在山中修行的禅师从皎洁月光下的林间小路上散完步，回到自己的茅屋时，正碰上有个小偷光顾。他怕惊动小偷，一直站在门口等候。

小偷找不到值钱的东西，返身离去时看到了禅师，正感到惊慌时，禅师说："你走老远的山路来探望我，总不能让你空手而回！"说着，脱下了身上的外衣，"夜里凉，你带着这件衣服走吧。"

说着，禅师就把衣服披在了小偷身上。小偷不知所措，低着头溜走了。

禅师看着小偷的背影，感慨说："可怜的人呀，但愿我能送你一轮明月！"

第二天，暖阳照耀。禅师睁开眼睛，看到昨晚披在小偷身上的那件外衣整齐地叠着，放在了门口。禅师非常高兴，喃喃说道："我终于送了他一轮明月……"

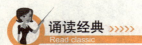

诵读经典 >>>>>
Read classic

The next day the warm sun shone. The monk opened his eyes and saw the cloak he had draped over the thief the previous night was neatly folded on the doorstep. The monk was very pleased and said, "I finally sent him a moon..."

第二天，暖阳照耀。禅师睁开眼睛，看到昨晚披在小偷身上的那件外衣整齐地叠着，放在了门口。禅师非常高兴，喃喃说道："我终于送了他一轮明月……"

妙语连珠 >>>>>
Sparkling discourse

★ Where there is sorrow, there is holy ground.
哪里有不幸，哪里就有圣地。

★ When you are the anvil, bear; when you are the hammer, strike.
当你是铁砧时，忍受；当你是铁锤时，锻造。

Ashore, the sage asked the young man in a tone of derision, "When you were submerged, how did you feel? Besides trying to go ashore, were you still considering other things?"

上岸后，圣人用揶揄的口吻问年轻人："潜入水下时，你有何感觉？除了想上岸，还考虑别的事吗？"

I Just Wanted the Air

A young man visited a **sage** ① for wisdom.

"Young man, please come with me." With the words, the sage silently walked towards the lake nearby.

Coming to the lake, the sage didn't hesitate to step into the lake and walked to the depths of the lake.

The young man had no **option** ② but to follow the sage.

The lake was getting deeper and deeper, the water **immerging** ③ the young man's neck.

However, the sage didn't mind the young man's frightened eyes and went farther.

The water finally **immersed** ④ the young man's head.

Shortly afterwards, the sage quietly turned around and returned to the lakeshore.

Ashore, the sage asked the young man in a tone of **derision** ⑤, "When you were **submerged** ⑥, how did you feel? Besides trying to go ashore, were you still considering other things?"

The young man replied immediately, "I just wanted the air."

The sage **instructed** ⑦ slowly, "It is the case! If you want to get wisdom, you should be just as you want the air as strongly as you sank in the water and can get wisdom."

生词有约

① sage

n. 圣人；圣人

② option

n. 选择；选择权

③ immerge

vt. 使浸入；使隐没

④ immerse

vt. 使沉浸；使没入

⑤ derision

n. 嘲笑

⑥ submerge

vt. 使淹没；使漫没

⑦ instruct

vt. 指导；教授

我只想得到空气

一位年轻人拜访圣人，求教智慧。

"年轻人，请随我来。"说着，圣人默默地向附近的湖走去。

走到湖边，圣人毫不犹豫地跨进湖里，向湖深处走去。

年轻人别无选择，只好跟随在圣人后面。

湖渐渐深了起来，水浸没到了年轻人的脖子。

然而，圣人毫不介意年轻人恐怖的目光，走得更远了。

水终于浸没了年轻人的头顶。

不久，圣人又默默地转回身，回到湖岸边。

上岸后，圣人用揶揄的口吻问年轻人："潜入水下时，你有何感觉？除了想上岸，还考虑别的事吗？"

年轻人马上答道："我只想得到空气。"

圣人慢慢地教诲道："正是这样！要想求得智慧，就要像沉入水下时想得到空气一样强烈，才能获得！"

诵读经典 >>>>>
Read classic

The sage instructed slowly, "It is the case! If you want to get wisdom, you should be just as you want the air as strongly as you sank in the water and can get wisdom."

圣人慢慢地教诲道："正是这样！要想求得智慧，就要像沉入水下时想得到空气一样强烈，才能获得！"

妙语连珠 >>>>>
Sparkling discourse

☀ Civilization is a movement and not a condition. A voyage and not a harbor.

文明是发展，不是状况；是航行，不是港口。

☀ Some small spirits, ashamed of their origin, are always striving to conceal it, and by every effort they made to do so, betray themselves.

有些小人羞于自己的出身，所以总是设法掩盖，但他们越是这样做，越是出卖了自己。

A Mysterious Valley

A rich man lives in his **enormous**[①] **villa**[②], enjoying the extremely **luxurious**[③] life.

Every day there are some strangers who take away a couple of boxes from his home. The rich man decided to follow them and came to a mysterious valley. Seeing they were about to throw the three boxes in the abyss, he demanded with surprise, "Please tell me what's in them."

The strangers answered indifferently, "They are the feelings that you have **abandoned**[④]."

"No, it's impossible!" The rich man disbelieved them and opened them.

In the first box there was his beloved one walking alone slowly along the beach at night.

His close friend was in the second box. After **bankruptcy**[⑤], he was longing for help and **consolation**[⑥] from the rich man.

His parents were seen in the third box. They have prepared a table of delicious food for dinner, waiting for him to reunion.

Seeing them, he felt that his heart was **lashed**[⑦] by a burning whip full of misery and guilt. He begged the strangers, "Please give them back to me. I have a lot of money. You can take as much as you want!"

However, the strangers told him with a serious look, "It's too late to take them back. The woman you loved never showed up again at charming night; your friend, having endured the long daytime, finally made out the stars with different distance; your parent bought a dog and found love

生词有约

① enormous
adj. 巨大的，庞大的
② villa
n. 别墅；郊区住宅
③ luxurious
adj. 奢华的；豪华的
④ abandon
vt. 遗弃；放弃

⑤ bankruptcy
n. 破产

⑥ consolation
n. 安慰；抚慰

⑦ lash
vt. 鞭打；攻击

and warmness from it."

After finishing their words, they threw the three boxes down to the abyss and disappeared.

With a lonely look, the rich man stood there still, gazing at the hollow of the valley in front of them…

神秘的山谷

富翁住在巨大的别墅里，享受着非常豪华的生活。

每天都有几个陌生人从他家里搬走几只箱子。富翁决定跟踪他们，随后来到一个神秘的山谷。他看到这些人正准备把三只箱子扔进深渊，便吃惊地问道："请告诉我，这些箱子里装的是什么。"

陌生人冷淡地回答说："它们是你抛弃的那些感情。"

"不，这不可能！"富翁不相信他们的话，就打开了那三只箱子。

第一只箱子里装的是他心爱的人夜晚独自在海滩慢慢地走着。

第二只箱子里装的是他的密友。公司破产后，他渴望富翁的帮助和安慰。

第三只箱子里装的是他的父母亲。他们做了一桌美餐等待他回家团聚。

看完后，他感到心像被火辣辣的鞭子抽打一般，充满了痛苦和愧疚。他哀求陌生人说："请把它们还给我吧。我有的是钱。你们要多少都可以拿去！"

然而，陌生人一脸严肃地告诉他说："太晚了，无法收回了。你爱的女人在迷人的夜晚再也没有出现。你的朋友熬过长长的白天后，终于看清了那些远近不一的星星。你的父母买了一条狗，从它身上找到了爱和温暖。"

说完，陌生人把三只箱子扔下山谷，就消失了。

富翁神情孤独，站在那里一动不动，凝望着眼前空荡荡的山谷……

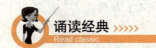

诵读经典 >>>>>
Read classic

Seeing them, he felt that his heart was lashed by a burning whip full of misery and guilt. He begged the strangers, "Please give them back to me. I have a lot of money. You can take as much as you want!"

看完后，他感到心像被火辣辣的鞭子抽打一般，充满了痛苦和愧疚。他哀求陌生人说："请把它们还给我吧。我有的是钱。你们要多少都可以拿去！"

妙语连珠 >>>>>
Sparkling discourse

★ There is strong shadow where there is much light.

凡是光多的地方，阴影也深重。

★ The true test of civilization is, not the census, nor the size of the cities, nor the crops, but the kind of man that country turns out.

文明的真正标准不在于人口数目、城市规模大小、出产粮食多少，而在于国家培养出何等人才。

Reduce to Bare Essentials

A young man went to see a wise man, saying that after graduation, he set many targets for himself, but years later he **accomplished**① nothing.

When he found the wise man, the latter was reading in the cottage by the river. With a smile, the wise man heard the young man's words, and said to him, "Come help me boil a kettle of water first!"

The young man saw a big pitcher standing in the corner, next to a small fire stove, but he found no firewood, so he went out for it.

He came back with some dead wood, filled up the kettle with water and put on the stove. He put some firewood in the stove and burned up, but because the pot was too large, when the **faggot**② burned out, the water did not boil. Then he ran off to get firewood. When he went back, the water had nearly turned cold. This time he became smart, so he was not eager to light the fire, but went out to look for some firewood again. Because the fire wood was well prepared, the water boiled pretty soon.

The wise man suddenly asked him, "If there is not enough firewood, how should you boil the water?"

The young man thought for a moment and shook his head.

The wise man said, "If so, pour out some water of the kettle!"

The young man nodded thoughtfully.

The wise man continued, "You had so many **aspirations**③ at first and set too many goals, just as the large

生词有约

① accomplish
vt. 实现；完成

② faggot
n. 柴把；枝条捆

③ aspiration
n. 抱负；渴望

182

kettle was filled with too much water but you didn't have enough firewood, so you couldn't boil the water, and if you wanted to make the water boil, you either emptied some of the water or prepared some firewood!"

The young man saw the light suddenly.

When he went back, he removed many listed targets from his plan, leaving only a few recent ones, while with spare time he studied all kinds of specialties.

A few years later, his goals were realized.

删繁就简

一个年轻人满腹烦恼,去找一位智者,说他大学毕业后,为自己树立了许多目标,但几年来一事无成。

他找到智者时,智者正在河边小屋里读书。智者微笑着听完年轻人的倾诉,对他说:"来,你先帮我烧壶开水!"

年轻人看见墙角放着一把极大的水壶,旁边是一个小火灶,但没有发现柴火。于是,他便出去找。

他在外面拾了一些枯枝回来,装满一壶水,放在灶台上。他在灶里放了一些柴,便烧了起来。可是,壶太大,那捆柴烧尽了,水也没开。于是,他跑出去继续找柴,回来时那壶水已经凉得差不多了。这次,他学聪明了,没有急于点火,而是再次出去找柴。因为柴准备充足,所以水不一会儿就烧开了。

智者突然问他:"如果没有足够的柴,你该怎样把水烧开?"

年轻人想了一会儿,摇了摇头。

智者说:"如果那样,就把水壶里的水倒掉一些!"

年轻人若有所思地点了点头。

智者接着说:"你一开始踌躇满志,树立了太多的目标,就像这个大水壶装了太多水一样,而你又没有足够的柴,所以不能把水烧开,要想把水烧开,你要么倒出一些水,要么先去准备柴!"

年轻人恍然大悟。

回去后,他把计划中所列的目标去掉了许多,只留下最近的几个,同时利用业余时间学习各种专业知识。

几年后,他的目标都变成了现实。

诵读经典 >>>>>
Read classic

You had so many aspirations at first and set too many goals, just as the large kettle was filled with too much water but you didn't have enough firewood, so you couldn't boil the water, and if you wanted to make the water boil, you either emptied some of the water or prepared some firewood!

你一开始踌躇满志，树立了太多的目标，就像这个大水壶装了太多水一样，而你又没有足够的柴，所以不能把水烧开，要想把水烧开，你要么倒出一些水，要么先去准备柴！

妙语连珠 >>>>>
Sparkling discourse

✪ If the only tool you have is a hammer, you tend to see every problem as a nail.

如果你拥有的工具只是一把锤子，你往往会把每个问题都看作是钉子。

✪ The greatness of a country doesn't depend on its size but on the quality of its citizens and the leadership.

一个国家的伟大并不看它的幅员大小，而要看它的公民和领导的素质。

One man greeted her and said, "We, the strongest and most able men in the village, couldn't climb up this mountain. How did you do this?"

一个战士跟她打招呼说："我们是部落中最强壮、最能干的男人，都爬不上山。你是怎么做到的呢？"

Mother's Strength

There were two warring tribes in the Andes, one that lived in the **lowlands**[①] and the other high in the mountains.

One day the mountain people invaded the lowlanders, and as part of their **plundering**[②] of the people, they **kidnapped**[③] a baby of one of the lowlander families and took the infant with them up into the mountains.

The lowlanders didn't know how to climb the mountain. They didn't know any clue of the path that the mountain people used while they didn't know where to find the mountain people or how to **track**[④] them in the steep **terrain**[⑤].

Even so, they sent out their best party of fighting men to climb the mountain and bring the baby home. The men tried one method of climbing after another. After several days of efforts, however, they had climbed only a couple of hundred feet. Feeling hopeless and helpless, the lowlanders decided that the cause was lost, and they prepared to return to their village below. As they were packing their **gear**[⑥] for the **descent**[⑦], they saw the baby's mother walking toward them. They realized that she was coming down the mountain that they hadn't figured out how to climb. And then they saw that she had the baby strapped to her back. How could that be?

One man greeted her and said, "We, the strongest and most able men in the village, couldn't climb up this mountain. How did you do this?"

The mother shrugged her shoulders and said, "It isn't your

生词有约

① lowland
n. 苏格兰东南部的低地

② plunder
n. 抢夺；战利品；掠夺品

③ kidnap
vt. 诱拐；绑架

④ track
vt. 追踪；循路而行

⑤ terrain
n. 地形；地势

⑥ gear
n. 工具

⑦ descent
n. 下降；下坡路

baby."

As long as you have love in your heart, no mountain you cannot climb.

母亲的力量

安第斯山有两个敌对的部落，一个部落住在低地，另一个部落住在高山上。

有一天，山上部落侵略山下部落。在对山下部落抢劫中，他们绑架了一户人家的婴儿，并把婴儿带上了山。

山下部落的人不知道怎么才能爬上山。他们不知道山上部落走的山道的任何线索，也不知道在哪里找到山上部落，更不知道怎样在陡峭的山地跟踪追击。

尽管如此，但他们仍然派自己部落中最优秀、最勇敢的战士爬上山，把孩子抢回来。战士们尝试了一个又一个方法。然而，努力了好几天后，他们仅仅爬了几百英尺。山下部落的战士们感到绝望无助，认为没有办法爬到山上去，准备回到山下的村庄。正当他们收拾工具准备返回山下时，只见那个婴儿的母亲正朝他们走来。他们意识到她下来的那座山正是他们不知道怎样爬的那座山。随后，他们看到了她背着那个婴儿。这怎么可能呢？

一个战士跟她打招呼说："我们是部落中最强壮、最能干的男人，都爬不上山。你是怎么做到的呢？"

孩子的母亲耸了耸肩，说："那不是你们的孩子。"

只要心中有爱，没有爬不过去的高山。

诵读经典 >>>>>
Read classic

The lowlanders didn't know how to climb the mountain. They didn't know any clue of the path that the mountain people used while they didn't know where to find the mountain people or how to track them in the steep terrain.

山下部落的人不知道怎么才能爬上山。他们不知道山上部落走的山道的任何线索，也不知道在哪里找到山上部落，更不知道怎样在陡峭的山地跟踪追击。

妙语连珠 >>>>>
Sparkling discourse

✪ Make your life a mission, not an intermission.
让你的生命成为使命，而不是一次停顿。

✪ Life is so brief and time is fleeting. Grasp it and it will be an opportunity; depict it and it will be a rainbow.

生命如此短暂，光阴飞逝如箭。抓住它，它就是机会；描绘它，它就是彩虹。

He called his three sons to him. "Here is some money," he told them. "You must each take one coin to buy something that will fill this room. The one who can do this shall have my fortune."

他把三个儿子叫到身边，对他们说："给你们一些钱，你们必须各自拿一枚硬币去买一件东西，这件东西要充满整个房间。谁能做到这一点，谁就可以拥有我的财产。"

Candlelight Wisdom

Once upon a time, there was an old **merchant**[①] who had three sons.

"To whom shall I leave my **fortune**[②]?" he wondered. "It must be the cleverest son. But which one is the cleverest?"

He called his three sons to him. "Here is some money," he told them. "You must each take one coin to buy something that will fill this room. The one who can do this shall have my fortune."

"It is a big room," said the eldest son.

"One coin will not buy very much," said the second son.

But the youngest son said nothing. He thought a while, and then he smiled. "Come, brothers," he said. "Let us go to the market."

The eldest son bought straw with his coin. But one coin bought only a bit of straw. Even when he had spread it as much as he could, the straw covered only a corner of the room.

The second son bought sand with his coin. But one coin bought only a bit of sand. Even when he had spread it as he could, the sand covered only half of the floor.

"What did you buy?" the elder sons angrily asked the youngest. "You don't have any straw or any sand."

"I bought this," said the youngest son.

"A candle!" cried the brothers. "What good is candle?"

"Watch," said the youngest son.

He lit the candle, and all at once the room was filled with

生词有约

① merchant
n. 商人；店主
② fortune
n. 财富；命运

188

light!

"Although you are the youngest, you are indeed the cleverest of my sons," the old merchant said.

烛光智慧

从前一位老商人有三个儿子。

"我要把自己的财产留给谁呢?"他想。"一定是最聪明的那个儿子。可是,谁最聪明呢?"

他把三个儿子叫到身边,对他们说:"给你们一些钱,你们必须各自拿一枚硬币去买一件东西,这件东西要充满整个房间。谁能做到这一点,谁就可以拥有我的财产。"

"那是一个大房间,"大儿子说。

"一枚硬币买不了多少东西,"二儿子说。

但是,最小的儿子什么也没说。他想了一会儿,然后微微一笑说:"让我们到市场上去吧。"

大儿子用他那枚硬币买了稻草,但一枚硬币只能买一点稻草。甚至当他尽可能多地将稻草铺开时,那些稻草只盖住了房间的一个角。

二儿子用他那枚硬币买了沙子。但是,一枚硬币只能买一点沙子。甚至当他尽可能铺开时,沙子只铺了一半地板。

"你买什么东西?"两个年长的儿子生气地问最小的儿子。"你既没有买稻草也没有买沙子。"

"我买的是这个,"最小的儿子说。

"蜡烛!"两个哥哥大声叫道。"蜡烛有什么用?"

"看,"最小的儿子说。

他点燃蜡烛,房间里马上充满了光明!

"尽管你年龄最小,但你的确是我最聪明的儿子,"老商人说。

诵读经典 >>>>>
Read classic

The eldest son bought straw with his coin. But one coin bought only a bit of straw. Even when he had spread it as much as he could, the straw covered only a corner of the room.

大儿子用他那枚硬币买了稻草,但一枚硬币只能买一点稻草。甚至当他尽可能多地将稻草铺开时,那些稻草只盖住了房间的一个角。

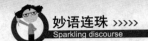

妙语连珠 >>>>>
Sparkling discourse

✪ The challenge of life is to overcome.

人生的挑战在于征服。

✪ Life is a grindstone. It depends us whether it grinds us down or polishes us up.

生活就是磨刀石。我们是被磨碎还是被磨亮，取决于我们自己。

> **Your Majesty, if the rays of the moon can warm a person, the sight of water can satisfy his thirst.**
>
> 陛下，要是月亮的光线能给人温暖，那看看水也能解渴。

The Sight of Water Can Satisfy the Thirst

One cold night the King called Nasreddin to him and said, "If you're able to spend this night in the courtyard with only your shirt on, I will give you one hundred gold coins!"

In the courtyard Nasreddin saw a stone mill. He began to push it around, faster and faster. When dawn came, he was sweating all over himself.

The King got up and was surprised to see Nasreddin **in high spirits**①. The King hated to lose one hundred gold coins, so he asked, "Was there a moon last night?"

"Yes."

"Then our **bargain**② is off," said the King. "If there was a moon, it was warm. In that case even I could have spent the night outside!"

A few months later, the King and his men went hunting. It was hot summer and at the edge of the desert it was like a **furnace**③. The King and his men were dying of thirst.

They turned toward Nasreddin's house in the hope of getting some water. Nasreddin was sitting on the edge of his well when he heard the voice of the King, "Nasreddin, bring some fresh water! Be quick and serve us!"

"Please make yourself at home," said Nasreddin.

"Where is the water?" cried the King.

"Right here, Your Majesty, you see?" Nasreddin pointed to the well.

"You only show me the water but don't give me a drink!" fumed the King.

"Your Majesty, if the rays of the moon can warm a person, the sight of water can **satisfy**④ his thirst."

生词有约

① in high spirits
兴高采烈；情绪高涨

② bargain
n. 交易；契约

③ furnace
n. 火炉；熔炉

④ satisfy
vt. 满足；使满意

191

看看水也能解渴

一个寒冷的夜晚，国王把纳斯雷丁叫到他的身边，说："要是你能只穿一件衬衣在院子里度过这一夜，我就送给你100枚金币！"

纳斯雷丁在院子里看到一盘石磨，便开始推着石磨转，越转越快。当黎明来临时，他汗流浃背。

国王起床后，看到纳斯雷丁精神抖擞，就吃了一惊。国王不愿意失去一百枚金币，就问："昨晚有月亮吗？"

"有。"

"那我们的交易无效，"国王说。"要是有月亮，天就很暖和。在那种情况下，就是我也能在外面过夜！"

几个月后，国王和他的随从们去打猎。那是一个炎热的夏天，沙漠的边缘天热得像火炉一样。国王和随从们渴得要死。

他们转身向纳斯雷丁家走去，希望搞点水喝。纳斯雷丁正坐在井沿上，突然听到国王的声音："纳斯雷丁，端些干净水！快来伺候我们！"

"请不要拘束，"纳斯雷丁说。

"水在哪里？"国王叫道。

"陛下，就在这里，你看到了吧？"纳斯雷丁指着井说。

"你只是让我看了水，却没有让我喝！"国王发怒说。

"陛下，要是月亮的光线能给人温暖，那看看水也能解渴。"

诵读经典 >>>>>
Read classic

In the courtyard Nasreddin saw a stone mill. He began to push it around, faster and faster. When dawn came, he was sweating all over himself.

纳斯雷丁在院子里看到一盘石磨，便开始推着石磨转，越转越快。当黎明来临时，他汗流浃背。

妙语连珠 >>>>>
Sparkling discourse

❂ The secret of living is to find the pivot of a concept on which you can make your stand.

生活的秘诀在于找到一个能够支撑你的思想支点。

❂ The aim of life is to develop oneself and realize one's nature perfectly.

生活的目标就是发展自我，并彻底认清自我。

The old man looked down at the youngster and replied, "I've thought a lot in my lifetime, and the secret can be summed up in four words."

老人看着小男孩答道："我在一生中想了许多，人生的真谛可以概括为四个词。"

画龙
点睛

A Wishing Well

An eight-year-old boy **approached**[1] an old man in front of a wishing well, looked up into his eyes, and asked: I understand you're a very wise man. I'd like to know the secret of life."

The old man looked down at the **youngster**[2] and replied, "I've thought a lot in my lifetime, and the secret can be **summed up**[3] in four words:

"The first is to think. Think about the values you wish to live your life by.

"The second is to believe. Believe in yourself based on the thinking you've done about the values you're going to live your life by.

"The third is to dream. Dream about the things that can be, based on your belief in yourself and the values you're going to live by.

"The last is to dare. Dare to make your dreams become reality, based on your belief in yourself and your values."

And with that, Walter E. Disney said to the little boy: Think, Believe, Dream and Dare.

生词有约

① approach
vt. 接近
② youngster
n. 年轻人；少年
③ sum up
总结；概述

许愿井

一个 8 岁的小男孩走到一眼许愿井旁边的一位老人身边，看着他的眼睛问道："我知道你是一个非常有智慧的人，我想知道人生的真谛。"

老人看着小男孩答道："我在一生中想了许多，人生的真谛可以概指为 4 个词：

与 **青春** >>>>> 有关的日子 *砥砺派*

"首先是思考，思考你生活的价值观。

"其次是信任，对自己的信任基于你已经找到自己一生依赖生存的价值观。

"再次是梦想，梦想那些可以基于你一生遵循的价值观和对自己的信任的事情。

"最后是勇敢，在你的价值观和对自己信任的基础上，勇敢地让梦想变成现实。"

最后，沃尔特·E·迪斯尼对这个小男孩说：思考、信任、梦想和勇敢。

诵读经典 >>>>>
Read classic

The last is to dare. Dare to make your dreams become reality, based on your belief in yourself and your values.

最后是勇敢，在你的价值观和对自己信任的基础上，勇敢地让梦想变成现实。

妙语连珠 >>>>>
Sparkling discourse

❂ Man is a reed that is the most fragile in nature, but he is a thinking reed.

人是自然界中最脆弱的一棵芦苇，但却是一棵会思考的芦苇。

❂ The orbit of life is unforeknowable, so no one can finish his autobiography in advance.

人生的轨道无法预知，谁也不能事先写好自传。

"Everything happens for the best," my mother said whenever I faced disappointment. **"If you carry on, one day something good will happen."**

"一切都会好的。"每当我面临失望时，母亲都会说，"如果你坚持下去，总有一天好事会出现。"

Everything Happens for the Best

"Everything happens for the best," my mother said whenever I faced disappointment. "If you carry on, one day something good will happen."

Mother was right, as I discovered after graduating from college in 1932, I had decided to try for a job in radio, then work my way to a sports announcer. I **hitchhiked**[①] to Chicago and knocked on the door of every station and got turned down every time.

In one **studio**[②], a kind lady told me that big stations couldn't risk hiring an inexperienced person. "Go find a small station that'll give you a chance," she said.

I thumbed home to Dixon, Illinois. While there were no radioannouncing jobs in Dixon, my father said Montgomery Ward had opened a store and wanted a local **athlete**[③] to manage its sports department. Since Dixon was where I had played high-school football, I applied. The job sounded just right for me. But I wasn't hired.

My disappointment must have shown. "Everything happens for the best," Mom reminded me. Dad offered me the car to job hunt. I tried WOC Radio in Davenport, Iowa. The program director, a wonderful Scotsman named Peter MacArthur, told me they had already hired an announcer.

As I left his office, I asked aloud, "How can a fellow get to be a sports announcer if he can't get a job in a radio station?"

I was waiting for the elevator when I heard MacArthur calling, "What was that you said about sports? Do you know

生词有约

① hitchhike
vi. 搭便车

② studio
n. 演播室；工作室

③ athlete
n. 运动员；体育家

anything about football?" Then he let me stand before a **microphone** ④ and asked me to broadcast an imaginary game.

　　The **preceding** ⑤ autumn, my team had won a game in the last 20 seconds with 65-yard run. I did a 15-minute build-up to that play, and Peter told me I would be broadcasting Saturday's game!

　　On my way home, as I have many times since, I thought of my mother's words: "If you carry on, one day something good will happen."

　　I often wonder what direction my life might have taken if I'd gotten the job at Montgomery Ward.

④ microphone

n. 扩音器，麦克风

⑤ preceding

adj. 在前的；前述的

一切都会好的

　　"一切都会好的。"每当我面临失望时，母亲都会说，"如果你坚持下去，总有一天好事会出现。"

　　1932 年大学毕业时，我才发现母亲说的没错。当时，我决定在电台找一份工作，然后通过奋斗，当一名体育播音员。我搭便车来到芝加哥，敲了每一家电台的门，每次都被拒之门外。

　　在一家演播室，一位好心的女士告诉我说，大电台都不可能冒风险去雇没有经验的人。"找一家小电台，它会给你一个机会的。"她说。

　　我搭便车回到家乡伊利诺伊州迪克森。迪克森没有无线电播音的工作。父亲告诉我说，蒙哥马利·沃德开了一家商店，想在当地雇一位运动员管理体育部。因为迪克森是我中学曾打过橄榄球的地方，所以我就提出了申请。这份工作对我正合适，但我还是被雇佣。

　　我的失望之情一定是露了出来。"一切都会好的。"妈妈提醒我说。爸爸将车给我，让我去找工作。我去了衣阿华州达文波特 WOC 电台试了试。节目主管是一个名叫彼得·麦克阿瑟的了不起的苏格兰人。他告诉我说他们已经雇佣了一名播音员。

　　我离开他的办公室时，大声问道："一个在广播电台都找不到工作的人怎么能成为一名体育播音员呢？"

　　我等电梯时，听到麦克阿瑟朝我喊道："你说的体育是怎么回事？你知道橄榄球吗？"于是，他让我站在麦克风前，请我为一场假想的比赛解说。

　　在前一年的秋天，我的球队在最后 20 秒内以 65 码的距离赢得了一场球。我对那场球赛做了 15 分钟的精彩解说。彼得告诉我可以为星期六的比赛解说！

　　在回家的路上，我想到了母亲的那番话，从此多次都是这样："一切都会好起来的。如果你坚持不懈，好事总有一天会到来。"

我常常想，如果得到了蒙哥马利·沃德的那份工作，我的人生会通向何方。

诵读经典 >>>>>
Read classic

On my way home, as I have many times since, I thought of my mother's words: "If you carry on, one day something good will happen."

在回家的路上，我想到了母亲的那番话，从此多次都是这样："一切都会好起来的。如果你坚持不懈，好事总有一天会到来。"

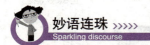

妙语连珠 >>>>>
Sparkling discourse

✪　All stupid things will be gradually melted in the reading of good books every day as if by a fire.

一切蠢事，在每天阅读好书的影响下，仿佛烤在火上一样渐渐地熔化。

✪　Reading in youth is like peeping the moon through a crack; at middle age, like looking over it in a courtyard; at old age, like playing it on a platform.

少年读书，如隙中窥月；中年读书，像庭中望月；老年读书，似台上玩月。

The Last Oak Tree

A farmer looked after his family and his land. Winter was coming soon, and he needed firewood to keep his family warm and cook their food.

The farmer **saddled**[①] his horse and rode to the forest, but all the trees had been cut down to build houses. He rode to the valley where the river ran, but all the trees had been cut down to make boats.

The only place left to look for was in the hills far away, so he rode all night to get there. When he arrived, all he found was a single, very great oak tree. It stood proud with big leaves, long branches, and fat roots. Very small **seedlings**[②] grew all around the tree.

The farmer raised his axe and started to cut.

"Wait," came a voice.

The farmer dropped his axe and looked around, but nobody was there. "Who said that?" asked the farmer.

"I did," answered the tree.

"But trees cannot talk," said the farmer.

"Yes, we can," said the tree.

"What do you want me to do?" asked the farmer.

The tree asked, "Why do you want to cut me down?"

"Because I need firewood to keep my family warm and cook our food," answered the farmer.

"But I am the last tree," cried the oak. "What will you do next year—when there are no more trees anywhere?"

The farmer thought long and hard. He looked at the seedlings around him and said, "I will cut these seedlings

生词有约

① saddle
vt. 给（马）加上鞍座

② seedling
n. 幼苗

down for firewood."

"They are not big enough to use as firewood," explained the tree. "Next year, when all the tree seedlings have grown, you can cut me down."

"But what will I do now?" said the farmer. "My family will starve and freeze to death without firewood."

The tree thought for a moment. "Use your wooden fence for firewood."

"But all my animals will run away," said the farmer.

"Build a stone wall to replace it," said the tree. "A stone wall will last for many years."

"That is a good idea," the farmer said. "But next year I will be back to cut you down." And the farmer left the last tree on the hill.

During the winter, the farmer used his wooden fence for firewood. The other farmers saw what he was doing. They could not find any firewood either, so they used their fences for firewood and replaced them with stonewalls. All the farmers' families kept warm and ate warm meals.

When fall came again, the farmer needed more firewood. He rode to the forest, but all he saw were seedlings. He rode to the valley where the river ran, but all he saw were more seedlings. He went to the hill where the last tree was standing. When he got to the top, he saw that the seedlings had grown into **saplings**[3]. He walked to the oak and raised his axe over his head.

"Wait," said the oak.

"What?" said the farmer.

"Why do you want to cut me down? I am the last tree that can bear seeds. If you cut me down, there will be no more trees to bear seeds."

The farmer put down his axe and said, "I need firewood to cook and keep my family warm."

"If you wait one more year," said the oak. "the saplings will start bearing seeds, and then you can cut me down."

"But what will I do for firewood this year?" the farmer

③ sapling

n. 树苗；小树

asked.

The tree thought for a moment. "You can use your wooden stable for firewood. Next year you can cut me down when the saplings start **bearing**④ **acorns**⑤."

④ bear
vt. 生产（农作物或水果）

⑤ acorn
n. 橡子；橡实

"I'll do it," said the farmer, "but next year I'll be back to cut you down." And the farmer left the last tree standing on the hill.

All during the freezing winter, the farmer used his wooden stable for firewood. The other farmers saw what he was doing. They could not find any firewood either, so they used their stables for firewood and replaced them with stables made of bricks. All the farmers' families kept warm and ate warm meals.

When fall came again, the farmer needed more firewood. He rode toward the forest, but there were not enough saplings to last through the winter, either. He went to the hill where the last tree was standing, and raised his axe over his head.

But the tree did not say a word.

The farmer stopped. He put down the axe and sat under the tree. "What else can I use for firewood?" he asked the tree.

The tree did not answer him.

The farmer thought for a moment. "I know. I can use the **toolshed**⑥. I'll build a new one of stone and use the old one for firewood." And the farmer left the last tree on the hill.

⑥ toolshed
n. （园艺工具等的）工具房；工具室

Every fall after that, the farmer would ride to the hill where the very great oak tree stood. He would sit under the spreading limbs and think of other things to use for firewood, instead of cutting down the tree.

And that oak tree is still there today, but it is no longer the last tree.

最后一棵橡树

农夫照看着家人和土地。冬天马上就要来了，所以他需要柴火让家人取暖做饭。

农夫跨鞍上马，向森林骑去。可是，所有的树都被砍倒用来建房了。他又骑到了大河流过的山谷，而所有的树都被砍倒用来造船了。

剩下要找的唯一地方就是远处的小山里。于是，他连夜骑马赶往那里。他到达那里时，只发现一棵孤零零的大橡树。大橡树傲然耸立，大大的树叶，长长的树枝，肥肥的根部。橡树四周长满了小树苗。

农夫举起斧子就要砍。

"等一下，"一个声音说。

农夫放下斧子，向四周看了看，没见一个人。"谁在说话？"农夫问。

"是我，"橡树回答说。

"可树不会说话，"农夫说。

"不，我们会，"橡树说。

"你要我做什么？"农夫问。

橡树反问道："你为什么要把我砍倒？"

"因为我需要柴火让家人取暖做饭，"农夫回答说。

"可我是最后一棵树，"橡树哭道，"当什么地方都没有树时，下一年你怎么办？"

农夫苦思冥想了好长时间。他向四周的树苗看了看说："我将这些树苗砍作柴烧。"

"它们作柴火还不够大，"橡树解释说，"明年，当所有树苗都长大时，你可以把我砍倒。"

"可我现在怎么办？"农夫说，"没有柴火，我的家人将会饿死冻死。"

橡树想了一会儿说："用你们家的木篱笆当柴火烧。"

"可我所有的动物会跑掉，"农夫说。

"砌一堵石墙代替，"橡树说，"石墙会顶好多年。"

"这是个好主意，"农夫说，"不过，明年我要回来把你砍倒。"说完，农夫就离开了小山上的最后一棵树。

冬天，农夫就用他家的木篱笆当柴火烧。其他农夫看到了他这样做。因为他们也找不到任何柴火，所以也将他们家的篱笆当柴火烧，用石墙代替了木篱笆。所有的农夫都暖暖和和，吃上了热饭。

秋天再次来临时，农夫又需要柴火。他骑马来到了森林，但他看到的都是小树苗。他又骑马来到了大河流过的山谷，他所看到的也是小树苗。他来到最后一棵树耸立的小山上。他到达山顶时，看到小树苗已经长成了小树。他走到橡树边，将斧子举到了头顶。

"等一下，"橡树说。

"什么事？"农夫问。

"你为什么要砍倒我？我是能产籽的最后一棵树。你把我砍倒，就不会有树产籽了。"

农夫放下斧子说："我需要柴火做饭、让家人取暖。"

"你要是再等一年，"橡树说，"小树就开始产籽了，然后你可以把我砍倒。"

"可我今年要什么作柴火烧呢？"农夫问。

橡树想了一会儿说："你可以用你们家的木马厩当柴火烧。当明年小树开始产籽时，你可以把我砍倒。"

"我会那样做的，"农夫说，"可明年我会回来把你砍倒的。"农夫离开了小山上的最后一棵树。

整个寒冬，农夫就用他家的木厩作柴火烧。其他农夫又看到了他这样做。因为他们也找不到任何柴火，所以就用他们家的木厩作柴火，用砖砌的马厩来代替它们。所有农夫的家人都暖暖和和，吃上了热饭。

秋天再次来临时，农夫又需要柴火。他骑马向森林走去，可是，小树还不够挨过整个冬天。他来到了最后一棵树耸立的小山上，将斧子举过了头顶。

可是，橡树没说一句话。

农夫停住手，放下斧子，在橡树下坐下来。"我还能用什么作柴火呢?"他问橡树。

橡树没有回答。

农夫想了一会儿。"我知道了。我可以用工具棚。我再建一个石头的，然后将旧木棚当柴火烧。"随后，农夫离开了小山上的最后一棵树。

从那以后，每年秋天，农夫就会骑马到那棵硕大无朋的橡树耸立的小山上去。他常常坐在蓬蓬勃勃的树干下，想起用其他东西来当柴火烧，而没有砍倒这棵树。

那棵大橡树如今仍在那里，但已不再是最后一棵树了。

诵读经典 >>>>>
Read classic

✪ He rode to the valley where the river ran, but all he saw were more seedlings. He went to the hill where the last tree was standing. When he got to the top, he saw that the seedlings had grown into saplings. He walked to the oak and raised his axe over his head.

他又骑马来到了大河流过的山谷，他所看到的也是小树苗。他来到最后一棵树耸立的小山上。他到达山顶时，看到小树苗已经长成了小树。他走到橡树边，将斧子举到了头顶。

✪ Every fall after that, the farmer would ride to the hill where the very great oak tree stood. He would sit under the spreading limbs and think of other things to use for firewood, instead of cutting down the tree.

从那以后，每年秋天，农夫就会骑马到那棵硕大无朋的橡树耸立的小山上去。他常常坐在蓬蓬勃勃的树干下，想起用其他东西来当柴火烧，而没有砍倒这棵树。

妙语连珠 >>>>>
Sparkling discourse

✪ Books introduce us into the best society; they bring us into the presence of the greatest minds that have ever lived.

书籍把我们引入最好的交际圈，它们带我们去见古往今来最伟大的思想家。

✪ Books are really man's loyal friends, as they can provide you with wings, sometimes flying to the faraway places, sometimes to the ancient times and sometimes even to the unknown future.

书确实是人类的忠实朋友，因为它们能使人插上翅膀，时而飞向远方，时而飞向古代，有时甚至飞向未知的未来。

The Sled against the Blizzard

Balto trotted head down in the darkness of a stinging **blizzard** ①. Behind him his ten teammates kept pace as he guided them into Nome, Alaska, and down a deserted street to the hospital.

"Halt!" Musher Gunnar Kasson croaked through ice-burned lips. Balto dropped into the deep snow at the door of the hospital. Kasson sank to his knees beside him. With tears welling from his near-blinded eyes, hands shaking from exhaustion, he pulled sharp chunks of ice from Balto's bleeding paws. "Balto," Kasson whispered into his neck fur. "Damn fine dog!"

It was 5:30 a.m. on February 2. Balto had saved lives.

The people of Nome were stricken with **diphtheria** ②, a deadly disease.

They were in desperate need of the **serum** ③ that would stop the "black death" that was killing a person a day in the sub-arctic town. When the railroad train carrying the serum had become snowbound in Nenana, 660 miles away, and the planes could not take off, the U.S. Signal Corps sent out a call for dog teams.

Mushers from miles around, including Gunnar Kasson, responded. They knew the assignment was dangerous, but they brought their strongest and most intelligent dogs to the snowbound outposts along the route to Nome.

At one post after another, a team would pull in, the serum would be passed on, and another team would pull out.

生词有约

① blizzard
n. 大风雪；暴风雪

② diphtheria
n. 白喉

③ serum
n. 免疫血清

The relay ran day and night for four days. Then Charlie Olson and his team of seven pulled into Bluff, 67.5 miles from Nome, in a roaring blizzard. He handed Gunnar Kasson the serum and warned him about the winds and cold.

At first Kasson decided to wait out the storm. But at ten o'clock that night, the blizzard showed no sign of stopping or even letting up. Kasson knew lives were at stake. He and his dogs took off into the icy tempest.

The next relay point was 34 miles away. As Balto led his team across the Topok River, an 80-mile-an-hour wind struck like a railroad engine and lifted clouds of snow into the air. Neither the dogs nor Kasson could see. But Balto never hesitated. He trotted on, following his own internal compass that guided him around drifts and out onto an ice-covered **lagoon** ④. Near the shore, Kasson sensed trouble. "Haw," he called.

④ lagoon
n. 环礁湖

Obeying reluctantly, Balto ran to the left, off the trail, and splashed into an overflow of water. Wet feet meant crippled dogs. In desperation Kasson drove the team into soft snow to dry their paws and was instantly lost in whiteness.

But Balto kept going. Picking his way, and making intelligent decisions, he trotted on at a steady pace. Twice the sled overturned and the dogs **tangled** ⑤. Twice Kasson righted the sled, straightened the traces, and let Balto lead the way. Fortunately, as they crossed Norton Sound, the wind got behind them. They covered the next 12.5 miles to Port Safety in eighty minutes.

⑤ tangle
vt. 使混乱

At the relay station, the lights were out. The musher and his team were asleep. Time would be lost waking them. Twenty-one miles away people were dying. Kasson made a decision. His dogs were running well. "Hup! Hup!" he called, and Balto kept going.

Along the seacoast the snow stopped. Kasson could see again. Two of his dogs were stiffening up. The temperature was thirty-six degrees below zero Fahrenheit. He stopped to quickly make rabbitskin boots for the dogs, and went on.

At last they pulled into Nome, exhausted but **undaunted**⑥. The dog relay teams had completed in five and a half days a trip that usually took the mail train more than twenty-five days. The next morning Balto's name appeared on the front page of every major newspaper in the United States. He was praised on the floor of Congress. Invitations for personal appearances poured in. Balto and Kasson toured from California to New York, stopping in big and little towns amid cheers and fanfare.

Balto has not been forgotten. His statue, made by R. G. Roth, stands in New York City's Central Park. Under Balto's name are these words:

*Dedicated to the **indomitable**⑦ spirit of the sled dogs that relayed antitoxins 660 miles over rough ice, across treacherous waters, through Arctic blizzards from Nenana to the relief of stricken Nome.*

⑥ undaunted
adj. 大无畏的；大胆的；刚毅的

⑦ indomitable
adj. 不屈不挠的；一往无前的

风暴雪橇

巴尔托在黑暗的暴风雪中向前奔跑，它身后有 10 队友在它的带领下跑进阿拉斯加州诺姆地区，然后沿着一条荒无人烟的街道跑向那家医院。

"停！"雪橇手刚纳·凯森用冻烂的嘴唇嘶哑地喊道。巴尔托一下子卧到了医院门口深深的雪地里。凯森也跪在了它身边，泪水从他那几乎失明的眼里涌了出来，他的手因极度疲劳而瑟瑟颤抖。他将冻结在巴尔托鲜血淋淋的爪子上的几大块锋利的冰渣拨拉下来。"巴尔托，"凯森贴在它的颈毛上低声说，"你真棒！"

这是 2 月 2 日早晨 5 点 30 分。巴尔托挽救了好多人的生命。

诺姆地区的人都严重感染了一种致命疾病——白喉。

他们急需能够制止这种黑死病的免疫血清，这种黑死病正在北极圈附近地区每天杀死一个人。当载着血清的火车在 660 英里外的尼纳纳地区被大雪封住，而且飞机也无法起飞时，美国信号公司便发出了招集狗雪橇队的紧急求援信号。

方圆几英里的雪橇手——包括刚纳·凯森——都纷纷响应。他们知道任务非常危险，所以他们把最强健、最聪明的狗带到了通向诺姆的、被大雪封住的边远居民点。

过了一哨又一哨，一个雪橇队来到一个居民点，将血清传给了另一个雪橇队，就这样由一个居民点传给另一个居民点。

这样夜以继日传递了 4 天。后来，查理·奥尔森带领他的由七条狗组成的雪橇队在呼啸的暴风雪中赶到了距离诺姆 67.5 英里的布拉福。他将血清传递给刚纳·凯森，并警告他要注意大风和寒冷。

最初，凯森决定等风暴停息再出发。但到了晚上十点钟，风暴还没有要停的迹象，甚至没有减弱的趋势。凯森知道现在是生死攸关的时刻。他和他那些狗就出发，进入到了冰冷的暴风雪中。

下一个交接点在 34 英里开外。当巴尔托领着它的队员穿过托宝克河时，风速高达每小时 80 英里，就像火车的发动机一样，将大块大块的雪掀到空中。凯森和他那些雪橇狗什么也看不见。但巴尔托义无返顾，继续跑着，凭着它自己的本能躲过了漂浮物，跑上了冰雪覆盖的环礁湖。接近湖岸边时，凯森才意识到了麻烦。"左转，"他大声叫道。

巴尔托很不情愿地服从命令，转向左边，偏离了车道，咕咚一声掉进了泛滥的湖水中。狗爪沾湿就意味着狗再也无力奔跑。无奈之际，凯森将雪橇赶到轻柔的雪中，以便擦干它们的爪子，但随即在茫茫雪野中迷路了。

但巴尔托仍在继续跑着。它小心翼翼，并作出了明智的选择。它步子平稳，雪橇翻倒了两次，其他的狗都乱了阵脚。凯森两次调正了雪橇，摆直了路线，然后又让巴尔托领路前行。幸运的是，当他们穿过诺顿湾时，狂风变成了顺风。他们用 80 分钟跑完了后来的 12.5 英里，到达了安全港。

传递站的灯全都灭了。雪橇手和他那些狗都在睡觉。再叫醒他们，时间就来不及了。死神正在逼近 21 英里外的人们。凯森当机立断，他这些狗都跑得很不错。"驾！驾！"他喊着，随后巴尔托又继续跑了起来。

海边的雪已经停了。凯森又能看见了。现在的温度是零下 36 华氏度。他的两只狗有点儿僵硬了。他停下来，迅速给狗套上了兔皮靴，然后又继续跑了起来。

最后，他们终于到达了诺姆，虽筋疲力尽，但无所畏惧。雪橇狗传送队用 5 天半时间完成了邮递火车 25 天才能完成的旅程。第二天早上，巴尔托的名字出现在美国各大报纸的头版上，它受到了国会的赞扬，各种邀请函雪片般飞来。凯森和巴尔托从加利福尼亚一路旅游到纽约，沿途在大小城镇都受到了夹道欢迎。

巴尔托没有被人们遗忘，由 R·G· 罗思完成的巴尔托雕像耸立在纽约市中央公园。在巴尔托的名字下面写着这样一段话：

献给勇往直前、不屈不挠的雪橇狗。为了拯救生命，它们踏过坚冰，越过危机四伏的水域，穿过北极大风暴，行进 660 英里，将抗生素从尼纳纳地区送到了灾情深重的诺姆地区。

诵读经典 >>>>>
Read classic

Dedicated to the indomitable spirit of the sled dogs that relayed antitoxins 660 miles over rough ice, across treacherous waters, through Arctic blizzards from Nenana to the relief of stricken Nome.

献给勇往直前、不屈不挠的雪橇狗。为了拯救生命，它们踏过坚冰，越过危机四伏的水域，穿过北极大风暴，行进660英里，将抗生素从尼纳纳地区送到了灾情深重的诺姆地区。

妙语连珠 >>>>>
Sparkling discourse

❂ A room without books is a body without soul.

没有书的房间就像没有灵魂的躯体。

❂ Books can either make us traveling all over the world or have a heart-to-heart talk with us though strange to us.

书能使我们足不出户而畅游千山万水，素不相识而促膝谈心。

The Coyotes in the Moonlight

Joe and I had just finished breakfast. We were having a last, slow cup of coffee. That's when we first saw the two **coyotes**①.

They stood watching our lonely cabin. They must have smelled the meat we had cooked. Winter food was hard to find on the snowy plain. We felt sorry for them. Soft-hearted Joe wanted to feed them.

"Go ahead," I said. "throw them some meat. But I bet they won't take it. **Ranchers**② put out poisoned meat for coyotes. They learn not to trust food that's offered."

But Joe cut off two **chunks**③ of meat and went outside.

At first the coyotes stood their ground. Joe got about thirty yards from them. Then they became excited. They backed slowly into the bush. They were too scared to make a stand. But they were too hungry to leave. Joe dropped the meat on the snow and started back to the cabin.

He was halfway back when coyotes raced to the meat. Each one **snapped up**④ some and ran into the bush.

Joe and I had come to Wyoming to look for gold. We had found this old log cabin just as winter caught us. We were safe there from the cold north wind and the snow.

The cabin sat at the foot of a mountain. We could see all around us for miles. But there just wasn't much to do. It was so lonely and silent. We said that coyotes' howling kept us company.

生词有约

① coyote
n. 郊狼

② rancher
n. 牧场主

③ chunk
n. 大块

④ snap up
迅速抓取某物

Until the sun came up, we would hear them. They would start with a few sharp **yaps**⑤. Then they got louder. Their song would always end in a long, sad howl.

Of all the wild animals that roam the Great Plains, I like coyotes best. It's easy to like these sly little wolves. You'll always hear them when the sun goes down on a winter day, singing to the land they love.

Joe and I were glad the two coyotes didn't forget us. They hunted on a trail down the river. Our cabin was near their trail. As they came by on the early morning, they always stopped.

Like I said, that winter they had a hard time finding food. The small animals they hunted were safe in holes under the snow. The coyotes were thin under their heavy fur.

The male was a rather large coyote. Also, he was kind of afraid. The female was small and brave. Whenever we saw them, she was in the lead. He kept a few steps behind. Maybe she was too hungry to be afraid.

She had learned that we had no dogs around. She knew we wouldn't hurt her. As she came close to the cabin, though, the male would stay behind. About twenty yards from the door she would stop. That was the line she would not pass. She just **trotted**⑥ back and forth until we opened the door.

Joe or I would go out with food. She would back up a little and wait. The male would go hide behind some bush. They waited until the cabin door closed. Then they would run for the food. And they would always share it!

Mostly the coyotes came to our cabin just after sunup. They often seemed tired. They had been hunting down by the river. When they were down there, they had to watch for poisoned food, guns, and traps.

One morning in March, our coyote friends failed to come.

We were worried. All that day we looked toward the river. We kept hoping they would turn up. But evening came, and we hadn't seen them. Other coyotes howled that night. But

⑤ yap
n. 吠叫

⑥ trot
vi. 小跑

our two friends didn't answer.

We went to the window many times the next morning. We were sure something ugly had happened. It was a cloudy, gray morning. The snow was nearly gone, and a sharp wind blew through the brush. We ate breakfast in silence. Joe was very sad. He had started the friendship with the coyotes. Now it seemed to have ended. The wind blew through and as I was staring out the window, something caught my eye.

"Look, Joe!" I cried. "You see what I see? Out there by that low rise?"

He ran to the door. "It's them!" he shouted. "Come on!"

We ran out. I didn't even put on a cap. Our coyotes were struggling toward the cabin. We soon could see they both were worn out.

The little female was dragging a terrible steel trap. Its sharp jaws bit into one of her legs.

But still she was not alone. Her mate held the trap chain in his teeth. He had helped her pull the heavy thing through the brush.

Had they come to find us? We had been friendly. They were not afraid of us. Surely they knew we would help.

As we came near, they stopped. He backed away to hide behind a bush. But she stood and watched us. Her tired eyes were shining.

"She may snap at you. Her leg looks real bad," I warned Joe.

Joe stooped and took hold of her furry neck. Softly, he talked to her.

Then he said, "Get at that trap now. I've got her even if she should **act up** ⑦."

It must have hurt when I took off the trap. But the little coyote didn't do a thing.

We went back to the cabin. The two coyotes came along. The female was again in the lead. She limped on three legs. They ate the food we put out. Then they went away.

From then on we saw the coyotes less often. Spring had

⑦ act up
耍脾气；捣蛋

come and changed their wintertime habits. They were getting ready to start a new family.

Joe and I went back to work. We were looking for gold again. We used the cabin only for sleeping now. There was no snow, so we couldn't see coyote tracks.

The spring rains stopped. The brush all turned green. Then one night we heard a little cry at the door. I jumped out of the bed and looked outside. There in the moonlight stood our little coyote. She had something in her mouth.

At first I thought it was a rabbit. Then saw she was carrying a coyote pup.

She stepped into the cabin and carefully laid the pup on the floor.

Suddenly, Joe exclaimed, "It's hurt! Its paw is bleeding." He picked up the pup and looked at the paw. I went to get hot water. "It doesn't amount to anything. Looks like something fell on its paw," he said.

But the mother had brought the pup to us. She wanted us to do something about it. So we did what we could to help. While we cleaned the foot with soap and water, the mother didn't move. She just whined as if telling us to hurry up. She had remembered us. But it was time to go. Joe put the pup down on the floor. The mother picked it up in her mouth. She ran off in the silver moonlight.

月光郊狼

我和乔刚吃过早饭，正慢慢地喝着最后一杯咖啡。就是在那个时候，我们第一次看到了那两只郊狼。

它们站在那里望着我们孤零零的小木屋。它们一定是闻到了我们做饭的肉香。冬天在雪原上是很难找到食物的。我们为它们感到难过。软心肠的乔想给它们东西吃。

"去吧，"我说，"给它们扔些肉。但是，我敢说它们是不会吃的。牧场主们经常为郊狼放下过毒的肉。它们已学会了不相信主动送给它们的食物。"

但是，乔还是切掉两大块肉，走了出去。

起初，那两只郊狼站在那里没有动。乔离它们大约有 30 码远。随后，它们跃跃欲试，慢慢地退回到了丛林里。它们太害怕不敢摆开架势，但它们太饿又不愿离开。乔将肉放在雪地上，开始返回小木屋。

他刚走回半路上，两只郊狼就飞奔到了那两块肉旁边，各自飞快地叼起一块肉，跑进了丛林里。

我和乔来怀俄明州淘金。正当冬天来临之际，我们发现了这个旧木屋。在那里，我们可以免受寒冷的北风和雪的袭击。

小木屋座落在一个山脚下。我们可以看到方圆几英里。但是，没有多少事做。是那样孤独和寂静。我们常常说，郊狼的嗥叫声陪伴在我们左右。

太阳升起前，我们常常听到它们的嗥叫声。它们开始叫时经常带着尖叫声，随后声音越来越响亮。它们的吠叫总是以一声悲怆的长嗥而结束。

在所有漫游在大平原的野生动物中，我最喜欢郊狼。喜欢上这些狡黠的小郊狼是很容易的事儿。当冬天的傍晚太阳落山时，你总是会听到它们对它们热爱的大地歌唱。

我和乔很高兴那两只郊狼没有忘记我们。它们沿着河边的一条小路猎捕。我们的小木屋就在那条小路附近。它们早上路过时总是会停下来。

像我所说的那样，那年冬天它们寻找食物非常艰难。它们要猎捕的那些小动物都安全地待在雪下的洞里。两只郊狼厚厚的皮毛下都瘦成了皮包骨头。

那只公狼个头大，同时也有点儿胆怯。那只母狼个头很小，却很勇敢。无论我们什么时候看到它们，小母狼总是打头阵。公狼常常站在后面几步远处。也许是母狼太饿才不害怕的吧。

母狼已经得知我们周围没有狗，知道我们不会伤害它。然而，当母狼走近小木屋时，公狼总是留在后面。在离门大约 20 码处，母狼常常会停下来，通常不会越过那条线，只是前后小跑着，直到我们把门打开。

无论是乔还是我总是带着食物出来。母狼常常会后退一点，在那里等待着。公狼藏进某个灌木丛后面。它们一直等到小木屋门合上，然后才向那食物跑去。而且它们总是两个一起分享！

两只郊狼大都是在太阳刚刚升起之后来到我们的小木屋边，好像总是非常疲惫。它们一直在沿着河边捕猎。到那里时，它们不得不提防着下过毒的食物以及枪和陷阱。

3 月的一天早上，我们的郊狼朋友没有过来。

我们忧心忡忡，整整一天都在向河那边张望，一直希望它们会出现。但是，夜晚来临了，也没有看到它们。那天夜里其他的郊狼嗥叫着。但是，我们的两个郊狼朋友没有回音。

第二天早上，我们一次次地走到窗边，相信一定是发生了什么不幸的事。那是一个灰暗多云的早晨。雪融化殆尽，风呼啸着穿过灌木丛。我们默默地吃着早饭。乔非常伤心。他已经跟那两只郊狼建立起了友情。现在好像这种友情要结束了。风吹过来，而当我望着窗外时，某个东西引起了我的注意。

"看，乔！"我大声叫道，"你知道我看见了什么？在那个的低洼地方？"

乔跑到门口，大声叫道："是它们！快点儿！"

我们跑了出去。我甚至连帽子都没有戴。我们的郊狼正挣扎着向小木屋走来。我们马上就看出它们俩已经筋疲力尽了。

小母狼拖着一个可怕的钢夹，钢夹的利齿咬进了它的一条腿。

但是，它不是孑然一身。它的同伴用牙咬着那个钢夹链，帮它拖着那个沉重的东西穿过了灌木丛。

它们是来找我们的吗？我们曾是好朋友。它们不害怕我们，肯定知道我们会帮助它们。

当我们走近时，它们停了下来。公狼向后退进了一个灌木丛。但是，母狼却站在那里望着我们，它疲惫的眼睛闪闪发亮。

"它也许会咬你。它的腿看上去的确是受伤了，"我警告乔说。

乔弯下腰，抱住它毛茸茸的脖子，对它轻轻地说着话。

随后，他说："现在要着手处理掉那个夹子。就是它耍脾气，我也得那样做。"

当我取下那个夹子时，一定伤着了它。但是，那只小郊狼什么也没有做。

我们回到了小木屋。两只郊狼也跟了过来。母狼又一次走到了前面，三条腿一瘸一拐地跳着。它们吃着我们摆出来的食物，之后就走了。

从那以后，我们看到两只郊狼的次数就少了。春天已经来临，改变了它们冬天的习惯。它们正准备建立一个新的家庭。

我和乔重新投入工作，再次寻找起了金子，现在只把那个小木屋当作睡觉的地方。因为没有雪，所以我们无法看到郊狼的踪迹。

春雨停止。灌木丛都开始泛绿。后来有一天夜里，我们听到了门边的一小声叫唤。我从床上跳起来，向门外望去，只见月光下站着我们的小郊狼，嘴里衔着一个什么东西。

起初我还以为那是一只兔子，后来才看到它是衔着一只小狼崽。

它走进了小木屋，小心翼翼地将小狼崽放在地上。

乔突然大声叫道："它受伤了！它的爪子还在流血。"他抱起那只狼崽，看着那只受伤的爪子。我过去端热水。"不要紧。看上去好像是什么东西掉在了它的爪子上。"他说。

但是，它的母亲将它送到了我们这里，想要我们对此做点儿什么。因此，我们就尽我们所能帮助它。在我们用肥皂和水清洗它的蹄子时，它的母亲一动不动，只是呜呜叫着，好像是在催我们要快点。它还记得我们。但是，到了该走的时候了。乔将小狼崽放在地上。它的母亲将它衔在嘴里，跑进了银色的月光中。

诵读经典 >>>>>
Read classic

❶ Then they became excited. They backed slowly into the bush. They were too scared to make a stand. But they were too hungry to leave.

随后，它们跃跃欲试，慢慢地退回到了丛林里。它们太害怕不敢摆开架势，但它们太饿又不愿离开。

✪ About twenty yards from the door she would stop. That was the line she would not pass. She just trotted back and forth until we opened the door.

在离门大约 20 码处，母狼常常会停下来，通常不会越过那条线，只是前后小跑着，直到我们把门打开。

妙语连珠 >>>>
Sparkling discourse

✪ There is no greater grief than to recall a time of happiness when in misery.

什么也没有比在悲惨中回忆起幸福的时刻痛苦。

✪ Each of us is the accumulation of our memories.

我们每个人都是我们记忆的积累。

To My Memories of the Past

One evening I sat in Miami's Pro Player **Stadium**[①] watching a baseball game between the Florida Marlins and the New York Mets. During the seventhinning stretch, I noticed a teenage boy and his father one row in front of me. The father was a Mets fan, by the looks of his cap; his son's bore the Marlins' logo.

The father began **ribbing**[②] his son about the Marlins, who were losing. The son's responses grew increasingly sharp. Finally, with the Marlins hopelessly behind, the boy turned to his father snarling, "I hate you! You know that!" Then he got up and took the steps two at a time toward the grandstand.

His father shook his head. In a moment he stood and squeezed out of his row of seats, looking both angry and **bereft**[③]. Our eyes met. "Kids!" he said.

I sympathized—after all, I was a father now, knowing how father and son felt. There was a time when I, too, had turned on the man who loved me most.

My father was a country doctor who raised Hereford cattle on our farm in southern Indiana. A white four-board fence around the property had to be scraped and painted every three years. The summer after my freshman year in high school, one June day my dad decided I should extend the fence.

We were sitting at the edge of the south pasture, my father thoughtfully whittling a piece of wood, as he often did. He took off his Stetson and wiped his forehead. Then he pointed to a stand of hemlocks 300 yards away. "From here to

生词有约

① stadium
n. 露天体育场

② rib
vt. 嘲笑；戏弄

③ bereft
adj. 凄凉的；孤寂的

216

there—that's where we want our fence," he said. "Figure about 110 holes, three feet deep. Keep the digger's blades sharp and you can probably dig eight or ten a day."

In a tight voice I said I didn't see how I could finish that. Besides, I'd planned a little softball and fishing. "Why don't we borrow a power auger?" I suggested.

"Power augers don't learn from work. And we want our fence to teach us a thing or two," he replied, slapping me on the back.

I **flinched**④ to show my resentment. What made me especially mad was the way he said "our" fence. The project was his, I told him. I was just the labor. Dad shook his head, then went back to his piece of wood.

I admired a lot about my dad, and I tried to remember those things when I felt mad at him. Once, when I'd been along on one of his house calls, I watched him tell a sick farm woman she was going to be all right before he left or he wasn't leaving. He held her hand and told her stories. He got her to laugh and then he got her out of bed. She said, "Why, Doc, I do feel better."

I asked him later how he knew she would get better. "I didn't," he said. "But if you don't push too hard and you keep their morale up, most patients will get things fixed up themselves." I wanted to ask why he didn't treat his own family that way, but I thought better of it.

If I wanted to be by myself, I would retreat to a river birch by the stream that fed our pond. It forked at ground level, and I'd wedge my back up against one trunk and my feet against the other. Then I would look at the sky or read or pretend.

That summer I hadn't had much time for my tree. One evening as my father and I walked past it, he said, "I remember you scrunching into that tree when you were a little kid."

"I don't," I said sullenly.

He looked at me sharply. "What's got into you?" he said.

Amazingly, I heard myself say, "What the hell do you

④ flinch
vi. 退缩

care?" Then I ran off to the barn. Sitting in the tack room, I tried not to cry.

My father opened the door and sat opposite me. Finally I met his gaze.

"It's not a good idea to doctor your own family," he said. "But I guess I need to do that for you right now." He leaned forward. "You think no one else is like you. And you think I'm too hard on you and don't appreciate what you do around here. You even wonder how you got into a family as dull as ours."

I was astonished that he knew my own thoughts.

"The thing is, your body is changing," he continued. "And that changes your entire self. You've got a lot more male hormones in your blood. And, Son, there's not a man in this world who could handle what that does to you when you're fourteen."

I didn't know what to say. I knew I didn't like whatever was happening to me. For months I'd felt out of touch with everything. I was irritable and restless and sad for no reason. And because I couldn't talk about it, I began to feel really isolated.

"One of the things that'll help you," my dad said after a while, "is work. Hard work."

As soon as he said that, I suspected it was a ploy to keep me busy doing chores. Anger came suddenly. "Fine," I said in the rudest voice I could manage. Then I stormed out.

I dug post holes every morning, slamming that digger into the ground until I had tough **calluses**⑤ on my hands.

⑤ callus
n. 茧子

One morning I helped my father patch the barn roof. We worked in silence. In the careful way my father worked, I could see how he felt about himself, the barn, the whole farm.

Just then, he looked at me and said, "You aren't alone you know."

Startled, I stared at him, squatting above me with the tar bucket in his hand. How could he possibly know what I'd been thinking?

"Think about this," he said. "If you drew a line from your

feet down the side of our barn to the earth and followed it any which way, it would touch every living thing in the world. So you're never alone. No one is."

I started to argue, but the notion of being connected to all of life made me feel so good that I let my thoughts quiet down.

As I worked through the summer, I began to notice my shoulders getting bigger. I was able to do more work, and I even started paying some attention to doing it well. I had hated hole-digging, but it seemed to release some knot inside me, as if the anger I felt went driving into the earth. Slowly I started to feel I could get through this rotten time.

One day near the end of the summer, I got rid of a lot of junk from my younger days. Afterward I went to sit in my tree as a kind of last visit to the world of my boyhood. I had to **scuttle** ⑥ up eight feet to get space enough for my body. As I stretched out, I could feel the trunk beneath my feet weakening. Something had gotten at it—ants, maybe, or just plain age.

I pushed harder. Finally, the trunk gave way and fell to the ground. Then I cut up my tree for firewood.

The afternoon I finished the fence, I found my father sitting on a granite outcrop in the south pasture. "You thinking about how long this grass is going to hold out without rain?" I asked.

"Yep," he said. "How long you think we got?"

"Another week."

He turned and looked me deep in the eyes. Of course I wasn't really talking about the pasture as much as I was trying to find out if my opinion mattered to him. After a while he said, "You could be right." He paused and added, "You did a fine job on our fence."

"Thanks," I said, almost **overwhelmed** ⑦ by the force of his approval.

"You know," he said. "you're going to turn out to be one hell of a man. But just because you're getting grown up doesn't mean you have to leave behind everything you liked

⑥ scuttle
vi. 疾跑

⑦ overwhelm
vt. 使不知所措

219

when you were a boy."

I knew he was thinking about my tree. He reached into his jacket pocket and pulled out a piece of wood the size of a deck of cards. "I made this for you," he said.

It was a piece of the heartwood from the river birch. He had carved it so the tree appeared again, tall and strong. Beneath were the woods "Our Tree."

Leaving the Miami Stadium that day, I saw the man and the boy walking toward the parking lot. The man's arm rested comfortably on his son's shoulder. I didn't know how they'd made their peace, but it seemed worth acknowledging. As I passed, I tipped my cap—to them, and to my memories of the past.

向过去致敬

一天晚上，我坐在迈阿密职业选手体育馆，观看弗罗里达马林队对纽约麦特队的一场棒球赛。在第七局中场休息时，我注意到坐在我前排的一个十几岁男孩和他的父亲。从帽子的外观可以看出，那位父亲是个麦特队迷，他的孩子戴的则是马林队的标志。

那位父亲拿正节节败退的马林队跟儿子开玩笑，儿子回答的声音越来越尖。最后，马林队已落后无望时，男孩冲着父亲大声吼道："我恨你！你知道！"随后，他站起来，三步并作两步朝大看台走去。

那位父亲摇摇头。过了一会儿，他也站起来，挤了出去，看上去既生气又孤寂。我们彼此看了一眼。"真孩子气！"他说。

我同情这位父亲——毕竟我现在也身为人父。我知道父子间是何感觉。我也曾伤害过深爱我的人。

我的父亲是一名乡村医生，在印第安那州南部我们的农场养了好多黑尔福德牛。围着牧场的白色木栅栏每三年得刮擦油漆一次。那年夏天，我刚上初一。6月的一天，爸爸决定让我扩建栅栏。

我们坐在牧场南边，父亲像往常一样一边想心事，一边削着木块。一会儿，他摘下斯泰森毡帽，擦了擦额头的汗，指着300码以外的一排铁杉树。"从这里到那里——我们的栅栏就要这样长，"他说，"估计要挖110来个坑，每个坑3英尺深。如果你的工具锋利，一天大概可以挖八、九个坑。"

我嘟声嘟气地说，我不知道该怎么完成。再说，我还打算玩垒球和钓鱼。"我们何不借把强力钻呢？"

"用强力钻干活学不到什么，我们想通过修栅栏学点儿东西。"他拍着我的背说。

我向后退缩，以示不满。尤其令我气愤的是他说"我们的"栅栏的那个架势。这是他的计划，我告诉他说，我只不过是苦力而已。父亲摇摇头，又继续削起了木块。

我很崇拜爸爸。我生他的气时，总是尽力回想有关他的那些往事。有一次，我陪他一起出诊。我看见他对一位患病的农妇说，他走之前，她一定会好起来，否则他就不会走。他握着她的手，给她讲故事。他逗她笑了起来，然后扶她起床。她说："哇，医生，我感觉好些了。"

后来，我问他怎么知道她会好起来。"我不知道，"他说，"但如果不给他们施加压力，并使他们精神振奋，大部分病人就会自己好起来的。"我想问问他为什么不那样对待自己的家人，但我还是不问为好。

如果我想独自待着，我便会爬到流入我家池塘的那条溪流旁的一棵桦树上，桦树在地面处叉成两股。我背靠着一根树干，脚抵在另一根树干上。随后，我仰望天空，或看看书，或装装样子。

那年夏天，我没那么多时间到树上玩。一天晚上，当我和父亲路过那棵树时，他说："我记得你小时候常爬上去玩。"

"我不记得了，"我沉着脸说。

他盯着我问道："你到底怎么了？"

令我吃惊的是，我居然听到自己说："你会在乎什么呀？"说完，我转身跑到仓房，坐在食物贮藏室里，尽力不哭出声来。

父亲打开门，坐在我对面。最后，我与他目光相遇。

"医治自己家人并不是个好主意，"他说，"但我想现在有必要这样做。"他往前倾了倾身。"你认为没有人像你一样。你认为我对你太严厉，也不关心你的一举一动。你甚至奇怪你怎么会出生在这样一个乏味的家庭。"

我对他竟知道我自己的想法感到非常吃惊。

"其实是你的身体在发生变化，"他接着说，"而这种变化又改变了你整个人。你血液中有了更多的男性荷尔蒙。孩子，世上没人能帮你处理你14岁时体内的这个变化。"

我不知道该说什么好。我知道我不喜欢发生在自己身上的这些事。几个月来，我感到与所有的一切都失去了联系。我无缘无故地发火、焦虑和伤心。而且，因为我无法诉说，所以我开始感到非常孤独。

过了一会儿，父亲说："其中有件事可以帮助你。那就是劳动。艰苦的劳动。"

他一说完，我就怀疑这又是他为了让我继续干那些杂活而耍的手段。我突然发起火来。"好，"我用最粗鲁的声音说完，便冲了出去。

我每天挖柱坑，把工具使劲插进土里，直到我的手上结了厚茧。

一天早上，我帮爸爸补仓房的屋顶。我们默不作声地工作着。爸爸一丝不苟。我可以看

221

出他对自己、对仓房和整个农场是何种感觉。

正在这时，他看着我说："你知道，你并不孤单。"

我吃惊地望着他手提柏油桶蹲在我的上方。他怎么知道我一直在想什么呢？

"想一想，"他说，"如果你从脚下画一条线，沿着仓库侧面一直画到地上，然后随意沿着它走，你将遇到各种各样有生命的东西。所以，你并不孤单。谁也不孤单。"

我想争辩，但他这种生命息息相通的想法让我感觉非常愉快，所以我又放弃了这一念头。

干了一夏天活，我开始注意到自己的肩膀变宽了，可以干更多的活了，甚至开始注意干好。我曾十分讨厌挖坑工作，但它似乎可以解开我心里的结，好像所有的愤怒随着掘土挖坑深深地埋进了地里。慢慢地，我开始感到我可以度过这段糟糕的日子了。

快到夏末的一天，我扔掉了许多小时候的玩艺儿，之后又回到树上，向我童年的世界告别。为了找到足够容纳我身体的空间，我不得不迅速向上爬了8英尺。当我舒展身体时，我感觉到脚下的树枝在颤抖。它已经枯朽了，也许是因为蚂蚁或岁月的侵蚀吧。

我用力推它。结果，树干折断，掉到了地上。随后，我把树全砍了当柴烧。

修完栅栏的那天下午，我发现父亲坐在牧场南边一块凸出的花岗岩上。"你认为这片草地没有雨水能维持多久？"我问。

"对呀，"他说，"你说能持续多久呢？"

"一星期吧。"

他转过身，深深地望着我。当然，我并不是真在谈牧场，其实我只想弄明白我的想法对他是否重要。过了一会儿，他说："你可能是对的。"他暂停了一下，补充道："你把我们的栅栏修得真好。"

"谢谢，"我说，他的赞许差点儿让我不知所措。

"你知道，"他说，"你将证明你是一个了不起的男子汉。但你长大了并不意味着就得放弃小时候喜欢的那些东西。"

我知道他是在说我的树。他伸手从夹克口袋里掏出一块纸牌大小的木片说："是我为你做的。"

它是用那棵桦树心材做的。他把那棵树刻在上面：它高大壮实，又出现在了我面前。树的下面刻着"我们的树"。

那天离开迈阿密体育馆时，我看见那对父子正向停车场走去。那位父亲的手舒坦地搭在儿子的肩上。我不知道他们是怎么和解的，但他们似乎找到了彼此都可接受的方法。我走过时，用手触了一下帽檐——向他们、也向我过去的记忆致敬。

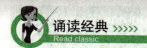

诵读经典 >>>>>
Read classic

If I wanted to be by myself, I would retreat to a river birch by the stream that fed our pond. It forked at ground level, and I'd wedge my back up against one trunk and my feet against the other. Then I would look at the sky or read or pretend.

如果我想独自待着，我便会爬到流入我家池塘的那条溪流旁的一棵桦树上，桦树在地面处叉成两股。我背靠着一根树干，脚抵在另一根树干上。随后，我仰望天空，或看看书，或装装样子。

妙语连珠 >>>>>
Sparkling discourse

★ A window of opportunity won't open itself.
机遇之窗不会自己打开。

★ Opportunities are like sunrises. If you wait too long, you miss them.
机遇就像日出。等得太久，就会错过。

The Old Man and the Stone

Something **furtive**^① about the way the little old man rummaged through the trunk of his sedan captured my attention. He cast a nervous glance over his shoulder, then lifted out something heavy, wrapped in cloth.

His unexpected arrival had broken my absorption with the **undulating**^② hills of Blue **Mesa**^③, in Arizona's Petrified Forest. I don't think he saw me as he labored across the road and out into the desert. Curious, I followed him at a distance.

He moved with difficulty, stopping now and then to catch his breath. Finally, he reached the hump of a small hill that formed the lower edge of Blue Mesa. He calculated the slope, then hefted his burden and started down. I hurried forward, but by the time I reached the top of the slope, he had already gained the bottom. He walked perhaps ten yards to the edge of a small gully, then knelt in the dirt and gently unwrapped his bundle.

The piece of petrified wood appeared to be about 15 pounds, a splintered chunk from the base of a tree, looking astonishingly wooden although it had turned to stone 225 million years ago. It glittered with crystals and gleamed green and red and blue from the smooth **jasper**^④ that had filled in the tree's living cells.

The old man bent down and stroked the stone lovingly. Then he lifted his eyes to the horizon and sat motionless for a long time. At length, he rose with a final caress of his stone. I

生词有约

① furtive
adj. 鬼鬼祟祟的
② undulating
adj. 连绵起伏的
③ mesa
n. 平顶山

④ jasper
n. 碧玉

scrambled down the hill. He glanced from me to his rock and back again, then smiled sheepishly.

"Beautiful rock," I said casually.

"I had to bring it back," he said, answering my unspoken question.

"When did you find it?"

"Sixty years ago. I was 13. My brother and I took it right about here and hid it in the car. My father was upset when he found it, but we were back in New York by then."

We fell easily into conversation. He'd carried that rock with him through a life full of strange turnings. He'd been a standout shortstop in high school, enlisted in the Army Air Forces in World War II, married a nurse, got divorced. He built houses, started a business, grew rich, lost it all in a real-estate crash, started over and made a second success.

Along the way, he found the love of his life at an ice rink. They married and raised four kids. One was a lawyer, one a geologist, one was raising a family of her own. Their fourth child stepped on a land mine in Vietnam. That had been the hardest loss he'd ever had to bear…until his wife died three years ago. Next to all of that, he said, his **emphysema**⑤ seemed hardly worth mentioning. The doctors didn't hold out much hope.

The **diagnosis**⑥ was what had decided him. All his life, he'd thought the rock was his. Now it seemed he had merely borrowed it. He vowed to return to the desert whose memory he'd harbored all his life and bring back the rock he'd loved with such a guilty **twinge**⑦ through the years.

The sun had set by the time we reached the end of his tale. He sighed a peculiar wheezing sound. He patted his stone one last time; then I helped him up the loose slope. We turned back at the rim of the hill. The rock was now only a black dot in the large darkness of the hillside.

In the deepening twilight, I could just make out the faint smile on my companion's face, a traveler caught between relief and loss within sight of his journey's end.

⑤ emphysema

n. 肺气肿

⑥ diagnosis

n. 诊断

⑦ twinge

n. 一阵难受

老人与化石

小老头在他轿车后面的行李箱里鬼鬼祟祟摸索的样子引起了我的注意。他回头不安地看了一眼，然后抱出一件用布包着的沉甸甸的东西。

他的意外到来，打破了我对亚利桑纳州石化林连绵起伏的蓝方山的沉迷。我现在仍然认为他当时在缓慢穿过大路进入沙漠时并没看到我。我感到好奇，就远远地跟在他后面。

他艰难移动，不时地停下来喘口气。最后，他走到了蓝方山边较矮的小山冈上，打量了一下山坡，然后扛起那个包，开始下山。我匆匆向前；但当我到达坡顶时，他已经到了坡底。他大概走到了小山谷边有 10 码远，随后跪在土里，轻轻解开他那个包。

那个石化林块看上去有十五磅左右，是一棵树的底部裂成的一个块。令人吃惊的是，尽管它 2.25 亿年前就已经变成了石头，它看上去还像木头。它闪着水晶般的光泽，由于原树的活细胞中充满了柔和的墨绿色，那块石化林闪着绿红蓝三种颜色。

那个老人弯下腰，爱抚着那块石头，随后抬眼望着地平线，久久地坐在那里，一动不动。他最后抱了一下石头，站起身。我从山上爬下来。他看看我，瞧瞧石头，然后又看看我，不好意思地笑了笑。

"美石，"我若无其事地说。

"我不得不把它送回来，"他说，同时回答了我没说出口的问题。

"你是什么时候发现它的呢？"

"60 年前，那年我 13 岁。我和哥哥就是在这里发现的，将它藏在了汽车里。父亲发现时非常不安，但我们那时已经回到了纽约。"

我们轻松地攀谈起来。他曾带着那块岩石经历了奇异曲折的人生。他中学时曾是一名出色的棒球游击手，'二战'时加入空军，娶了一名护士，后来他们又分道扬镳。他建房，开公司，成了大款，在一次房地产危机中一败涂地，随后重新开始，又取得了第二次成功。

后来，他在一家溜冰场找到了自己一生的爱情。他们结婚，生了 4 个孩子。一个是律师，一个是地质学家，一个在养家。他们的第 4 个孩子在越南踩上了地雷。那是他必须得承受的最重大的损失……直到他妻子 3 年前撒手而去。他说，除此以外，他的肺气肿好像不值一提。医生们没抱多大希望。

诊断决定了他的一生。一生中，他曾想过那块岩石就是他的。现在好像仅仅是借借而已。他发誓要回到沙漠，他曾将整个一生珍藏在了那里；他要送回那块岩石，这么多年他都是带着内疚的心情爱着它。

我们听完他的故事，太阳已经落山了。他发出了奇异的喘息声。他最后一次拍了拍那块石头；随后，我搀扶他走上那个松软的山坡。我们又转向那个山边。那块石头如今在山坡硕大的黑暗中只剩下了一个黑点。

在越来越深的幽昏中，我只能分辨出同伴脸上淡淡的微笑，那是一个旅人在旅程快到尽头时处于轻松和失落之间的微笑。

诵读经典 >>>>>
Read classic

✪ Something furtive about the way the little old man rummaged through the trunk of his sedan captured my attention.

小老头在他轿车后面的行李箱里鬼鬼祟祟摸索的样子引起了我的注意。

✪ In the deepening twilight, I could just make out the faint smile on my companion's face, a traveler caught between relief and loss within sight of his journey's end.

在越来越深的幽昏中，我只能分辨出同伴脸上淡淡的微笑，那是一个旅人在旅程快到尽头时处于轻松和失落之间的微笑。

妙语连珠 >>>>>
Sparkling discourse

✪ Laurels don't make much of a cushion.

桂冠不是用坐垫做出来的。

✪ The difference between a helping hand and an outstretched palm is a twist of the wrist.

援助之手和摊开之掌的区别就是转一下手腕。

画龙
点睛

The Memory of the Blackberries

Just as I began a new job in New York, I had to learn another important job: father. At the office we had three new projects in the works, and at home I had a young son who was growing fast and needed me. To say I felt stretched is an understatement. This was never more dear than one Thursday when, for the second time in a week, I was packing for a business trip. "I know how important your job is," my wife, Ellen, said. "But it would be nice if you could be home more often."

I knew she was right. My son, Luke, was turning three, and I didn't like being away so much either.

"Yesterday," Ellen said, "Luke wandered around the house saying, 'Where is my dad? Where is he?'"

Ellen wanted to discuss this further, but there wasn't time. "Honey, I really have to make this plane," I said. "Let's talk tomorrow when I get back."

In Chicago my meeting ended early, and I suddenly had a couple of hours to kill. So I called on Dan, an old family friend who had retired to the area to be near his grandchildren.

Dan had once farmed in Indiana, where my father was a country doctor. Now, as we sat at his kitchen table, he began to reminisce about what a fine man my dad had been. "He'd get you well no matter what it took," Dan said. "I don't think there was a soul in that country who didn't love your father."

Then, to my surprise, Dan **confided**[①] that after he'd

生词有约

① confide
vt. 承认

228

recovered from **prostate**② cancer, he had developed a serious depression that he just couldn't lick. "I didn't care about getting better," he said. "But your daddy got me through it."

His remembrance touched me, and I put my hand on his shoulder. "He cared about his patients a lot," I agreed.

Indeed, I knew how devoted my father was to his patients. But I also knew that his devotion and hard work came with a price—a price that seemed high to his family.

Dad was a tall, lean man whose sky-blue eyes could see straight through anything. But despite his no-nonsense gaze and way of speaking, he was always easy to talk to.

We lived on a farm, not because we were farmers but because many of Dad's patients were. They often paid in livestock instead of cash, so he found a farm to put his fees out to graze.

There was no denying my father's love of hunting, however, and he always kept birds dog. I would train them until they were ready to hunt. He left that chore to me, he said, because he didn't have the patience. Yet what he did not want to do often seemed to hinge on what I might learn from doing it myself.

My dad taught me everything. He showed me how to use a handsaw and mark a right angle, for instance—skills that enabled me to cobble together a raft for the pond beyond our meadow. One corner ended up out of line, but Dad helped me launch it without comment on its fault.

His best way of helping was to ask questions that allowed me to realize things myself. When I was afraid I'd have to fight a guy at school who was **hassling**③ me, my father asked, "Can you take him?"

"I think so."

"Then you don't have to. Here, stand up and give me a shove."

He made me push him until I nearly knocked him down. "See, you just have to give him an idea of how strong you are. What if you try that and see if he doesn't back off?" I did, and

② prostate

n. 前列腺

③ hassle

vt. 使苦恼

it worked.

That was the kind of help I needed from Dad. But the summer I turned 13, he virtually disappeared from my life, and I didn't know what to do.

So many people were sick, and Dad was gone most of the time seeing patients. He was also building a new office and trying to earn enough to pay for an X-ray machine. Often the phone would ring while we were at supper and I'd hear him say, "Be right there." Then Mom would cover his plate with a pie tin and put it in the oven to wait.

Many times he'd be gone for an hour or more. Then his car would crunch on the gravel drive, and I'd run downstairs to sit with him while he ate. He'd ask about my day and gave me whatever advice I had to have about the farm. But that was about all he had energy for.

As that year went on, I worried about him, and I worried about me. I missed his help. I missed joking around and just being together. Maybe he doesn't like me as much as he did, I thought. Maybe I've done something to disappoint him. He'd been helping me become a man, and I didn't think I had a prayer of getting that done without his guidance.

The pond beyond the meadow was ringed with reeds and cattails. I liked to fish there. I'd never caught a big one, hooking only sunnies and a few catfish. But big fish were in there. I'd seen them jump, making a glistening **turbulence**④ in the mist of early morning. Sometimes the ripples would carry so far they'd reach the shore.

That summer I used to sit on my raft and think of ways to lure my father back. My mother wanted us to take a vacation, but he **nixed**⑤ that because he had so much work.

One day my mother and I stood in the kitchen and talked about him. "See if you can get him to go fishing," she finally said. "Even just one evening off will help."

The next day I began my campaign to get Dad down to our pond. I planned to make a fire, roast ears of corn and fry up whatever we could catch. The problem was getting my

④ turbulence
n. 波动；动乱

⑤ nix
vt. 否决；禁止

father to change into old clothes and take off a few hours.

Finally one Friday I simply bullied him into it. I met his car when he came into the mudroom, where we changed our work clothes. "We're going fishing," I said. "And that is that."

And we did! As we stood on the pond's edge casting into the fading sunlight, I was still amazed that I'd persuaded him to do it. Soon I went to gather wood for a fire. We hadn't had any luck yet, but we could still roast the corn and talk.

While I worked, I watched him cast into a deep hole near a fallen red oak. "Please let him catch a fish," I whispered to myself. "Any fish—just let him catch something."

Almost as if my thought had raised the fish to the lure, a bass struck his line. "Whoa, boss!" he yelled, and the moss-colored fish took to the air. It looked **humongous** ⑥ and put up a good fight as Dad expertly reeled it into his net, then brought it to me by the fire.

⑥ humongous
adj. 其大无比的

"Hey, Dad," I said. "How about that!"

He looked young, happy and proud. I **dredged** ⑦ his fish in cornmeal and fried it over the fire. We sat on a stone eating our supper.

⑦ dredge
vt. 撒；疏浚

"That was some meal," he said when finished. "I don't know when I've liked anything more."

My father made a pot of coffee while I went to the edge of the meadow where the briers were borne down with ripe blackberries. I picked up our dessert and carried back in my baseball cap. We had the berries with our coffee and watched the sun make dazzling colors in the western sky. My father ate slowly, one berry at a time, savoring each. Then out of the blue he began telling me how much he cared about me.

"You know, son, you're going to be a success in life," he said. "I know that because I never have to ask you to do something twice. But more than that, you're a good kid."

The expression on his face was of such warmth and pride that I felt utterly blessed.

Times like this were all too rare as my father's practice grew ever larger. But whenever I needed to, I'd reach back to

231

that moment by the pond, remembering how good it felt when Dad was with me.

"Yes, sir," Dan said, interrupting my memories." Your father was some fine man. And his medicine wasn't just pills and shots. He thought a lot about people. He could always understand what someone was going through."

"Yes. Sometimes he did," I said, looking momentarily away.

Then Dan told me: "When I was at my worst, I said to him, 'Doc, give me one reason to beat this depression.' And do you know what he said?"

Dan stared across the table until I re-established eye contact. "He said, 'Blackberries and how wonderful that is. To pick a handful of blackberries, sit down with someone you love very much and eat them. Think of that and tell me life's not worth the fight. You have a wonderful wife and three fine kids. Take some time with them. It's family we live for—not just ourselves.'

"That's what he said, and I've never forgotten it," Dan finished. "I think it saved my life."

My hands were quivering. All I could do was stare back at him. I was feeling so many emotions that I could muster not one word.

On the plane home I closed my eyes and thought about me and my dad. I knew what that day by the pond had meant to me. But I had never known what it meant to him. Now, in my mind's eye, I could see him standing at the edge of the water, the bass on his line, so full of joy. How wide the ripples spread, I thought. How far they reach.

Suddenly I found myself staring out the airplane window, hoping that the flight would get in on time. I planned to be home before dark for a change—to play in the yard with my son in the fading light of day.

黑莓的回忆

我刚刚在纽约开始新工作的同时，就不得不去学另一项重要的工作，就是为人之父。在办公室我们有 3 项新的工作规划，在家里我有个长得很快的小儿子需要照顾。单单说我紧张繁忙，不足以描述我的情况。有一个星期四，我收拾行装准备出差，是我一周内的第二次出差了，再没有比这事儿更令人沮丧了。我的妻子爱琳说："我知道你的工作有多重要，但要是你能在家多呆些时间就好了。"

我明白她是对的，我们的儿子鲁克眼看就要 3 岁了，我也不愿意总在外面出差。

"昨天，"爱琳说，"鲁克在房子里转来转去反复念叨着：'爸爸呢？爸爸在哪里呀？'"

爱琳还想往下说，但没有时间了，所以我说："亲爱的，我的确得去赶这一班飞机了。等我明天回来再接着谈吧。"

我在芝加哥的会议提前结束，我突然有了两三小时的空闲时间，因此我去看望了家庭的老朋友丹。为了和孙子孙女们住得近些，他退休后就住在附近。

丹原来在印第安纳州务农，我父亲曾在那里当乡村医生。那天我和丹坐在他家的厨房餐桌旁。他开始回忆我的父亲是个多么好的一个大好人。"无论花费多大精力，他都要把病人治好，"丹说，"我相信在农场那一带没有人不敬重你的父亲。"

随后，出我意料的是，丹还承认，他的前列腺癌治愈之后，曾患上严重的抑郁症久治不愈。"我并不在意是否能治好这病，"他说，"但是，你父亲最终却帮助我战胜了抑郁的心情。"

他的回忆深深地触动了我。我将手放在丹的肩上，赞同道："他一直都非常关心他的病人。"

的确如此。我知道父亲为病人付出了多少心血，但我也知道他的奉献精神和辛勤工作都得到了报偿———一种似乎高于他家庭的报偿。

爸爸的身材清瘦高挑，天蓝色的眼睛仿佛可以洞察秋毫。尽管他的神情和语气都很严肃，但和他谈话却会感觉轻松愉快。

那时，我们住在农场，并非因为我们是农民，而是因为爸爸的病人都住在那里。村民们看完病通常是以牲畜充当医疗费。于是，爸爸就找了一块农场，供放牧之用。

然而，不可否认，爸爸喜欢打猎，并且一直养着几只猎犬。这些猎犬由我负责驯养到可以狩猎为止。他说，之所以将这些琐事留给我去做，是因为他缺乏耐心。其实，他是否愿意做一件事往往决定于：如果让我去做那件事，是否我会学到一些东西。

爸爸教我学会了很多东西。他教我使用手锯和标明直角的方法，这些技术使我能在草场那边的池塘捆扎了一个小木排。木排有一端不成直线，他帮我纠正过来，并不责备我的过错。

　　他帮助我的最好方式就是向我提出问题，让我去心领神会。当我想和经常在学校跟我作对的家伙打架时，爸爸问我："你打得过他吗？"

　　"我想我应该打得过。"

　　"其实你不需要和他打架，站起来，使劲推我。"

　　我推了他好几下，几乎把他推倒。"瞧，你只要让他知道你有多强壮就行了，试一试这种方法，看他是不是会让步。"我依言行事，果然奏效。

　　那正是我需要爸爸所给予的帮助。但是，我13岁那年夏天，他几乎从我生活中消失。我真不知如何是好。

　　生病的人那么多，爸爸大多数时间都要出去为人看病，而且他还开了一家新诊所，设法挣足购置X光机的钱。电话铃经常在我们吃晚饭时响起，我总是听他说："我马上就到。"妈妈总是将他的饭菜放进锅里热着，等他回来。

　　通常他都要一小时或更长时间才能回来。听到他的汽车驶上砾石车道时发出的声音，我就赶紧跑下楼，趁他吃饭时和他聊聊天。他常常问我当天的情况，告诉我应该知道的一些牧场知识，他也只有精力和我谈这些了。

　　渐渐地，我对爸爸，对自己感到有些担心。我失去了他的帮助，失去了和他共享快乐的机会，而只是每天住在一起而已。"也许他不像以前那样喜欢我了。"我想。"也许是我做了什么让他失望的事儿。"他过去一直在帮助我成为一个真正的男子汉。我认为，没有他的指引，我的愿望是不会实现的。

　　在草场那边的池塘周围环绕着芦苇和香蒲，我喜欢去那里钓鱼，但从来没钓到过大鱼，只钓到过太阳鱼和鲇鱼。但是，池塘中确有大鱼，我曾看到过它们跳出水面时在清晨的薄雾中飞溅起银色的水花，有时水中泛起的涟漪会波及到岸边。

　　那年夏天，我常常坐在自制的木排上，想着将爸爸吸引回我身边的各种方法。妈妈希望全家外出做一次旅行。爸爸却因工作繁忙而拒绝了。

　　一天，我和妈妈在厨房又谈起了他。"看看你是不是能拉他出去钓鱼，"她最后说，"即使是外出消遣一个傍晚也好啊。"

　　第二天，我开始实施拉爸爸去池塘的计划。我要生起篝火，在上面烤玉米和我们钓上来的战利品。问题的关键是要让爸爸换上便装，轻松几个小时。

　　终于，在一个星期五，我把他拉去钓鱼了。那天，他进了泥土小屋时，我看见了他的车。我们在屋里换上了衣服。"我们要去钓鱼，"我说。"就这么回事。"

　　我们真的去钓鱼了！当我们在夕阳下站在池塘边甩杆时，我仍不敢相信自己真的说服了爸爸。过了一会儿，我去捡木柴准备生火。虽然我们并没有钓到任何东西，但我们也可以一边烤玉米一边聊天。

　　我一边捡木柴一边看着爸爸将鱼杆甩进了一棵被伐倒的红橡树旁边的深水坑里。"让他钓到一条鱼吧，"我小声念叨着，"什么鱼都行，让他钓着点儿东西就行。"

好像水中的鱼听到了我的恳求似的，一条鲈鱼咬钩了。"哇，太棒了！"爸爸兴奋地喊道，只见青苔色的鲈鱼悬在半空中，个头大极了。鱼奋力挣扎了几下，爸爸熟练地将它放进网里，然后递给了坐在篝火边的我。

"嗨，爸爸，"我说，"这鱼儿真够大的！"

爸爸看上去年轻、快乐而自豪。我在鱼上撒了玉米粉，放在篝火上烤。后来，我们就坐在一块石头上吃起了晚餐。

"真是一顿美餐，"饭后，爸爸说，"我不知道还有比这个更美妙的了。"

爸爸煮上了一壶咖啡。我到草场边的刺莓丛中去摘黑莓。花托上的黑草莓都熟透了，沉甸甸地压了下来。我采摘了一大堆，装在棒球帽里，带回去作为我们的饭后甜食。我们一边喝着咖啡，一边吃着黑莓，一边看西下的太阳光变幻着不同的色彩。爸爸慢慢地咀嚼着黑莓，一个个细细品味着，突然向我表述起他对我的关怀来。

"孩子，你的一生会很成功的，"他说，"我这样说是因为每次我让你干什么事，我从来不必说第二遍，而更重要的是，你是一个好孩子。"

他当时的神情是那样温柔而自豪，让我感到非常愉快。

后来，随着爸爸业务范围的逐渐扩大，这种在一起游玩、谈心的机会就越来越少了。但是，每当我需要时，就会重新想起池塘边的那段时光，回忆和爸爸在一起时有多么快乐。

"是的，"丹打断了我的回忆说。"你的父亲真是一个好人，他给人治病不仅仅是让人吃药、打针，他总为别人想得十分周到，总是善解人意。"

"对，他有时确实如此，"我说着，暂时移开了视线。

接着，丹告诉我说："我病情最严重时，曾问你的父亲：'医生，能告诉我一个战胜抑郁症的方法吗？'你猜他怎么说？"

丹看着我，直到我们的目光再次接触，才又继续说道："他说：'黑莓，多好啊。去摘一大捧黑莓，和你最爱的人坐在一起品尝其中的滋味。设想一下这样的情形，你还会告诉我生活不值得你去和病魔抗争吗？你有贤惠的妻子，还有三个好孩子，多花一些时间和他们在一起吧，我们是为家人，而不只是为自己，活在这个世界上。'"

"他当时就是这样对我说的，至今我仍然记得非常清楚，"丹最后说道，"我觉得是他这番话挽救了我的生命。"

我两手颤抖，呆呆地望着丹，我当时的情绪是那样复杂，一句话也说不出来。

在返程的飞机上，我闭上眼睛回想着我和父亲在一起的情景。我知道池塘边的那个傍晚对我的意义，却从不知道父亲的想法。现在，在我脑海里，我可以看到他站在池边，鱼竿上挂着鲈鱼，充满快乐之情。我想，那涟漪扩散得多宽广，多远啊。

突然，我发现自己望着机窗外，希望飞机能按时着陆。我要在天黑之前赶回家，和儿子在暮色中到院子里嬉戏。

诵读经典 >>>>>
Read classic

❂　Dad was a tall, lean man whose sky-blue eyes could see straight through anything. But despite his no-nonsense gaze and way of speaking, he was always easy to talk to.

爸爸的身材清瘦高挑，天蓝色的眼睛仿佛可以洞察秋毫。尽管他的神情和语气都很严肃，但和他谈话却会感觉轻松愉快。

❂　I'd seen them jump, making a glistening turbulence in the mist of early morning. Sometimes the ripples would carry so far they'd reach the shore.

我曾看到过它们跳出水面时在清晨的薄雾中飞溅起银色的水花，有时水中泛起的涟漪会波及到岸边。

妙语连珠 >>>>>
Sparkling discourse

★　Man can climb the highest summit, but he cannot dwell there long.
人可以爬上最高峰，但无法在那里住得太久。

★　We can ward an elephant, but cannot dodge a fly.
我们可以躲开一头大象，却躲不开一只苍蝇。

A Seven-Dollar Dream

"Wanted: Violin. Can't pay much. Call..."

Why did I notice that? I wondered, since I rarely look at the classified ads.

I laid the paper on my lap and closed my eyes, remembering what had happened many years before, when my family struggled to make a living on our farm. I, too, had wanted a violin, but we didn't have the money...

When my older twin sisters began showing an interest in music, Harriet Anne learned to play Grandma's upright piano, while Suzanne turned to Daddy's violin. Simple tunes soon became lovely melodies as the twins played more and more. Caught up in the rhythm of the music, my baby brother danced around while Daddy hummed and Mother whistled. I just listened.

When my arms grew long enough, I tried to play Suzanne's violin. I loved the **mellow**① sound of the firm bow drawn across the strings. Oh, how I wanted one! But I knew it was out of the question.

One evening as the twins played in the school **orchestra**②, I closed my eyes tight to capture the picture firmly in my mind. Someday, I'll sit up there, I vowed silently.

It was not a good year. At harvest the crops did not bring as much as we had hoped. Yet even though times were hard, I couldn't wait any longer to ask: "Daddy, may I have a violin of my own?"

"Can't you use Suzanne's?"

"I'd like to be in the orchestra, too, and we can't both use

生词有约

① mellow
adj. 圆润的

② orchestra
n. 管弦乐队

the same violin at the same time."

Daddy's face looked sad. That night, and many following nights, I heard him remind God in our family devotions, "...and Lord, Mary Lou wants her own violin."

One evening we all sat around the table. The twins and I studied. Mother sewed, and Daddy wrote a letter to his friend, George Finkle, in Columbus, Ohio. Mr. Finkle, Daddy said, was a fine violinist.

As he wrote, Daddy read parts of his letter out loud to Mother. Weeks later I discovered he'd written one line he didn't read aloud: "Would you watch for a violin for my third daughter? I can't pay much, but she enjoys much, and we'd like her to have her own instrument."

When Daddy received a letter from Columbus a few weeks later, he announced, "We'll be driving to Columbus to spend the night with Aunt Alice as soon as I can find someone to care for the livestock."

At last the day arrived, and we drove to Aunt Alice's. After we arrived, I listened while Daddy made a phone call. He hung up and asked, "Mary Lou, do you want to go with me to visit Mr. Finkle?"

"Sure," I answered.

He drove into a residential area and stopped in the driveway of a fine, old house. We walked up the steps and rang the door chime. A tall man, older than Daddy, opened the door. "Come in!" he and Daddy heartily shook hands, both talking at once.

"Mary Lou, I've been hearing things about you. Your daddy has arranged a big surprise for you!" Mr. Finkle ushered us into the parlor. He picked up a case, opened it, lifted out a violin and started to play. The melody **surged**③ and spoke like waterfalls. Oh, to play like him, I thought.

Finishing the number, he turned to Daddy. "Carl, I found it in a pawnshop for seven dollars. It's a good violin. Mary Lou should be able to make beautiful music with it." Then he handed the violin to me.

③ surge
vi. 汹涌澎湃

I noticed the tears in Daddy's eyes as I finally comprehended. It was mine! I stoked the violin gently. The wood was a golden brown that seemed to warm in the light. "It's beautiful," I said, barely breathing.

When we arrived back at Aunt Alice's, all eyes turned as we entered. I saw Daddy wink at Mother, and then I realized everyone had known but me. I knew Daddy's prayer, and mine, had been answered.

The day I carried my violin to school for my first lesson no one could imagine the bursting feeling in my heart. Over the months I practiced daily, feeling the warm wood fit under my chin like an extension of myself.

When I was ready to join the school orchestra, I trembled with excitement. I sat in the third row of violins and wore my white orchestra jacket like a royal robe.

My heart beat wildly at my first public performance, a school operetta. The **auditorium**④ filled to capacity and the audience buzzed while we softly tuned our instruments. Then the spotlight centered on us, and a hush fell as we started to play. I felt sure everyone in the audience was watching me. Daddy and Mother smiled proudly at their little girl who held her cherished violin for the whole world to admire.

④ auditorium
n. 礼堂

The years seemed to run more swiftly then. And by the time my sisters graduated, I found myself in the first-violin chair.

Two years later, I graduated. I packed my cherished violin in its case and stepped into the grown-up world. Nurse's training, marriage, working in the hospital, rearing four daughters filled my years.

More years passed. My violin made every move with us, and I carefully stored it away when we unpacked-briefly remembering how much I still loved it and promising myself to play it soon.

None of my children cared about the violin. Later, one by one, they married and left home...

Now here I was with the newspaper want ads. I forced

239

my thoughts to the present and read again the ad that had **transported** [5] me back to childhood memories. Laying aside the paper, I murmured, "I must find my violin."

I discovered the case deep in the recesses of my closet. Opening the lid, I lifted the violin from where it nestled on the rose-velvet lining. My fingers caressed its golden wood. I tuned the strings, miraculously still **intact** [6], tightened the bow, and put **rosin** [7] on the dry horsehairs.

And then my violin began to sing again those favorite tunes that had never left my memory. How long I played I'll never know. I thought of Daddy, who did all he could to fill my needs and desires when I was a little girl. I wondered if I had ever thanked him.

At last I laid the violin back in its case. I picked up the newspaper, walked to the phone and dialed the number.

Later in the day, an old car stopped in my driveway. A man in his 30s knocked on the door. "I've been praying someone would answer my ad. My daughter wants a violin so badly," he said, examining my instrument. "How much are you asking?"

Any music store, I knew, would offer me a nice sum. But now I heard my voice answer, "Seven dollars."

"Are you sure?" he asked, reminding me so much of Daddy.

"Seven dollars," repeated, and then added, "I hope your little girl will enjoy it as much as I did."

I closed the door behind him. Peeking out between the drapes, I saw his wife and children waiting in the car. A door suddenly opened and a young girl ran to him as he held out the violin case to her.

She hugged it against her, then dropped to her knees and snapped open the case. She touched the violin lightly as it caught the glow of the late-afternoon sun, then turned and threw her arms around her smiling father.

⑤ transport
vt. 把……带入特定境地

⑥ intact
adj. 完整无缺的

⑦ rosin
n. 松香

七美元的梦想

"求购小提琴，出价不高。请打电话……"

我为什么偏偏注意这则广告呢？连我自己也搞不清楚。平时我很少注意这类广告。

我把报纸放在膝间，闭上双眼，往事便一幕幕浮现在眼前：那时全家人含辛茹苦靠种地勉强度日。我也曾想要一把小提琴，但家里买不起……

我的两个孪生姐姐爱上了音乐。哈丽特·安妮学弹祖母留下的那台竖式钢琴，苏珊娜学拉父亲的那把小提琴。由于她们不断练习，因此没过多久简单的曲调就变成了悦耳动听的旋律。陶醉在音乐中的小弟弟禁不住随着音乐的节奏翩翩起舞，父亲轻轻哼唱，母亲也不由自主吹起了口哨，而我只是注意听着。

我的手臂渐渐长长了，也试着学拉苏珊娜的那把小提琴。我喜欢那绷紧的琴弓拉过琴弦时发出的柔媚圆润的声音。"噢，我多么希望能有一把琴啊！"但我明白这是不可能的。

一天傍晚，我的两个孪生姐姐在学校乐队演出时，我紧紧地闭上眼睛，以便把当时的情景深深地印在脑海里。"总有一天我也要坐在那里，"我暗暗发誓。

那年年景不好。收成不像我们所盼望的那样好。尽管岁月如此艰难，但我还是急不可待地问道："爸爸，我可以有一把自己的小提琴吗？"

"你用苏珊娜那把不行吗？"

"我也想加入乐队，但我们俩不能同时用一把琴。"

父亲的表情显得非常难过。那天晚上以及随后的许多夜晚，我都听到他在全家人晚间祈祷时向上帝祷告："……上帝啊，玛丽·露想要一把自己的小提琴。"

一天晚上，全家人都围坐在桌边，我和姐姐们复习功课，母亲做针线活，父亲给他在俄亥俄州哥伦布市的朋友乔治·芬科写信。父亲曾说，芬科先生是一名出色的小提琴家。

父亲一边写一边把信的部分内容念给母亲听。几周后，我才发现信中的这一行字他没念："请留神帮我三女儿寻一把小提琴好吗？我出不起高价，但她喜欢音乐，我们希望她能有自己的乐器。"

又过了几周，父亲收到哥伦布市的回信。他对大家说："只要我能找到人帮忙照看家畜，我们就一起去哥伦布市，到爱丽斯姑姑家过一夜。"

这一天终于到来了。我们全家人驱车前往爱丽斯姑姑家。到那以后，父亲打了个电话，我在旁边听着。他挂上电话后问我："玛丽·露，你想和我一起去看芬科先生吗？"

"当然想，"我答道。

父亲将车开进一个居民区，停靠在一座古色古香的楼房前的车道边上。我们登上台阶，按响了门铃。开门的是一个比我父亲年纪大的高个子的先生。"请进！"他和父亲亲切握手，两人马上攀谈了起来。

"玛丽·露，我早就听说过你的一些情况。你的父亲为你准备了一件礼物，一定会让你大吃一惊。"说完，芬科先生将我们领进客厅，便开始拉了起来。乐曲时而激越高亢，时而像瀑布飞泻。"噢，要是像他那样拉该多好啊！"我心里想。

一曲终了，他转过身对我的父亲说："卡尔，这是在一家当铺里找到的，才花了 7 美元，是一把好琴。这下玛丽·露就可以用它演奏优美的乐曲了吧。"说完，他将琴递给了我。

看到父亲眼里的泪水，我终于明白了一切。我有了自己的小提琴！我轻轻地抚摸着琴。这把琴是用金色灿烂的棕色木料制成的，在阳光的映照下显得是那样温暖。"多么漂亮啊！"我激动得透不过气来了。

当我们回到爱丽斯姑姑家时，所有人的目光都投向了我们父女俩，只见父亲正向母亲挤眼。这时，我才恍然大悟，原来只有我一个人还蒙在鼓里。我知道我和父亲的愿望已经得到实现。

我带着那把小提琴到学校上第一堂课的那天，当时那种万分激动的心情是谁也无法想象的。随后的几个月，我天天坚持练琴，感到抵在颌下那温暖的琴木就像我身体的一部分。

加入校乐队时，我激动得浑身颤抖。我身着白色队服，俨然女王一般。我坐在小提琴组的第三排。

首次公演是学校演出的小歌剧，当时我的心狂跳不止。礼堂里座无虚席。我们乐队成员轻轻地调试音调，观众席里还在叽叽喳喳说个不停。舞台聚光灯射向我们，台下立刻鸦雀无声。我们开始了演奏。我确信观众的目光都在注视着我。我的父母亲也都在看着他们的小女儿，嘴边挂着自豪的微笑。他们的小女儿怀里抱着她那把心爱的琴，让全世界都来赞赏它。

岁月似乎过得太快了。两个姐姐双双毕业后，我便坐上了首席小提琴的席位。

两年后，我也完成了学业，将心爱的小提琴放回琴箱，步入了成年人的世界。先是接受护士培训，然后是结婚成家。在医院工作的几年里，我先后生了 4 个女儿。

以后的许多年里，我们每次搬家，我都带着这把琴。每次打开行李布置居室时，我都要小心翼翼地将琴存放好，忙里偷闲时，想着我仍是多么爱它，同时对自己许愿说，用不了多久还会用这把小提琴演奏几首曲子。

我的几个孩子没有一个喜欢小提琴的。后来，她们相继结婚，离开了家。

现在我的面前摆着这张征求广告的报纸。我尽力不再去回首往事，将这则引起我对童年回忆的广告又看了一遍后，放下报纸，喃喃自语道："一定得把我的琴找出来。"

我在壁橱深处找出了琴箱，打开盖子，将安卧在玫瑰色丝绒衬里中的小提琴拿出来。我的手指轻轻地抚摸着金色的琴木，令人惊喜的是，琴弦仍然完好无损。我调试了一下琴弦，紧了紧琴弓，又往干巴巴的马尾弓上抹了点松香。

接着，小提琴又重新奏出了那些铭记在我心中最心爱的曲子。也不知究竟拉了多长时间。我想起了父亲，在我童年时代是他竭力满足我的一切愿望和要求，对此我不知道自己是否感谢过他。

最后，我把小提琴重新放回箱子里，拿起报纸，走到电话边，拨响了那个号码。

当天晚些时候，一辆旧轿车停靠在我家的车道旁。敲门的是个 30 来岁的先生。"我一直都在祈祷着会有人答复我登在报纸上的那则广告。我的女儿太希望有一把属于自己的小提琴了，"他一边说，一边查看我那把琴。"要多少钱？"

我知道，不管哪家乐器行都会出好价钱的。但此时此刻，我听到自己的声音回答说："7美元。"

"真的吗？"他这一问，倒使我更多地想起了父亲。

"7美元，"我又说了一遍，接着补充道："希望你的小女儿也会像我过去那样喜欢它。"

他走后，我随即关上门，从窗帘缝里看到他的妻子和孩子们正等候在车子里。车门突然打开，一个小姑娘迎着他双手托着的琴箱跑过来。

她紧紧地抱住琴箱，随后双膝跪倒在地，"吧嗒"一声打开箱子。她轻轻地抚摸着红彤彤的夕阳映照下的那把琴，转过身，搂住了面带微笑的父亲。

诵读经典 >>>>>
Read classic

⭐ I laid the paper on my lap and closed my eyes, remembering what had happened many years before, when my family struggled to make a living on our farm.

我把报纸放在膝间，闭上双眼，往事便一幕幕浮现在眼前：那时全家人含辛茹苦靠种地勉强度日。

⭐ She hugged it against her, then dropped to her knees and snapped open the case. She touched the violin lightly as it caught the glow of the late-afternoon sun, then turned and threw her arms around her smiling father.

她紧紧地抱住琴箱，随后双膝跪倒在地，"吧嗒"一声打开箱子。她轻轻地抚摸着红彤彤的夕阳映照下的那把琴，转过身，搂住了面带微笑的父亲。

妙语连珠 >>>>>
Sparkling discourse

⭐ A book is a mirror: if an ass peers into it, you can't expect an apostle to look out.

书是一面镜子：如果一只驴向里面窥视，你不可能指望正往外看的是一名圣徒。

⭐ Books are a delightful society. If you go into a room filled with books, even without taking them down from their shelves, they seem to speak to you, to welcome you.

书是令人愉快的伙伴。如果你走进一个摆满书的房间，即使不把它们从书架上拿下来，它们也仿佛在向你说话，欢迎你的到来。

A Hawk across the Sky

The hawk hung from the sky as though suspended from an invisible web, its powerful wings outstretched and motionless. It was like watching a magic—until, suddenly, the spell was shattered by a shotgun blast from the car behind us.

Startled, I lost control of my pickup. It **careened**① across the gravel shoulder until we stopped inches short of a barbed-wire fence. My heart was pounding as the car raced past us, the steel muzzle of a gun sticking out the window. I shall never forget the gleeful smile on the face of the boy who'd pulled that trigger.

"Geez, Mom. That scared me!" said Scott, 14, sitting beside me. Then my son's face clouded. "Look! He shot that hawk!"

While driving home along Arizona's interstate 10 to our cattle ranch, we had been marveling at a magnificent pair of red-tailed hawks swooping low over the Sonoran Desert. **Cavorting**② and diving at breathtaking speeds, the beautiful birds mirrored each other in flight. Then one hawk changed its course and soared skyward, where it hovered for an instant over the interstate. That's when the gun blast turned their play into an explosion of feathers.

Horrified, we watched the red-tail spiral earthward straight into the path of an 18-wheeler. Air braker screeched, but it was too late. The truck struck the bird, hurling it into the median.

Scott and I ran to the spot where it lay. Because of the

生词有约

① careen
vi. 歪歪斜斜地行进

② cavort
vi. 嬉戏

hawk's small size, we decided it was probably a male. He was on his back, a shattered wing doubled beneath him, the powerful beak open, and round, yellow eyes wide with pain and fear. The **talons**③ on his left leg had been ripped off, and where the brilliant fan of tail feathers had gleamed, only the red feather remained.

③ talon
n. 猛禽的锐爪

"We gotta do something, Mom."

"Yes, " I murmured. "We're got to take him home."

As Scott reached for him, the terrified hawk lashed out with his one remaining weapon—a hooked beak as sharp as an ice pick. Scott threw his leather jacket over the bird, wrapped him firmly and carried him to the pickup. From somewhere high in the sky, we heard the plaintive, high-pitched cry of the other hawk. "What will that one do now, Mom?"

"I don't know," I replied. "I've heard they mate for life."

At the ranch, we tackled our first problem: restraining the flailing hawk without getting hurt ourselves. Wearing welding gloves, we laid him on some straw inside an orange crate and slid the slats over his back.

Once the bird was immobilized, we removed splinters of bone from his shattered wing and then tried bending the wing where the main joint had been. It would fold only halfway. Through all this pain, the hawk never moved. The only sign of life was an occasional raising of the third lid over fear-glazed eyes.

Wondering what to do next, I called the Arizona-Sonora Desert Museum. "I know you mean well," the curator said sympathetically, "But **euthanasia**④ is the kindest thing."

④ euthanasia
n. 安乐死

"Destroy him?" I asked, gently stroking the auburn-feathered bird secured in the crate.

"He'll never fly again with a wing that badly injured," he continued. "Even if he could, he'd starve to death. Hawks need their claws as well as their beaks to tear up food."

As I hung up, I knew he was right.

"But the hawk hasn't even had a chance to fight," Scott argued.

Fight for what? I wondered. To huddle in a cage? Never to fly again?

With the blind faith of youth, Scott made the decision for us. "Maybe, by some miracle, he'll fly again," he said. "Isn't it worth the try?"

So began a weeks-long vigil during which the bird never moved, ate or drank. We forced water into his beak with a syringe. But the pathetic creature just lay there, scarcely breathing. Then came the morning when the red-tail's eyes were closed.

"Mom, he's...dead!" Scott cried.

"Maybe some whiskey," I said. It was a technique we'd used before to coax an animal to breathe. We pried open the beak and poured a teaspoon of the liquid down the hawk's throat. Instantly his eyes flew open and his head fell into the water bowl in the cage.

"Look, Mom! He's drinking!" Scott said, with tears sparkling in his eyes.

By nightfall, the hawk had eaten several strips of steak, sprinkled with sand to ease digestion. The next day Scott removed the bird from the crate and wrapped his good claw around a fireplace log where he teetered and swayed until the talons locked in. As Scott let go of the bird, the good wing flexed slowly into flight position, but the other was rigid, protruding from his shoulder like a **boomerang**⑤. We held our breath until the hawk stood erect.

⑤ boomerang
n. 回飞镖；飞去来器

The creature watched every move we made, but the look of fear was gone. He was going to live. Now, would he learn to trust us?

With Scott's permission, his three-year-old sister, Becky, named our visitor Hawkins. We put him in a chain-link dogrun ten feet high and open at the top. That way he'd be safe from bobcats, coyotes, raccoons and lobos. In one corner we mounted a **manzanita**⑥ limb four inches from the ground. The crippled bird perched there day and night, staring at the sky, watching, listening, waiting.

⑥ manzanita
n. 熊果树

In time, Hawkins's growing trust blossomed into affection. We delighted in spoiling him with treats like baloney and beef jerky soaked in sugar water. Soon, the hawk whose beak was powerful enough to crush the skull of a desert rat had mastered the touch of a butterfly. Becky fed him with her bare fingers.

Hawkins loved to play games. His favorite was tug of war. With an old sock gripped tightly in his beak and one of us pulling on the other end, he always won, refusing to let go even when Scott lifted him into the air. Becky's favorite was ring-around-the-rosy. She and I held hands and circled Hawkins's pen, while his eyes followed until his head turned 180 degrees. He was actually looking at us backward!

We grew to love Hawkins. We talked to him. We stroked his satiny feathers. We had saved and tamed a wild creature. But now what? Shouldn't we return him to the sky, to the world where he belonged?

Scott must have been wondering the same thing, even as he carried his pet around on his wrist like a proud falconer. One day he raised Hawkins's perch just over the bird's head. "If he has to struggle to get up on it, he might get stronger," Scott said.

Noticing the height difference, Hawkins assessed the change from every angle. He jumped—and missed, landing on the concrete, hissing pitifully. He tried again and again with the same result. Just as we thought he'd given up, he flung himself up at the limb, grabbing first with his beak, then his claw, and pulled. At last he stood upright.

Each week after that, Scott raised the perch a little more, until Hawkins sat proudly at four feet. How pleased he looked—puffing himself up and preening. But four feet was his limit; he could jump no higher.

Spring brought warm weather and birds. We thought Hawkins would enjoy all the chirping and trilling. Instead, we sensed a sadness in our hawk.

One morning we found him perched with his good wing

extended, the other quivering helplessly. All day he remained in this position, a piteous, rasping cry coming from his throat. Finally we saw what was troubling him: high in the sky over his pen, another red-tail hovered.

His mate? I asked myself. How could it be? We were at least 30 miles from where we'd found Hawkins, far beyond a hawk's normal range. Had his mate somehow followed him here? Or, through some secret of nature, did she simply know where he was?

"What will she do when she realizes he can't fly?" Scott asked.

"I imagine she'll get discouraged and leave," I said sadly. "We'll just have to wait and see."

Our wait was brief. The next morning Hawkins was gone.

Questions tormented us. How did he get out? The only possibility was that he'd simply pulled himself six feet up the fence, grasping the wire first with his beak, then his one good claw. Next he must have fallen ten feet to the ground.

How would he survive? He couldn't hunt. Clinging to his perch and a strip of meat with one claw had proven nearly impossible. Our crippled hawk would be easy prey. We were heartsick.

A week later, however, there was Hawkins perched on the log pile by our kitchen door. His eyes gleamed with a brightness I'd never seen before. And his beak was open. "He's hungry!" I shouted. The bird snatched a package of baloney from Scott's hand and ate greedily.

Finished, Hawkins hopped awkwardly to the ground. We watched as he lunged, floated and crashed in short hops across the pasture, one wing flapping mightily, the other a useless burden. Journeying in front, his mate swooped back and forth, scolding and whistling her encouragement until he reached the temporary safety of a mesquite grove.

Hawkins returned to be fed throughout the spring. Then one day, instead of taking his food, he shrank back and squawked. Suddenly he struck at us with his beak. The hawk that had trusted us for nearly a year was now afraid. I knew he was ready to return to the wild.

As the years passed, we occasionally saw a lone red-tail gliding across our pastures, and my heart would leap with hope. Had Hawkins somehow survived? And if he hadn't, was it worth the try to keep him alive as we did?

Nine years later, when Scott was 23, he met an old friend in Phoenix who had lived near our ranch. "You won't believe this," he said. "but I think I saw your hawk roosting in a scrub oak down by the wash . He was all beat up with a broken wing just like Hawkins."

"You gotta go take a look Mom," insisted Scott.

The next day I drove north until the dirt road became zigzagging cattle trails and finally no trails at all. When a barricade of thorny mesquite trees stopped me, it was time to walk. Finally an opening through the maze led me down to a sandy wash. It was the perfect feeding ground for a hawk.

I searched for hours, but saw no trace of Hawkins. Finding him, I thought, was too much to hope for. It was getting cold when I sensed I was being watched. Suddenly I found myself looking straight into the eyes of a large female red-tail. Roosting in a mesquite less than 15 feet away, she was perfectly **camouflaged**⑦ by autumn foliage.

⑦ camouflage
vt. 掩饰

Could this magnificent creature have been Hawkins's mate? I wanted so much to believe she was, to tell Scott I had seen the bird that had cared for her mate, scavenged for his food and kept him safe. But how could I be sure?

Then I saw him.

On a branch beneath the dark shadow of the large bird hunched a tattered little hawk. When I saw the crooked wing, the proud bald head and withered claw, my eyes welled with tears. This was a magic moment: a time to reflect on the power of hope. A time to bless the boy with faith.

Alone in this wild place, I learned the power of believing, for I had witnessed a small miracle.

"Hawkins," I whispered, longing to stroke the ragged feathers, but daring only to circle him. "Is it really you?" My answer came when the yellow eyes followed my footsteps until he was looking at me backward and the last rays of sunlight danced on his one red feather.

Then, finally, I knew—and, best of all, my son would know. It had been worth the try.

鹰击长空

那只鹰悬挂天空，好像吊在一个看不见的网里，张开有力的翅膀，纹丝不动，如在表演魔术一般。我们都看得入了迷。突然，从我们后面那辆汽车边传来一声枪响，惊破了所有的一切。

我大吃一惊，开着的小货车也一时失控，歪歪斜斜地冲上路肩，差点儿撞在一排铁丝网上。我的心怦怦狂跳，后面的车从我们旁边飞驰而过，猎枪钢管伸出窗外。我永远忘不了那个开枪的男孩脸上那副扬扬得意的笑容。

"天啊，妈妈。吓死我了，"坐在我旁边的斯科特说。随后，我这14岁的儿子面露忧色。"看！他射中了那只鹰！"

我们当时正在一边沿着亚利桑那10号州际公路开车回牧场，一边欣赏一对矫健的红尾鹰在索诺拉沙漠上空翱翔。两只美丽的鹰以惊人的速度飞腾俯冲，一高一低，一左一右，配合得天衣无缝，然后其中一只改变方向，向上升腾，在州际公路上盘旋了一会儿。就是这时，枪声把它们的嬉戏变成了羽毛四飞的劫难。

我们惊骇地看着红尾鹰盘旋下降，跌到路上，一辆18轮大拖车正开过去。空气刹车戛然煞住，但为时已晚，大拖车撞到鹰身上，把它抛到了马路中间。

我和斯科特向鹰跌落的地方跑去。它体形很小，我们相信是一只雄鹰。只见它躺在地上，腹部向上，一只严重受伤的翅膀折在身下，尖嘴张开，圆圆的黄眼睛睁得老大老大，充满痛苦和恐惧，左爪已经撕裂，尾巴上一整排美丽光亮的羽毛只剩下一条红色的。

"我们得想想办法，妈妈。"

"对，"我轻声说，"我们得带他回家。"

斯科特伸手去抱那只受伤的鹰，它用唯一还可以运用的武器——像冰锄般锋利的钩形鹰嘴——猛啄。斯科特把皮夹克盖在鹰的身上，紧紧裹着他，把他抱到小货车上。这时，从高空中传来另一只鹰的尖叫声和哀鸣。"那一只现在会怎样，妈妈？"

"不知道，"我说，"听说鹰是从一而终的。"

　　回到牧场，我们要解决的第一个难题是怎样使那在不断挣扎的鹰安定下来而我们自己又不致受伤。我们戴上焊工手套，把他放在铺了干草的橘子箱里，然后用板条压着它的背。

　　鹰给我们制服了，不能动弹。我们替它把伤翼的碎骨拿掉，设法顺着主关节把翼弯曲，但翼只能屈到一半。它虽很痛苦，却一动不动。唯一能使我们知道它仍活着的是他偶尔会翻起眼睛，露出恐惧的目光。

　　我不知道下一步该怎么办。于是打电话给亚利桑那 - 索诺拉沙漠博物馆。"我知道你是一片好心，"馆长同情地说，"但安乐死是最仁慈的做法。"

　　"毁了它？"我问，一面轻轻抚摸困在木箱里的那只赤褐色羽毛的鹰。

　　"鹰翅受了那么重的伤很难再飞了，"他继续说，"就算它能再飞，也会饿死。鹰需要爪和嘴撕咬食物。"

　　我挂上电话，知道他说得对。

　　"但这只鹰连挣扎奋斗的机会也没有，"斯科特争辩说。

　　"为什么奋斗？"我暗忖道，"蜷缩在笼子里？永不再飞？"

　　斯科特本着年轻人盲目的信念，替我们作出了决定。"也许奇迹会出现，它能再次起飞，"他说，"难道这不值得试试？"

　　于是，我们开始一周又一周地守护着它，但它一动不动，不吃不喝。我们用注射器把水灌进它的嘴，但这只可怜的东西只是躺在那里，好像没有呼吸似的。后来有一天早上，红尾鹰两只眼睛闭上了。

　　"妈妈，它……死了！"斯科特喊道。

　　"用威士忌试试，"我说。以前我用过这方法使动物恢复呼吸。我们把它的嘴掰开，将一茶匙酒灌进它的喉咙。它的两只眼睛马上睁开，头掉在笼里的小碗里。

　　"看，妈妈！它在喝水！"斯科特眼含泪水说。

　　到晚上，鹰已经吃了几小块牛排肉，肉上撒了些沙帮助它消化。第二天斯科特把鹰从木箱里拿出来，替它把没受伤的那只爪环着壁炉边的一条柴枝。它起初摇摇摆摆，后来爪抓住了木头，站稳了。斯科特放手时，它那只没受伤的翅膀慢慢折成飞行的姿势，另一只则很僵硬，好像飞去来器似的从肩膀上突出来。我们屏息等待，鹰终于站直了。

　　它注视着我们的一举一动，但已无恐惧之色。它活了下来，但能学会信任我们吗？

　　斯科特让 3 岁的妹妹贝基替这客人取名霍金斯。我们把它放在一个 10 英尺高的铁丝栏裹，上面打开，那样它就不会受到野豹、郊狼、浣熊和大灰狼侵袭。我们在一角离地 4 英寸处装了一根熊果树枝。鹰日夜都栖息在那里，仰望天空，注视、倾听、等待。

　　霍金斯对我们越来越信任，后来更对我们产生了感情。我们乐于偶尔宠它一下，喂它香肠片和浸了糖水的牛肉干。不久，这只嘴强劲有力可以啄碎沙漠鼠头盖骨的鹰变得像蝴蝶般温柔。贝基可以就用手指拿食物喂它。

　　霍金斯喜欢玩游戏。它最喜欢玩拔河。我们让它用嘴紧紧咬住旧袜子的一端，我们其中一人拉着另一端。它总是赢，就算斯科特把它整个扯了起来，它还是死咬着不放。贝基则最喜欢玩团团转。她和我手抓着手，绕着霍金斯的笼子走。霍金斯的眼一直盯着我们，头可以整个扭转一百八十度。实际上它是从背后看我们的！

我们渐渐爱上了霍金斯。我们和它说话，抚摸它光滑的羽毛。我们救了它，也驯服了一只野禽。但现在该怎么办呢？我们是不是应该把它送回天空，让它回到它原来的世界呢？

斯科特有时像一个猎鹰训练员，自豪地把他的宠物紧在手腕上四处走。但他一定也在想着同一个问题。有一天，他将霍金斯的栖木提高到了刚高过头。"如果它要费一番劲力才可以上去，就可以把它锻炼得强壮些，"斯科特说。

霍金斯注意到栖木的高度改变了，就从不同角度去观察提高了的栖木。它跳起来——没够着，跌落在混凝土地上，可怜地嘶叫着。它一试再试，还是够不到。就在我们以为它会放弃时，它飞身扑到栖木上，先用嘴咬紧，然后用爪，再把身体拉了上去。最后它终于站直了。

以后每个星期，斯科特都把栖木提高一点，直到霍金斯得意地坐在离地 4 英尺处。它踌躇满志，用嘴梳理羽毛。但它不能跳得比四英尺更高了，这已是极限。

春天带来了温暖的天气和各种鸟。我们原以为霍金斯会喜欢听到鸟的啭鸣声和啁啾声。但正好相反，我们感觉到它非常忧伤。

一天早上，我们发现它站在栖木上，张开没受伤的那只翅膀，受了伤的那只则在无力地抖动。它整天都保持这个姿势，喉咙中发出可怜而刺耳的叫声。后来，我们才知道是什么原因：在它笼子上方的天空，另一只红尾鹰在盘旋。

"是它的伴侣？"我问自己。怎么可能呢？我们离发现霍金斯的地方至少有 48 英里，远超过鹰的飞程。是不是它的伴侣竟神奇地跟着它来到了这里？还是由于大自然中一些我们不知道的原因，它的伴侣自然就知道了它在什么地方？

"如果它的伴侣发现它不能飞，会怎样做？"斯科特问。

"我想它也会失望地离去，"我难过地回答说，"我们只有等等看。"

我们不用等多久。第二天早上，霍金斯飞走了。

有许多问题困扰着我们。它是怎样出来的？唯一的可能是它扑上栏杆 6 英尺高处，先用嘴咬住铁丝，然后用没受伤的爪子钩住。最后，它一定是从 10 英尺高的栏顶上跌到了地上。

它怎能生存呢？它不能猎食。用一只爪同时抓住栖木和一块肉，差不多是不可能的。我们那只残废了的鹰很容易就会成为别的猛兽猛禽的猎物。我们感到非常沮丧。

但一星期后，霍金斯又飞到了我们厨房门外的柴堆上，两眼闪着我们从来没有见过的光彩。它张开嘴。"它饿了！"我喊道。鹰从斯科特手里抢走了一包香肠片，狼吞虎咽地吃起来。

然后，霍金斯笨拙地跳到地上。我们看着它在草地上向前一冲，飘动了一下又落下来，每次飞短短的距离。它一只翅膀拍得很有力，另一只却是无用的累赘。它的伴侣在前面来回飞扑，时而责备它，时而啸叫鼓励它，直到它飞抵一棵牧豆树的临时庇护所。

整个春天，霍金斯都回来找我们喂食。然后有一天，它没有拿它的食物，反而向后退缩，还发出粗响的叫声。它突然用嘴攻击我们。它过去一年很信任我们，现在却害怕了。我知道它已准备好回到荒野去。

以后多年，我们偶然会看到一只孤独的红尾鹰在我们牧场的上空飞翔，我心里会突然充满希望。霍金斯会不会竟然神奇地活下去了？如果它活不下去，我们这样救了它又是否值得？

时隔 9 年后，斯科特 23 岁了。他在凤凰城见到一个以前住在我们牧场附近的老朋友。"我知道你不会相信，"朋友说，"但我想我是看到你的鹰栖息在洼地那边的矮橡树里。它断了一只翅膀，样子憔悴，就像霍金斯那样。"

"你得去看看，妈妈，"斯科特坚持说。

第二天，我就开车北上，直到泥路变成弯弯曲曲的小径，后来连小径也没有了。一棵有刺的牧豆树挡住我的去路，我只好下车步行。最后，我走过纵横交错树林中的一片空地，来到沙洼地。这里是鹰理想的觅食地。

我找了几个小时，都看不到霍金斯的踪影。我觉得找到它的希望太渺茫了。气温逐渐下降，我觉得好像有什么在监视我似的。突然，我发现在我眼前的是一只大红尾雌鹰的眼睛。它栖息在不到 15 英尺外的一棵牧豆树上，似乎完全隐没在秋天的红叶里。

这只雄伟的鸟会是霍金斯的伴侣吗？我很想相信它就是，这样就可以告诉斯科特我见到了一直照顾霍金斯的伴侣，为它觅食，保护它。但我怎能肯定呢？

随后，我见到了它。

在大鹰阴影下的一根树枝上，弓身站着一只羽毛破乱的小鹰。我一看到那屈折的翼、傲慢的秃头和萎缩的爪，两眼立即盈满泪水。这是一个美妙的时刻：是反省希望的力量的时刻。也是祝福那个充满信心的孩子的时刻。

我独立荒野，明白了信心的力量，因为我看到了一个小小的奇迹。

"霍金斯，"我轻声说，很想去抚摸它蓬乱的羽毛，却只敢绕着它转，"真的是你吗？"它黄色的眼睛盯着我的脚步，直到它把头扭转 180 度来望着我，夕阳的余辉在它那唯一的一条红羽毛上闪耀，我才找到了答案。

然后，我终于知道——而最重要的是我儿子会知道——救它的确是值得的。

诵读经典 >>>>>
Read classic

❂ With an old sock gripped tightly in his beak and one of us pulling on the other end, he always won, refusing to let go even when Scott lifted him into the air.

我们让它用嘴紧紧咬住旧袜子的一端，我们其中一人拉着另一端。它总是赢，就算斯科特把它整个扯了起来，它还是死咬着不放。

❂ On a branch beneath the dark shadow of the large bird hunched a tattered little hawk. When I saw the crooked wing, the proud bald head and withered claw, my eyes welled with tears. This was a magic moment: a time to reflect on the power of hope. A time to bless the boy with faith.

在大鹰阴影下的一根树枝上，弓身站着一只羽毛破乱的小鹰。我一看到那屈折的翼、傲慢的秃头和萎缩的爪，两眼立即盈满泪水。这是一个美妙的时刻：是反省希望的力量的时刻。也是祝福那个充满信心的孩子的时刻。

妙语连珠 >>>>>
Sparkling discourse

❂ Books are the ship crossing the sea of time.

书籍是横渡时间大海的航船。

❂ It is better to place the books in the study than to stuff the money into your pocket.

书房里摆满书籍远比钱包里塞满钞票要好。